VENUS AND JUPITER

BRIDGING THE IDEAL AND THE REAL

ERIN SULLIVAN

The Wessex Astrologer

Published in English in 2021 by
The Wessex Astrologer Ltd
PO Box 9307
Swanage
BH19 9BF

For a full list of our titles go to www.wessexastrologer.com

© Erin Sullivan 1996

Erin Sullivan asserts her moral right to be recognised as
the author of this work

Cover design by Jonathan Taylor

A catalogue record for this book is available at The British Library

ISBN 9781910531617

First published in 1996 by the CPA Press in England under
ISBN 1900869044

No part of this book may be reproduced or used in any form or by any means
without the written permission of the publisher.
A reviewer may quote brief passages.

To Howard Sasportas, in loving memory

Table of Contents

Part One: Venus Aphrodite - Dual Goddess

Eros and Aphrodite: love and creation 1
  The Origin of Things 5
  Eros - the creative source 11
  Erotomania 21
  The birth of Aphrodite Urania 26
  Love and strife 30
The dual goddess: Urania and Pandemos 36
  Aphrodite's children 39
  Sappho - Aphrodite's minion 41
  Eros, Aphrodite and the astrological Venus 48
  Dual goddess, dual ruler 53
  Libra and Taurus - mind and body 57
The projection of the ideal 63
  Incubation of the creative seed 68
Aspects of love and creation: Venus to the planets 70
  Venus and Mercury 74
  Venus and the Moon 80
  Mars and Venus 95
  Jupiter and Venus 98
  Saturn and Venus 103
  The outer planets and Venus 107
  Uranus and Venus 110
  Neptune and Venus 113
  Pluto and Venus 116
  Unaspected Venus 122
Bibliography 126

Part Two: The Justice of Zeus and the Astrological Jupiter

Introduction 128
The background of mythology 133
    The rationalisations of myth 142
    Freud and the myth of Oedipos 147
    Myth and astrology 152
    The birth of Zeus-Jupiter 155
    Jupiter's reign 157
    Jupiter and the god of ecstasy 170
    Stranger in a strange land: the traveller 175
    Jupiter and the saviour complex 181
Jupiter in aspect to the natal planets 186
    Sun and Jupiter 186
    Jupiter and Mercury 194
    Jupiter and Venus 200
    Jupiter and Mars 205
    Jupiter and Saturn 213
    Jupiter and the outer planets 219
    Jupiter and Uranus 220
    Jupiter, Neptune, Pluto and everything 227
    Jupiter and Neptune 233
    Jupiter and Pluto 235
Bibliography 237
Acknowledgements 237

Part One:
Venus Aphrodite – Dual Goddess

This seminar was given on 27 February, 1994 at Regents College, London, as part of the Spring Term of the seminar programme of the Centre for Psychological Astrology.

Eros and Aphrodite: love and creation

The noise of the overhead projector is awful. Besides, today we don't really need it. I will use the white-board to illustrate things when we want to get into some graphics, notes or specifics. I just couldn't bear, for some reason, having that machine in here today. Maybe because transiting Saturn is square my natal Venus, the idea of putting a machine to that planet just does not appeal to me aesthetically.

Today, there is a lot of material we are going to explore, and, as usual, I'd like to outline what to expect. I will start off with some of the origins, mythology, and stories about the concept of love and creation – because the fundamental aspect of Venus is not just simply about relationships and falling in love and that kind of human experience, but also has something much deeper embedded in the symbolism. Venus and all her attributes and attendants symbolise the source of the font of creativity.

To fully appreciate the astrological Venus, we'll go back to the Greeks, to the Goddess of Love, Aphrodite. Though in the form which we'll talk about today, Aphrodite is full-blooded Greek, her mythic history is a complex amalgam of other Eastern goddesses which predate her by a considerable period of time – Babylonian, Chaldean, Sumerian, and so forth. So, if we think of a global mythology, a "monomyth", as Joseph Campbell called it (from James Joyce's *Ulysses*), she is a descendant of the goddesses Ishtar and Astarte. But by the time she arrives in Greece, there is already a very well-developed philosophy and mythology centred around Aphrodite. Venus is, of course, the Roman name for the Greek Aphrodite. Embedded in the symbols in the horoscope is a phenomenal amount of information – deep, underlying, archetypal material which isn't necessarily available upon gazing at the symbol of Venus, but does lie in that symbol. And, once we begin to work with it and look deeply into that symbol, essentially invoking Venus, all of that rich underlay of information and material is available – not consciously, but it does begin to rumble up through the layers of consciousness.

This is the magic of astrology. We become privy to information that is not readily available through any other medium. The knowledge comes through subtle means. Looking at symbols, reading a lot and talking to other people, we literally call up the images of gods and goddesses, activating the mythic realm. Thus, you can read all you want about Venus, but do remember that some of the informationthat you are going to get will come through your own source and be filtered through your relationship with the divine. So, therefore, any teachings, or anything that we can offer or share with each other, are minimal, because there is so much there that underlies the whole concept of Venus as a planet in the horoscope.

This glyph is going to represent different things to various people, depending on their interest, focus, background, and education. Obviously, to an astrologer it is a symbol for the planet as an archetype for a human experience, or as agency for an aspect of our innate human condition, or an indicator of mundane or physical things which Venus rules, like purses, fashion, the hormone system, and so on. To an astronomer, it is merely the symbol for the planet Venus, one of ten solar system shorthand glyphs – no magic there! – and, to a metallurgist, it's the symbol for copper. To a semiologist, it is the symbol for the feminine (while the symbol for Mars represents masculine/male), and so forth.

Aphrodite is the eldest of the Greek Pantheon. At her Greek-origin birth, she is attended to by the oldest of the gods – Eros himself. The creation myth I use is found in the *Theogony*, dating from the 6th century BCE, by Hesiod, a misogynistic Boeotian farmer. The origins of all the Greek hierarchy and theocracy are found in this fabulous poem. Origin myths almost always involve incredible tragedies and splits, and there was always something about the feminine that was very frightening and threatening, perilous, even. In fact, if you ever read the origin myths in the *Theogony*, you'll find in it the myth of the creation of woman. The story of Pandora's Box, of course, is renowned, but it's not commonly known that in his poem, Hesiod employs the various gods to bestow upon her enhancements of their own characteristics. For instance, Aphrodite is called to give her beauty and grace, and Hermes to instill in her "the mind of a thief and the morals of a bitch". Hmmm. So much for Hesiod's opinion of womankind. Anyway, back to Aphrodite.

From this small digression, we can see that there is a certain social bias and cultural distortion, I think, evident in the myths as they have been received, but their depth and quality is phenomenal and they do talk about something deep and mysterious. They are largely similar in archetypal content and globally consistent throughout a number of mythologies. The spontaneous emergence of a myth cannot lie, because it's not as if there was collaboration among the scribes or transmitters of the myths (that we know of), or a bunch of historians sitting down comparing notes – that happened much later. Myth is something that seems to emerge spontaneously out of the collective of the people who experienced their world.

The relationship that the archaic people had with their world was considerably different to the one we have today. Today, we are so much more rational and compartmentalised and Uranian that we have tremendous problems with coping with our self-consciousness. We may have become overly conscious – our capacity to deal with our awareness has resulted in tremendous floods of collective anxiety. This phenomenon of "consciousness" has, in fact, provided analysts, therapists, and astrologers with a tremendous practice, working with people who wish to come to understand why it is that we are so anxious about things which are so very simple. However, as Joseph Campbell said in his book, Myths to Live By, "The latest incarnation of Oedipus, the continued romance of Beauty and The Beast, stands this afternoon on the corner of 42nd Street and Fifth Avenue, waiting for the traffic light to change."

In the archaic world it is unlikely there was such a thing as neurosis. There was such a thing as life-anxiety and primal fear, and forms of insanity, but it had very little to do, in fact absolutely nothing to do, if my reasoning is correct, with worrying about how one appeared in the world. The consciousness had primarily to do with being in relationship with the world. It had to do with the gods and it had to do with nature, and nature and the gods were in some way in harmony and in relationship with each other and with humans. There was no volition, no ego; there wasn't a individualistic sense of the "I am" as we know it today, and there wasn't a whole lot of stress around self-awareness, either. What on earth is this lineage of stories that were told and retold, and why do we continually retell, in accord with our own culture and our own time, the concepts of the ancient and archaic world? Likely because they hold immutable truths. Though they are "true" on a feeling level, they are arguably accurate in the sense that we take "true" to be in the scientific model.

We know little about why these images were born out of the collective mind from archaic times, but I think the fact that we continue to live out, in our daily human experience, stories that are so old that we don't know the origins, tells us something about the nature of our species. It seems that there was a rush to get things written down after the advent of literacy in around the 6th century BCE. It is rather like the times we are in now, at the end of this millennium – masses of information flooding the collective. I was first drawn to classical studies in the mid-eighties because I was beginning to sense that we were in times not unfamiliar in my own consciousness – thus there must be more to NOW than met the mind. As there was then, in 5th century Athens, the seat of Western civilization, there seems now to be a flood of information happening, and a deep, soulful disenchantment. New laws, both social and natural, were being uncovered at an astounding rate, creating an atmosphere of social, moral, and theological mania as an entire culture was caught up in the attempt to rationalize and explain, understand and know, what was at hand. In Yeats' poem, "The Second Coming", he himself voiced this same anxiety:

> Things fall apart; the centre cannot hold;
> Mere anarchy is loosed upon the world,
> The blood-dimmed tide is loosed, and everywhere
> The ceremony of innocence is drowned;
> The best lack all conviction, while the worst
> Are full of passionate intensity.[1]

So, in the period of, say, from about 400 to 300 BCE, there was a renaissance, a flourishing of ideas, which form the origins of our current separation from nature and myth. The struggles that the Greek philosophers of the time endured, to try and rationalise (a key word here) the concept of the gods and the behaviour of human beings, is akin to our own current collective and individual anxiety today. The culture at that time was separating so acutely from the gods of the times, and was so stressful, that there was then, as there is now, a renewed interest in the mythological past.

Today, we are still in a quandary about who came first, gods or men. That dilemma in itself is an indication of our psychological split – trying to figure out what came first, the gods or us – and it's a question to which we are unlikely to find an answer. I think it's best here, even if it's just for the pleasure of hearing interesting tales, to tell you the origins of Eros and Aphrodite.

The Origin of Things

The Greek creation myth of the origin of the world has Chaos as the primal state. Chaos doesn't mean a terrible mess or disorder, as it is commonly used today to convey a disorganized desk, or someone's behaviour. Literally, it means a gap, a "yawn", implying that there is something unbounded and open, something going on very deep and mysterious which we don't understand. Now, out of Chaos, from some spark of incentive or necessity, Earth is brought forth – and

---

[1] W. B. Yeats, *The Second Coming,* MacMillan, Papermac, 1973, p. 211.

along with Earth, Tartarus, which is a place under the earth. This became a specific realm in Hades, in the Greek mind. The next offspring was Eros, which is Love, and Erebos, which is the gloom of Tartarus, and, finally, Nyx, which is Night. And this is it, this is the beginning of everything. The idea that the Genesis of all things is Chaos is not original to the Greeks. It's not exclusive in their worldview either. There are many parallels that are found in the Egyptian, Sumerian, and Babylonian stories, and also Native American mythologies, African, Tibetan, and Hindu. They all have a "chaos" out of which is born matter, and out of that *prima materia* are born Love and Darkness and the elements of nature, which begin to cohere after that.

"Chaos" in Greek is a rich array of elemental forces all in place, but without form or differentiation. Jung called this phenomenon a *pleroma* – a full void. Chaos, in this sense, is all things in a hiatus, waiting for something, living in a sense of intelligent suspension. This happens often in the creative process, as we shall see. In preparation for this seminar, anticipating today's material, I was poring over the bookshelf, and just "happened" to open at the right place, out of twenty volumes in a collection of works, a quote by Jung. He described the *pleroma* in this way. He says that "....in the pleromatic, or, as the Tibetans called it, Bardo state, there is a perfect interplay of cosmic forces, but with the creation, that is the division of the world into distinct processes in space and time, events begin to rub and jostle one another."[2]

And so this fertile chaos, then, in accord with the myth, spontaneously created company, and its parts and elements began to separate and constellate in ways to form complex identities – Love, Tartarus and Night – so the infernal and the earthy entities mentioned are all part of the result of this fertility experience of chaos. In other words, chaos is a full void, a pleroma, a waiting, where elements exist but are not differentiated into forms and things. The elemental forces are so totally merged in the state of chaotic origin

---

[2] C. G. Jung, *Collected Works,* Vol. 11, Bollingen Series XX, Princeton University Press, 1969, para. 620.

that it could be looked at as a state of ideal immersion. It really is the source of everything – chaos is the genesis of all things.

In the sense that we are using chaos, it is rather like the quantum level of experience, wherein energy and mass are not differentiated and are one – a unified force of energetic potential. The creation of Eros early on in the sequence makes perfect sense to me. Not only does he balance the other rather gloomy siblings of Tartarus, but also, it follows that he would be needed for further creation. In fact, Eros might be cited as the cause of Love or Creation, as well as the impetus of all life, of everything. This is a very old philosophical concept. But I think it makes sense that there would be a need to understand what it is that happens, that is so mysterious, that forces something to create, whether it's a bud out of a dead branch in the spring, or the birth of an animal, or the birth of a child. The need to comprehend creation has given rise to the richest stories in our mythic history!

There was a time, believe it or not, when there was no concept of paternity – women just swelled up and gave birth and that was it, nobody even questioned it, didn't even care, it seems. It was just all part of the pleroma, the full void out of which came something. In a personal sense, this myth is analogous to our own individual experience of waiting for something to happen. There are many times when we feel full of ourselves and complete, as if we are ready for something new, a new creation, but it's very uncomfortable, for it simply isn't happening. It's' often at this time that we are most uncomfortable with our sense of completeness, that we are, in fact, most aware of our need for a new experience, and something does actually get born out of that sense of fullness. For instance, if you feel depressed, sometimes it can be a precursor to a creative burst – often creation is preceded by depression.[3]

When you become consumed by the inner process, an incredibly all-consuming, full void occurs, and you begin to collapse into it. It really is a process of self-insemination, incubation and delivery, so really, I would think that the origin of all things as chaos is a

---

[3]Marie-Louise von Franz, *Creation Myths,* Spring Publications, Dallas, Texas, 1972.

beautiful way for the primitive mind to have expressed this sense of expectation and knowledge, of things to come, so to speak.

Eros, then, is the *deus ex machina* – he arrives, apparently, as the embodiment of a fully matured experience, in what appears to be a flash, an instant. Indeed, we can actually see this process occur in things which have a very short lifespan – some kinds of flowers, a bud, certain bugs, etc. One night you can go to sleep, and upon awakening the next day, there it is, you missed its birth, but it happened. It's spontaneous. It appears to be a flash, but, in fact, obviously because intellectually we know this, it's been incubating in secret. So, it's like that with us when we create – we get something new, a new idea – we incubate things in the womb of our psyche and that is the mysterious process that goes on around an erotic experience.

Audience: Would you say that Eros, as a god, has any morals? Do you think that the function of Eros as a creator can run amok? What if the feeling of divine inspiration is really a ridiculous fantasy, and days, months, even years are spent wasting time on an idea, product, or relationship?

Erin: Ah, yes, this is a very real problem. The whole process of creativity and love is fraught with potential disaster, which is why many people eschew the risks involved in love or creativity. The god Eros is primordial, amoral, and completely without boundaries – he is present in all things. I would call it the "cosmic attractor". This aspect of Eros is something quite disembodied and it could be thought of as a kind of omnipresent, unifying principle which needs a focus, or an object or a soul to move through. If we feel, for instance, a force of enchantment or an undifferentiated longing for truth, or beauty, or love, or an experience, and we feel a fusion with the divine, it's kind of like being infected or inseminated with pure Eros. The feeling is indefinable, inexpressible, and it is a transcendent experience. So, if these are the qualities of your inner experience and your feeling, I would think that this is an indication that you have been overcome by Eros. The necessity of an intermediary or a "representative" of Eros seems high – indeed, as usual, the Greeks had a story for that – the birth of Aphrodite seems like it was absolutely necessary in order for Eros to be channelled, or focussed, if you will. We will see that Venus Aphrodite is our human way of experiencing Eros in a much more embodied, accessible form.

Still, though, your concern about Eros running amok is valid – we have all experienced times when our creative impetus set us racing down the "wrong" path, to spend time, money, love or energy on a fruitless – literally a nonproductive – quest. Sometimes it is necessary to do nothing, or the wrong thing, or simply to experience raw energy! And as for creation, nobody knows what came first. It always has something to do with a mysterious seed, a spontaneous emergence and a series of magical births.

With respect to relationships and love: Clearly there is a preverbal experience of belonging. There is some kind of precedent to our adult feelings of love and relationship. There is a deep, primordial knowledge that it is possible to bond and fuse with another – if not bodily, then spiritually. The desire to fuse completely with a loved one is very common and the undifferentiated longing for union is something psychologists call the prebirth experience or womb memory, and I'm sure that it is partially true. In fact, I'm positive that it is true and that is where the horoscope is very interesting, because if you look at Neptune as a symbol for the "cosmic womb", and you look at the Moon as the physical womb, the birth mother – in the relationship between the two bodies, you can often see how much and how deep is this longing to return to that space of transcendental experience where two hearts beat as one. The Moon and Neptune are good indicators of what that kind of undifferentiated erotic experience is about. It's about wanting to get into a space of absolute and complete participation with Nature, of total fusion with the source of life itself – the amniotic Eros. No wonder there is so much in modern (post-Freudian) psychology about mother complexes. I am sure we all have very serious mother complexes, without which we would never seek to create, love, or be anything at all!

However, I am equally certain that this longing is not just a womb experience. I have no formulated dogma about reincarnation, but there has to be something about the experience of the soul that's brought in here. There an innate drive toward cohesion and embodiment of intangibles – mental or spiritual. The ancients saw Eros as the divine expression of that attraction, cohesion, and formation of relationship – the interaction and balance of things. I mean, this mood of Eros is considered by the great philosopher, Plato, as a type of divine madness. There were four forms of madness, one of which he called erotic madness. And he says of this madness, "This is the best form of divine possession, both for the subject himself and for his associate (that is, his beloved), and it is when he is touched with this madness that the man whose love is aroused by the beauty in others is called a lover."[4]

Now, Plato didn't necessarily mean a lover in the sense we might take it today, but a lover was a person infused with Eros and therefore in his school of thought, a potential philosopher – the lover of wisdom. It's marvellous what these poor fellows had to do to desexualize their Erotic experience, but I'm inclined to think this myself: that an attack of Eros doesn't always bring about a desire, obviously, to read the classics or to write an opera or a good novel. However, conversely, a desire to embrace higher wisdom or truth is an attack of Eros. So he whole experience surrounding an Erotic attack is about wanting to transcend the physical world, and sometimes this is done through physical means. So, it's like being awakened by beauty – really, if we are suddenly impassioned by some observation, mood, or sensation of something terribly sublime, it usually does trigger off a high-level experience in the intellectual mind. In order to experience this sublime attack in the physical world, it usually means descending out of the ideal into the common, and when we get into Aphrodite's job, as it were, we'll see how she facilitates these different levels of experience.

But whether or not Eros promoted a higher state of consciousness and brought about ultimate peace and harmony to the soul, or drove a person mad, was entirely determined by the direction that the Erotic possession took. By the time we arrive at Plato's ideals and the Greek philosophers, culture is rapidly moving toward the concept of

---

[4]Plato, *Phaedrus,* trans. Walter Hamilton, Penguin Classics, 1973, para. 260, p. 56.

individual control and volition. The idea that we can do something about matters both worldly and divine, and not offend either man or God, preoccupied the Greeks. Plato believed that there were ideals of perfection that existed in an ethereal realm – perfect forms of all earthly reality, which existed in a plane beyond the mortal world. Now, that sounds quite astrological as well, because how often have you looked at a horoscope and thought, "Well, this is absolutely fantastic, this is beautiful, this is brilliant – if only I didn't have to interpret it!" In itself, the horoscope is the perfect statement. However, finding the words to articulate what it is that you are seeing is very difficult, and then we get caught up in all sorts of things like ego and all the differentiation of the intellect.

Eros – the creative source

We can't stay in Eros. We have to move toward separation, differentiation, articulation, until we get so split and subjective and compartmentalised that sometimes beauty is lost. So, I think that just contemplation of these visions of ideals is something that is less confusing to us on some very, very important level. But the ideal forms – Plato called them *archetupos,* the origin of "archetype", the first stamp, the imprimatur of the thing, whatever it is – are the contents of our own psychic chaos, waiting to be quickened by Eros and facilitated to birth by Aphrodite.

Whatever it is, in our world, whether it's the table (they go on and on in the dialogues about tables and what kind of tables and what did the first table look like and is this a close enough replica to the ideal table – it's really quite amusing) or anything else, what Plato was about was that anything that's down here, that we can deal with in the material world, is, basically, a cheap replication of the ideal form somewhere "up there", in the heavens. And, at all costs, preparation or the terminus of life, in other words death, required the contemplation of these higher things, the perfect forms. The love of wisdom, of philosophy was Eros in its highest state. In other words, falling in love with the Ideal could bring one closer to perfection, to truth and beauty and wisdom. This was a view largely based on the concept that everything incarnate or tangible was, at best, only a hopeful replication of the Ideal, and should be treated as such.

It was entirely possible that the possession by Eros could also lead one to some very sordid experiences. In Platonic terms, Eros was both a dark daemon, and an exaltation of the soul, but it took effort on the part of us and our consciousness to direct Eros' influences towards the higher experience of ideal love – that is, love of things intangible, like philosophy, Truth, Beauty, Wisdom and the Good. Therefore the love of a beautiful person, albeit in the eye of the beholder, should stimulate the lover to things higher – to things at a loftier level, rather than to descend into the bowels of primordial chaos. The fact is all life was inseminated by Eros – the desire to explore the higher realms or the desire to go deeply into the physical realm of the body – the same primal force powered both motivations. The power of Eros/love is shown by the fact that these philosophical issues were taken so seriously. They were very, very, serious concerns, and some of the greatest minds in our literary history have bothered themselves with these concepts, and worried about them, and have constantly tried to come to terms with passion, and love, and romance. It really is one of the most mysterious things.

In archaic times, they knew that the experience of things outside themselves were agencies of the gods – there was no question. There was no split between mind and body, psyche and soma – none. This state was what the French mythographers called *participation mystique,* wherein a symbiotic relationship with man and nature existed, and were in absolute and complete sympathy. These people knew, rather than believed, that the experience of the divine and the daemonic were the manor of the gods, and they took great care to respect episodes of possession by the gods, or states of *enthios,* where the god enters in to the body and takes possession. This is literally what *enthios* means – it's the root for enthusiastic – *enthusiasmos* means to be taken over and have the god enter you and you become one with the god. So, they believed that this possession or enthusiasm was considered to be a possession of the gods. By the way, passion, excitement, or any extreme state, especially in women, was legislated against around the late 1700's. It was against the law and you would be put into a madhouse if you expressed passion on any level, whether that was high-level excitement and joy and wonder or daemonic and dark melancholy. Whichever extreme you went through, it was considered evil, and it was part of being possessed.[5]

Maybe it is, maybe it is about being possessed by Eros. In the ancient world there was a kind of respect for madness, because in the course of an episode, it was assumed that the divine had entered the body through the soul. For instance, when Cassandra alighted from Agamemnon's chariot after he came home from Troy, the people were afraid because she was "god-filled" – an oracle. So, they were a little afraid of it, but very respectful of it, too, because they had to assume that this person was, by far and away, more made up of the god than themselves, and you don't fool around with that. They were respectful. The Erotic experience of being seized by a divine passion or creative "furore" is a form of benevolent, divine madness.

Clearly, Eros was a powerful figure. His capacity to seize and compel was highly regarded, and in cases of daemonic possession, to be feared beyond all other forces. A truly divine possession and erotic stimulation is an extremely high-level experience. It's what you do with it, I think, that really counts. Now, it is a form of madness, isn't it? Haven't we all been enthused with a sense of new creativity? I've got this project I mean to do, or a painting, or an idea, or a book, or a dress to make, or a bookshelf, or whatever it is that's going to be made. All creativity is preceded by a fantasy time about how it – whatever it is – is going to be so beautiful that people are going to be stunned and transformed when they look at it, or read it, or hear it, or experience the thing.

Is it ever really quite like that when it finally happens? That's what Plato worried about a lot. Why is it that, in my mind, everything is so fantastic, and then when I see it outside, it's really very ordinary? Maybe that's the problem of trying to translate Eros into the common form of life. Anyway, we are all subject to this form of madness. In a classical tragedy by Sophocles, *The Antigone,* the chorus, wails – they're always wailing about something – "Be

---

[5]Michael Foucault, Madness and Civilization, Vintage Books, Random House, 1965.

careful, it looks really bad out there, it's really awful and what are we going to do?" The chorus seems to act as the shadow, or more like the realists. Meanwhile, the play is carrying on, but you have the chorus droning on about how dreadful it is and how doomed the future will be. About Eros, the chorus says: "Love (Eros) unconquered in fight. Love who falls on our havings. Ye rest in the bloom of a girl's unwithered face. You cross the sea. You are known in the wildest lairs. Not the immortal gods can fly, nor men of the day. Who has you within him is mad. You twist the minds of the just, wrongly pursue, and are ruined."[6]

Well, all right, I suppose. How often have we heard somebody, if not our own selves, bemoan an attack from Eros? The many descriptions are as ageless as the classic play quoted above. "I don't know what's come over me... I can't seem to get a grip on myself... It's bigger than both of us... I couldn't help it... The devil, the god, the wind, made me do it..." I mean, those are pretty feeble explanations for anything! The more contemporary excuses commonly touted now are Fate or Karma – actually, they are older, but we hear a lot about them now. "We did this in a past life, so we must make it up in this one," and so forth. We've got all sorts of ways of explaining something that can't be explained. The explanations are flimsy, they're without content and they're totally irrational.

So, we're really no further along than the Greeks who claimed that one's wits were taken away by Zeus, or their minds mazed by Hermes, or in the throes of Aphrodite's curse whenever they did anything odd or extreme. They blamed the gods, perhaps rightly. We still want to talk like that – nothing's changed. Or has it? Citing Eros as the charismatic energy behind love isn't quite enough. I think we more clearly understand now that Eros is the main mover of elemental forces which need to be channelled through a medium. That's the problem that we have in translating the ideal, the divine, into the profane, moving from the sacred to the profane.

---

[6]Sophocles, *The Antigone,* trans. Elizabeth Wyckoff, *The Greek Tragedies, Vol. 1,* University of Chicago Press, 1960, Ln. 781-90.

How do we get from up there to down here? That medium may come, in fact, in the form of a goddess or a god, and it strikes me that because Eros was so quick to attend the birth of Aphrodite, we might as well say that it's Aphrodite and dispense with all argument. I'd be willing to do that because Venus is the representative in our horoscope that articulates complex issues which arise out of love and creation. Therefore it is the Goddess of Love, Aphrodite/Venus, who acts as the channel force or medium for the undifferentiated erotic experience.

So, let's say Eros is the prime motivator and moves through Aphrodite. Now, that still leaves us in a pretty big realm. What has Aphrodite the goddess got to do with me and my horoscope, for example? I might need to think about how my own natal Venus behaves and interacts with other planets in my chart, and how I could individualize and personalize a collective Ideal – an exalted, divine condition – and bring it into my imagination, my personality, and through into my life. So, we're really talking about various levels. Possibly, it wouldn't hurt to compartmentalise things a bit. So, we have the divine by inspired feeling, then the profane or worldly shape it needs to be embodied in, which, as we shall see, are both reflected in dual faces of Aphrodite/Venus.

Before delving into the aspects of love as we find them in the dual goddess, Aphrodite /Venus, let's carry on a little bit more about Eros. An artist, for example, in the throes of creative *angst,* at times might feel tortured, besieged, maddened, infuriated, with his or her craft – that is the difficulty of translating the ideal into the manifest. It makes perfect sense. At times it is absolute hell, I assure you, and at others sublime. Such tension is the stuff of life, however. Sculptors always say that they aren't doing anything but releasing a form imprisoned in rock. It preexists within the stone or marble. It's in there to be uncovered, so the sculptor chips away very carefully to release the figure from its prison. Painters say that they are the medium for the image, writers are cramped by the inadequacy of words and the limits of earthbound creativity, and so on. The message is: Art or creation is discovery – it's not design.

There's skill, expertise, and craft; now Aphrodite plays a role in that as well. You tend to think that there's something about Venus that makes things rather prettily, that has to do with craft. She was reduced to the Goddess of Art and Craft at one time, but it's better to have something very pretty rather than ugly and uncrafted, depending on your eye. So, the source of the creative energy itself is vast and raw, but its channel is quite narrow and refined – and the results are dependent on the mastery of the execution of Eros' will, which is Aphrodite's realm. So, these creative impulses are refined and personalised by Aphrodite/Venus, who is really the goddess of both love and aesthetics – all things appear to come from the origins of chaos through this pleroma or full void and then through Aphrodite in her higher form, Aphrodite/Urania. See how the hierarchy came into being:

CHAOS
EROS
GAIA
OURANOS
APHRODITE URANIA
APHRODITE PANDEMOS

So, we're constantly translating things from one level to another, to another, to another, until we get right down to the specific. It is highly productive to do some exercises on translating the ideal to the very specific, down to the real business of what you want to think about, feel, do or whatever. It's a good exercise to try and move things from that place "up there", where it's all perfect and you know that it's all luminous and shimmering with inspiration, and yet it's so exhausting to actually make it real. So, it's a good exercise – you can practise it on your own – it will put you in touch with your own source of creative inspiration. Make a list of the "ideals" in your heart or mind, and then across from the "ideal", put the "real" – in other words, that which actually happens in your experience of life.

Creativity, for example is not just the fine arts, it is not about being a painter, or the writer of arias, or elegant mathematical formulae, or anything like that. It's really about spontaneously generating yourself, giving birth to yourself – it's about not committing suicide when the going gets really tough. That's creative! That's the most basic creativity you can produce. Sometimes it's just about staying alive. That's when you get Eros in to say to him, "OK, cosmic attractor, everything's going to be fine. Just stay where you are and pretty soon I'll get that inspiration again and give birth to something new."

There's a lot to be said about creation which has very little to do with art. There's far too much stereotype overlaid on creativity. I think one of the great misdemeanours of articulation, separation, and differentiation, is to say that there are artists and there are scientists, for example. So it doesn't allow a scientist who feels intuitive and creative and floaty and irrational, to think magically – he or she is constrained by the dicta of scientific methodology. However, increasingly, we are allowing our scientists to merge with the magical world and experiment more freely. And, similarly, this divisive thinking does not allow the artists, for example, to be rational and logical.

Audience: I have never felt like a creative person. I have Venus in Capricorn in the 5th house, and I think the Saturn energy blocks my Venus energy.

Erin: Is Venus square to Neptune?

Audience: Yes, in fact, Venus is square the exact midpoint of Saturn/Neptune. They are in the 2nd house.

Erin: Based on that alone, there is a complex of relationships going on. Your Saturn/Neptune is disposited by Venus, and Venus and Saturn are in mutual reception, and Saturn is in Venus' house. This is an incestuous type of relationship in which all the planets are involved in a feedback loop. It is easy to see why you consider yourself uncreative. However, the configuration itself does not deny creativity, but hampers your ability to see what you do as creative! Creativity is a lifestyle, not a painting. It strikes me that your childhood (5th house) was emotionally malnutrient and dry – that your innate sense of value and worth was never acknowledged.

Possibly you were an "investment" of your parents, most likely your father, and expected to be just like them. It is difficult for you to see your playful side and recognize a talent because, though you may be talented, if it isn't reinforced by the parents and established in early life, then you would feed back that primal rejection and think it is you!

The 5th house Saturnian, Capricorn Venus is bound to think itself "noncreative" because of the status quo stereotype you have assimilated from your parental experience, and reinforced by our culture. Frankly, I think you could be terribly creative at solving problems – unravelling other people's vague and nebulous problems and sorting them out. When you are posed with a series of choices and confusion from a friend, do you find that you can see the picture very clearly and organize the friend into a better situation? Venus in Capricorn is creative in a practical way. Remember that Saturn is the midwife of Venus, and you are more likely to respond to creativity if it is real, that is, if you can find a practical outlet, a solution, a proper vehicle for creative thinking. This is a perfect resonance with Venus Pandemos – the earthy, practical, tangible manifestation. But is it also in aspect to Uranus? Isn't Uranus at the opposition point?

Audience: Yes, it is a T-square, and my Sun is in Aquarius.

Erin: So, there is a dramatic split between the Urania and Pandemos urges. You have both aspects of Venus very strongly configured. There is Saturn the realist, Neptune the romantic, and Uranus the elitist idealist! All honing your Venus in practical, and insecure, I might add, Capricorn. So, your imagination is fine, your romanticism is fine, it's self-acceptance that is taking a bit longer to develop. Now that you see this aspect alive in your chart, can you bring it to a better perspective within your self? Can you not see that, when you are faced with a complex set of problems, you can figure them out better than anyone else? And management is terribly creative if you use your innovative mind and stop thinking of yourself as suffering under the Saturnian yoke of inadequacy.

All the agencies are there: creativity, innovation, imagination, and practical awareness of your boundaries and limits. Success can come from this. You don't have to be burning with fire to create or be creative, nor do you have to be up in the aethers, nor swimming around, awash in feeling. There are not always lightning bolts and burning bushes with every revelation – the ones that last are the ones which creep slowly to the fore and have substance.

We really need to rethink creativity. At any rate, all of these things that we are talking about are bound up in the same impulse. The force that drives individuals to bond and merge in meaningful ways in relationships, is the very same impulse that urges individuals to create.

This whole business of being creative and experiencing creation has to do with the erotic force underlying the impulse to stay alive, to live – to have *libido,* life-force. Both creation and procreation are motivated by Eros. We may not realise it, but when we love a subject, when we love something like an idea, or an activity or project, or a learning experience, we too invoke Eros. Eros turns us on, it stimulates us and inseminates us with the need to know, to understand and learn. So far, I've not mentioned sexuality, but the fact is that though sex is about erotica, erotica is not about sex. It's so incredibly important to realise that the idea of functioning in an erotic world is so different to the one that we're usually taught – at least, the world that I was taught. We weren't taught about Eros and education, we weren't taught that there was something that could be done with these feelings, these longings to merge and fuse and bond, other than find a relationship. Fortunately, times have changed, but people haven't and it takes generations to wash out a stereotype.

There is a lot of inconsistency in myth, because it is atemporal. For example, there are variants on the Eros myths – one of which says that Eros was born first, and that's the one I just gave you. It's the oldest. One which was developed much later, has Eros as a son of Aphrodite (which means that somehow we evolve archetypes through cultural imperatives). You may get wind of this if you do a broad spectrum of myth-reading, because there are sources for Aphrodite giving birth to Eros herself. That's fine, I don't mind that – it's a nice picture. Another variant has Aphrodite and Zeus as parents to Eros. Yet another, that's not as common, says Eros is the son of

Aphrodite and Ares. Now, that's nice, too, that makes a lot of sense, but again, it's very frail. Myself, I think the oldest story, the one found in Hesiod's *Theogony,* is a much more resonant myth – that is, Eros being first to arrive as the cosmogonic life-force, and from thence the quickening of the elemental and natural forces.

Now, before I go into the origins of Aphrodite, I thought it might be a good idea if we talked a bit about what I've been saying. What do you think about all that – about the impulse and origin? Does it strike anybody as something they might have experienced or felt themselves? Divine inspiration?

Audience: It sounds like our Aphrodite – or Venus – doesn't know that Eros exists, or if she does, that it is somehow 'outside', or beyond, or has to do with someone or something outside one's own self. Until a creative urge is actually manifested, would we know about the function of Aphrodite as the medium for this raw energy? It seems to me that Aphrodite is more interested in sensuality than in spirituality. Venus in the chart is usually focussed on relationships, or money, or the more physical, sensual aspect of our nature. This adds a new dimension to Venus – where values are not just learned, acquired and paid lip service to, but are lived in all aspects of our lives – that our product, if you will, is the measure of our values.

Erin: Actually, that's a really good observation. Eros is bigger than Aphrodite, and perhaps isn't recognised as an entity or agency, whereas Aphrodite is more quickly latched onto, hence the generally received view of Venus in the horoscope being representative of only that which is common, or manifest. But she has two distinct sides, as we shall find out in a minute. There is a factor of Eros that is akin to electricity, raw energy. To have an electrical wire just hanging out is rather dangerous, so instead they're all nicely woven together and covered with plastic with a little cap on and proper connectors, male and female connectors. You plug it into the wall and the electric impulse flows into the appliance, otherwise you're dead. It is sort of like that. It's like the power of the original force that has to have, in the terms of electricity, its pulse stepped down. So, you step it down and bring it into control.

Living in different parts of the world demonstrates this voltage simile. If you go over to North America, it's 120 volts, here it's 220, so you blow out your machinery if you don't have the right transformer. So, it's really like Aphrodite acting as a transformer for a very highly charged, very powerful, potentially deadly energy. The force is completely amoral, it has nothing to do with anything except creation. And running amok, it can create havoc. It does in the form of erotic possession, where there isn't a nice, safe, well insulated conduit that's well attached to the source of the power and has the proper instrument for being used.

Erotomania

We do have erotic possession. I watched a Channel 4 production on what they now call erotomania, which is the phenomenon of "stalking". They are just beginning to think about legislating it in England, and in the U.S. they've formed an entire force around this business of stalking. Its source is the great number of superstars that exist in North America, and the fact that some of their fans are so obsessed that they will spend their whole lives stalking them, knowing everything about them, living their lives, appearing all the time, and, as in the case of John Lennon, killing them. This is very dangerous. When somebody is seized by erotic possession – one of Plato's divine madnesses – and is incapable of containing it, he or she has become so infused with this super-high charge of Eros that all boundaries between unconscious and conscious dissolve and the person becomes completely mad.

Another example of erotic madness is Van Gogh. His was a form of erotic madness, not because he cut off his ear and sent it to a woman, but because it was in his artistic soul to go mad from the creation impulse. He was so involved, so possessed, and lacked such poor insulation and control, that the conduit wasn't very strong. So when he was filled with the sense of creative desire, he began to lose all contact with reality as we need it in order to function in a socially organised world. He was, in fact, a sufferer of erotic madness. Nothing to do with the woman, it had to do with creation. So, the cutting off of his ear was the terrible anger that would come into him because couldn't create properly. Perfection could not be met. You could watch his work, from the beginning of his career to the end, become more and more amazing, as far as I am concerned. He just got further and further out, and much more in touch with the cosmos than the sunflowers. In "Starry Night", you can see Van Gogh's return to Eros, his return from sanity – the "profane" ability to render a cosmic, erotic image into a beautiful painting which does not give you the feeling of madness when you look at it. However, this is where he rose (or fell) into full possession by Eros, and became mad.

Sometimes love destroys. It's mysterious and if we look at Venus in a composite chart or in synastry, we might get a bit of a hint of what it is about that particular love that destroys. Sometimes the act of falling in love causes one to lose one's sense of self and identity and sense of wholeness. Ego identification and articulation of self, and differentiation from "the other", are in fact impeded by love. That's erotomania. It's a phase, a really pleasurable phase in love, and, in fact, people who are in long-term relationships go through periods of it. They look back, say they've been married for thirty years, and say, "Do you remember 1956, that was when I completely lost all sense of my identity, and you were the one that was in control, and it was awful!" And you can go through phases. Those who have, say, sequential relationships, in which there is a full circle over a period of three, four, five years, maybe, will also recognize the stage of loss of identity. It's absolutely necessary in the formation and reformation stages of romance.

But it can be dangerous, and that is also possession by Eros. The feelings are not differentiated, the force does not become creative, you do not paint great paintings, you do not think philosophy. You think about the other, all the time. And that is obsession. And you fall apart. You lack identity and lose your shape, you become cosmic chaos. You see, in one sense it would be great if we could just lie around and think about the beloved all the time and be fed by tubes, and people would talk quietly as they tiptoed around the room. But not very often and not very likely are you going to be hospitalised for this and looked after. Your beloved is going to yell at you to stop it, and there's going to be a lot of articulation and differentiation that emerges out of strife.

The birth of Aphrodite is the product of a terrible split, a very big strife. And so, there's always something about love, in its pure, unadulterated, undifferentiated and unchannelled form, that is potentially dangerous. You do not hold onto a hot wire, it's just commonsense. But, we're attracted to it – very attracted. There's something about walking by a wire that doesn't have an end on it, and thinking, "I wonder if it's hot." Once, I went with my younger daughter, who's very adventurous, and her boyfriend, or husband now, to Stonehenge, and I have a set of four pictures – amazing photographs, because they are click, click, click, click – a sequence that describes the seductiveness of danger beautifully.

We were really bored, so we were sitting around, smoking cigarettes and sitting by this fence. How many of you have been to Stonehenge? OK. There's a whole flock of sheep on one side of this fence that surrounds the megaliths, and we were sitting next to it. A small child ran up to the fence and touched it and yelled and ran away. Aha, it's an electric fence. And so we all looked at each other, and I said, "Right, we'll touch it and see what it's like." And it was really funny, because Ralf, Yesca's husband, wouldn't do it! Then, he said he would do it if we did. Anyway, I did it and it was quite intense, actually. It was a very brief, but highly effective shock, which affects the joints. Then I took the sequence of photos of my daughter touching it. The first was a picture of her reaching out, nervously, then I got a picture of her with her hand, fingers, actually squeezing it, and her face is all alight, she is yelling and her hair standing on end; and then another picture as she pulls away. The fourth shot shows her collapsed in a heap, laughing on the ground. We were just in stitches – we couldn't resist it.

But it's impossible, if you have any sense of adventure at all, not to do something like that. I mean, what does it feel like? You want to do something like that, to get very close to danger. Nobody wants to die, but everybody wants to know what it's like. That's why we like to go for the dangerous thing – the thing that gives us the greatest charge, that really excites our senses. It could be racing car driving, it could be mountain climbing, it could be skiing along the crest of an avalanche (which is not usually very successful), it could be surfing. In the case of people who are introverted and less physical, it could be thinking. Thinking will take you to the edge as well. Little children like to repeat words over and over again that make them lose their knowledge of the meaning. People do play mind games that take them right out to the edge of knowledge, where they don't know anything any more. You can do it through chanting, you can do it through all sorts of ways to take yourself to the edge and lose it. It's all part of Eros.

That takes us right back – not to chaos, because chaos is complete and total absorption into the undifferentiated chasm of the unconscious. I don't know how one comes back from that one. That really is like slipping right over the event horizon into the black hole. You can go into erotic seizure, into possession, and come out of it. It's nice if it can be channelled. Sometimes pain will produce great art, sometimes loss or longing. When we talk about projection, sometimes we can have a beloved who doesn't even know we exist. But it's a great hook for creativity, like Dante's Beatrice. He never spoke to the girl, and the vision of her on the bridge was enough to write *Heaven, Hell* and *Purgatory!* So you know that much about that type of erotic possession. I have to say, if we want to experience a very high charge, and we allow it to take place, that's where it's coming from, and it does stimulate and create everything. It's the source of all creation.

Audience: Eros sounds like an outer planet, as if the forces of the unconscious, or the "beyond" consciousness, are involved in some way. I have noticed that people who have Venus in aspect – strong aspects, especially conjunctions, squares and oppositions – to Uranus, Neptune or Pluto, are more inclined to the extremes of the experiences you are describing. Could it be that they are more inclined to Eros in its raw form?

Erin: Well, sort of. Your observations are correct in that Venus and the outer planets have a communication link which can give them a greater range of expression of Eros – one which goes outside the realm of the mundane. Venus is more connected to the cosmic level of relating – imagination, romanticism, deep and hidden feeling levels – when it is in aspect to Uranus, Neptune or Pluto. You'll find that most people have several aspects from Venus to other planets, and very often to the outers as well. Venus needs more grounding when it is only aspecting an outer planet. A level of excitation exists with Venus/outer planet links that stimulates highly individualistic ways of experiencing Eros.

When I delineate the aspects of love, of Venus and the other planets, we will see how profoundly true that is. The power of the outer planets in connection with Venus produces some of the most divine and the most daemonic of cosmic attractions. There's a relationship between the stepping down of an archetype into a stereotype, and the common explanation for the outer planets is that they cannot be accessed or used, if you will, except through the medium of the inner planets. As you get older the outer planets become increasingly more personal, so that there is a shift in midlife, of the concept of the outer planets and how they are experienced. You mature into them. The Uranus half-cycle is the astrological demarcation of the advent of midlife. It occurs somewhere between thirty-seven and forty-two, depending on the generation.

That's the first step of conscious awakening to the unlived life. So you do wake up. Then, Neptune comes next, and then Pluto. Pluto is last – sometimes never. Some people never, ever wake up to Pluto power. They are possessed by it, as opposed to using it – the same as Eros, the same kind of perfect analogy.

Audience: So, the difficulty in expressing the realm beyond Saturn, the realm of imagination and unconscious, has another connotation? And the frustration of the outer planets results in a lot of *angst* and crisis and emergency? Could Venus not play a role in mediating or alleviating that existential anxiety?

Erin: Indeed, that's why the outer planets can be so frustrating, because what is brilliance and inspiration and original thought without it being manifest in some way? We all know people who are fabulously talented and brilliant, yet cannot manifest or render their brilliance and inspiration into a tangible medium. Therefore, we might look to Venus to see how idealism can be made into realism. The creation of the "higher octaves" in esoteric astrology tells us something significant about inner planets mediating the powers of outer planets. For instance, Neptune is the higher octave of Venus, and there is a very strong connection between Venus and the idealism of Neptune, but Venus has a strong relationship to Uranus, as well, considering that Ouranos, the sky, was her father. And Venus' relationship with Pluto is terribly seductive, compelling and erotic.

The birth of Aphrodite Urania

Now we will talk a bit about Aphrodite, the different myths, and how she has eternally affected artists, writers, poets, and so forth. She has been, and remains, the inspiratrix of artists and writers and philosophers and poets, great thinkers, as well as the everyday person. The birth of Aphrodite is an extremely emotive tale; it's actually quite horrific when you think of the implications within the myth. However, poets, and artists and lovers and creators all still praise the gifts of Aphrodite – the Goddess of Love, Patroness of the Arts, and the Creator of Aesthetics. And yet the birth which is reiterated in Hesiod's *Theogony* is filled with violence and blood-guilt and power struggles. The irony of the violent birth of the Goddess of Love isn't actually lost when we come to appreciate fully the complex relationship between conflict and creation, conflict and creativity, conflict and love, Eris (strife) and Eros (love).

To continue on from where we left off with the myth: After Chaos had created Gaia and her siblings, she brought forth her own consort. She was lonely, so she created Ouranos to surround and contain her – the Heavens. One assumes, perhaps, that this was assisted by Eros – but that's only my imagination, because in the poem, it actually says, "without love". Hesiod says, "And Earth bore Starry Heaven first to be an equal to herself, to cover her all over and to be a resting place, always secure for all the blessed gods.[7]

---

[7]Hesiod, *Theogony,* trans. Dorothea Wender, Penguin, London, 1973, ln. 127.

And so there was an equality and a deeply bonded relationship between Heaven and Earth. It's the most wonderful way of expressing the complete participation between the things that are above and the things that are below, and there is no separation between them. One imagines their union as essentially the ultimate alliance between opposites, the collaboration of the abstract and the concrete, the ephemeral and the temporal, Sky and Earth.

The intimate association of Heaven and Earth embodies the primal relationship, the absolute, basic, fundamental, archetypal relationship. It is an archetype which has served over aeons to symbolize the ideals of love and creative manifestation. The two of them bore many children. It was pretty random at first, a sort of chaotic, haphazard attempt at procreation which produced all sorts of bizarre kinds of creatures. According to myth, they were primarily anthropomorphic representations of psyche and nature, like the winds and the hills and memory, and things like that. It was a way of creating order out of chaos, if you will, by storytellers. But the most significant and humanoid of the offspring were the Titans, the youngest of whom was Kronos, good old Saturn – one of my favourites. He was to play the greatest single role in the evolution of the Greek theocracy. In *Saturn in Transit,* I dwell on this very heavily, so to speak.[8] His fateful birth began the turn of the wheel towards the inevitable arrival of Aphrodite.

After the birth of the Titans, there were the Cyclopes, three creatures with a single eye in the middle of their foreheads, and some really wild guys – the Hekatonchires, which simply means they had fifty heads and one hundred hands apiece. Now, these were so frightening and horrible that Ouranos refused their birth. He did not want to see them. They were completely and absolutely *persona non grata* – he did not like the way they looked, he did not want to have them around, they were not beautiful. They were something gross, ugly, primitive, and frightening, and so he repressed them in the womb of the Earth. These monsters represent our uncivilized aspects, part of

---

[8]Erin Sullivan, *Saturn in Transit: Boundaries of Mind, Body and Soul,* Arkana, Contemporary Astrology Series, Penguin, London, 1991, *passim.*

our own self which remains hidden, buried or unborn and thus, threatening in its primitiveness.

Gaia, like any normal woman after her term has passed, is desperate to give birth to these offspring. It's dreadfully uncomfortable for her, and, in the poem, Hesiod writes, "But she, vast Earth, being strained and stretched inside her, groaned, and then she thought of a clever, evil plan. Quickly she made grey adamant and formed a mighty sickle and addressed her sons." Essentially, what she did was to propose a plan to all of the sons, of whom only "...crooked Kronos, growing bold..." was fearless enough, and very likely ambitious enough, to agree to it.[9]

And, what happened was this: She placed in his hand a sickle, an attribute which he is known for today. This sickle plays a very important role in something that today we can very easily relate to. Having given this awful tool, she then lures Ouranos into a loving compromise, and, "...Unsuspecting Ouranos, longing for love, lay round the Earth." And at that moment Kronos reaches up and castrates him. The result is that the blood from the castration falls upon the Earth and the semen into the Sea of Cyprus, which quickens and spontaneously produces Aphrodite. And so she is a parthenogenic birth, like Athena, who springs full-born from the head of her father.

Aphrodite is spawned from Ouranos' semen and the Sea of Cyprus. She has no parents. That she is midwived by Saturn I find quite revealing. Saturn is the planet which can embody the ineffable and magical imagination and bring it to the world of the real. Saturn is the midwife of creativity, and through his harsh and patricidal act, brought Aphrodite or Venus into the real realm, to the world of form where we have tangible things. In creating the horizon and splitting the world parents, he brought to life the forces of love and creativity – as well as fury and retribution in the form of the Erinyes, the Furies, Aphrodite's triplet sisters – who, later in culture, become "internalised" as our conscience, our moral avengers.

---

[9]Hesiod, *Theogony, op. cit.*, In. 169.

Earlier, in the front, you were saying about how Uranus, Neptune and Pluto are somewhat analogous to the concept of Eros in that you can't do anything with them unless you work very hard and you bring them into the realm inside Saturn's orbit. Well, Saturn is the boundary, isn't it? The boundary between us and the world; our skin; the boundary of consciousness between the inner and outer planets; and the boundary of our experience of ourselves relative to that which is outside ourselves. It is Saturn who created the horizon which divides above and below and is a symbolic image for the conscious and the unconscious, the personal and the collective, and so forth.

Too, when that act was complete, Saturn created and ruled the Golden Age. He split time, he became the chronocrator when he permanently severed Heaven and Earth. Saturn's time was finite, whereas the "time" before him was infinite into the past, and the time after the ending of the Golden Age has continued on. Kronos is the originator of the split we now blame Descartes for! The archetype of the separation of nature and culture (earth and heaven) existed long before Descartes said, "I think, therefore I am." Opposites must exist before they can be unified. Indeed, an opposition is a split conjunction, in astrological language.

In fact, the whole aspect of relationship is one that we have to conceive of as the union of opposites, because there was no conscious awareness of such a thing as an "opposite until this main event. The main event produces Aphrodite, but it also produces the Furies (and we'll get into this a bit later). About Aphrodite's birth, Hesiod says, "...The genitals, cut off with adamant and thrown from land into the stormy sea, were carried for a long time on the waves. White foam surrounded the immortal flesh and in it grew a girl. At first, it touched on holy Cythera and from there, it came to Cyprus, circled by the waves, and there the goddess came forth."[10]

So, it's interesting that we should have someone as sinister as Kronos as the midwife of the Goddess of Love. But it also is this recollection, if we have a recollection of mythological time, of an origin that is much deeper than the separation from the mother and the severing of

---

[10]*Ibid.*, Ln. 190 ff.

the umbilicus. It goes way beyond birth, there's something bigger going on. It's not just about being expelled from the womb and severed from the mother and stuffed into a nappy, and a little blanket and then, forever after, longing to get back into the safety of the dark, nurturing womb. There's something much bigger going on, and I think that the archetypal severing is part of what it is that has required that we rationalise and find ways of explaining the longing to unite and to get back to absolute relationship with all things. But as human beings, it usually has to do with getting together with another person and having and sharing something.

Love and strife

This sort of archetypal divorce, or split of Heaven and Earth, is something that we all suffer from terribly, in a collective sense, because we are aware of it environmentally. We're aware of it psychologically and politically, but it also affects us in our personal, individuated psychology, in our longing for relationship and our unwillingness sometimes to accept relationship for what it is. Often we are in the "I thought it was going to be like this," or "Why isn't it like that?" or "Why are we doing this?" state of mind. It's pretty normal behaviour. But it also helps if we can realise that there are major precedents in the past, long back in archaic memory.

Of course, once born, we are the embodiment of all that ever was, so clearly we carry deep in some cellular memory this experience of split or separation or loss of participation with nature. We long for it to heal. This feeling of sadness and loss is so very easily translated into a relationship, and it might make it a bit easier on you or your client or me to understand that this is quite normal if acknowledged as an archetypal state of being. You are not human if you don't experience it. That's the problem with mortality – we're incomplete, we're always wanting something more – until you die, you'll want it. And that's life, and maybe because there have been so many separations and splits and evolutions and civilizations that have taken place, it makes sense that we should feel uncomfortable and unhappy all by our little selves.

But, there is a way of repolarizing and internalising, I think, because, buried very deeply in this grisly tale is a very cruel truth: that Venus was born out of strife and out of the irrevocable split of Heaven and Earth. The concept of Romantic Love as we know it today originates in the primal fantasy of fusion between opposites, which automatically implies that there is a self and there is an other. So, obviously, if that's the case, then we must always want to be with the other, whatever that is. I think it has a lot to do with basic, fundamental relationship anxiety – this archetypal castration, if you will. I suppose, if you want to bring it into a Freudian framework, it has a lot to do with a male anxiety about castration, or loss of male power in the union with the female, and also the idea that woman can possess or deny man. So, the relationship anxiety is always there on some level.

Also, I think that we can look at it on the dark side, on the negative level. We mortals have been split off and severed from the ideal world of the gods, heaven – which, by the way, is considered to be masculine – and then trapped on Earth, which is considered to be feminine!

However, another way of looking at this split is that Heaven "released" Earth, that there was something about the release of nature from the ideals of the Uranian world that meant it was possible to begin to manifest creativity in a practical way. We actually began to take form, and the form of civilisation – in other words, the evolution, creation and development of people and creativity – actually began at that point. As long as there is fusion, then there is no differentiation. As soon as you get differentiation, you get the possibility of creation.

On one hand, we can say, "Oh gosh, isn't it horrible that mummy and daddy are now forever split," and we're going to always be anxious about our parents dying or getting a divorce, or us not having a perfect relationship. You can also say that there is some kind of benefit here,. In the separation of the two things, we are actually allowed to have both worlds – we can live in the ideal world and translate it into the practical world. This is a lot more fun, but it does help explain something which is uncomfortable, and in fact has been written off as plain old neurosis. I'm not quite sure that I can accept it as simply neurosis.

The genesis of the goddess who rules equally over the sacred and the profane, Aphrodite, can at will strike one's heart with either despair or elation. This whole feeling of despair and elation occurs in that primordial castration, the severing of the archetypal father from the archetypal mother. That is a natural split. That we believe that Love will unite Heaven and Earth again, and heal the archetypal wound of elemental separation of the great mother and the great father, is the foundation of the artist's and the lover's eternal plea.

So, it does serve in a positive way, this longing to get back to nature or to get up into the heavens. It serves because it stimulates a tremendous creative force. Even in translation, Hesiod's poem reveals a real, stark power. It's a very brutal and transparent illustration of pretty basic motives and elemental forces in our nature. But it provides very fertile material for modern psychology. I guess Freud was the first physician-psychologist who began to employ the idea that myth had something to do with our current life. Joseph Campbell brought the world of myth to our modern world via the televised programs called *The Power of Myth*. And, of course, Jung developed myth, fairy tales and archetypes to the stage that new ideas are constantly emerging. Marie-Louise Von Franz' treatment of origin myths across cultures and their function in creativity is unparalleled in her book, *Creation Myths*.[11]

We have reclaimed some of our lost sources by doing that, and now that astrology is embracing its origins in myth, too, it helps to bring that into better focus. But I think that these are horrific tales – I mean, they really are something, if you read consistently in all the myths, just awful. The Hindu myths are equally amazing, with beheadings, arm severings, and all sorts of dreadful things going on; and as for the Greeks, it's just a constant round of shape-shifting, eating children or sleeping with one's mother, or poking out one's eyes. It is filled with fantastic goings on, but myth acts in the oldest

---

[11] Von Franz, *Creation Myths, op. cit.*

sense of the word as a catharsis, and it was another way of curing an illness – to experience *katharsis*, which means purge.

That was Aristotle's thesis. If one is obsessed, out of balance, then one could experience catharsis by vicariously experiencing the reenactment of something archetypal and mythological. I think that the repression of the horror and the shock factor of myth, which we don't like to acknowledge today, has resulted in its mass irruption into the collective consciousness as horrific crimes against humanity. There have always been horrific crimes against humanity, but it is now pandemic. We don't like nasty myths or Black Forest fairy tales anymore, but men are shooting children in their schoolrooms.

The Greeks used myths and heroic sagas for their cathartic qualities. They employed it later in the fifth century, using the stories boldly and with profound insight and sensitivity in the highly psychologically sophisticated tragedies – trilogies of plays enacted annually in the Theatre Dionysos. It's something that we can bemoan today because we collectively only think of Venus, for example, as the beautiful Botticelli painting of her emerging from the waves, riding to shore on a half-shell. Eros has since degenerated into the simpering Cupid figure on Hallmark gift cards – that's all we commonly have in the form of myth.

There are no Valentine cards with depictions of the great castration taking place, and the birth of Aphrodite. There's a whole market out there for anybody who wants to be seized by it – you could do a whole series of really gory, Greek greeting cards from the ancient world. "Have a nice day!" I think we're all too sunny. But I do my workshop on the shadow and have lots of fun with that as well.

[Great roars of laughter and pandemonium for several minutes – people in the audience acting out the myth and generally behaving as if in a Monty Python production.]

Oh, that seems to have struck a chord!

Something both terrible and wonderful has been lost in all of that, hasn't it? Maybe that's why people act it out much more frequently in the collective now. Maybe that's why we have dreadful mass killings and dreadful crimes. I think the start of cinematic cathartic horror was the House of Hammer horror movies. They were great because, although they were really scary, they were ludicrous as well. They were very Greek because they were so dramatic and so ridiculous, with their masks and noises and creatures that creep (you could even see the seams and things they wound them up with – it was great theatre). The problem is that we now have virtual reality. And, it is as if we are heading back into *participation mystique*, without any real redeeming feature when it comes into the reality of fear.

There is no mystique in the participation. It's no longer cathartic, it actually seeps into the brain and we lose contact with the separation, that necessary separation, between myth and daily life. That could be dangerous – the fact that the mass media has seized upon the cathartic qualities. Rather than sequestering it in a ritual *temenos* – a kind of secular sacred space – it is now fed to us as daily life activities. This has a very different psychological effect, a kind of narcotising effect, where we become increasingly desensitised to the sordid and dark side of the psyche.

Alfred Hitchcock was very conscious of the cathartic function of film; he was very Aristotelian. He was really the founder of the psychological thriller movie, and his whole thesis was, "Look, you get a bunch of people in the theatre, they watch really scary things, it takes care of a whole aspect of their nature, they go home and it's fine." I think that's really true, we go to the theatre to do that, and certainly, in the ancient times of the Theatre Dionysos, that was what it was about. Now I think it's over, but last week I saw Diana Rigg play *Medea* at Wyndhams in the West End. It was an absolutely amazing production. The set was terrifying – it took care of the lot for me. I've seen *Medea* several times, produced in as many ways, but that was the best.

How many people have watched *Maharabhat* – that amazing, mythical carry-on of India? I had just arrived in London, and it was early in 1990 and I was writing Saturn – or, rather, actively not writing it – and I turned on the television to break the difficulty of writing block. Just as the screen resolved, this colourfully dressed woman lay back, and gave birth to this huge stone. I thought, "OK, I can't get away from this – I run away and there it is." I sat there in amazement for ages, watching this huge stone roll down with everybody running after it – it was perfect.

In my mind, there's no split between myth and reality, because wherever you go, there it is. You think, "How does this pertain to me?" Obviously, it pertains, because if we've lost something, we've also gained something from it. It's quite interesting here, because we're talking about the birth of Aphrodite. In the continuation of this poem of Hesiod's, he says, "...Her name is Aphrodite among men and gods because she grew up in the foam [*aphros* means foam in Greek – she is 'foam-born']. Eros is her companion. Fair desire followed her from the first, both at her birth and when she joined the company of the gods. From the beginning, both among gods and men, she had this honour and received this power. Fond murmuring of girls and smiles and tricks and sweet delight and friendliness and charm."[12]

Now, I write that off as pure Greek misogyny – that's ridiculous. It may be a classic, but I can't accept that that was all that Aphrodite was good for, for women to doll themselves up with beautiful jewellery and trick men into behaving badly and distract them from their philosophical pursuits, which is basically what they were saying.

Audience: But were not the women better educated? I read somewhere that concubines were polymaths and were hired to teach the children and to accompany the men to functions, engaging them in high-level conversations and generally being their equals if not their actual superiors.

Erin: Yes, very true. Generally the women in the ancient world were confined to the *oikos* – the household – and the running of the immediate and extended family, but a special group of women existed called Hetairai. The essential thing about the Hetairai is that they were often better educated than the men – it's true. The Hetairai

---

[12]Hesiod, *Theogony, op. cit.,* Ln. 205.

were generally not Athenian citizens, and were often slaves or freed women. They were absolutely necessary for the education and civilisation of men, and they were often teachers in the ancient world – the meaning of Hetairai is virtually untranslatable in our cultural language. The word "concubine" has an entirely different connotation. Perhaps the Japanese Geisha would be a bit closer, as they were trained in many skills as well.

The dual goddess: Urania and Pandemos

Attributes, characteristics, realms and domains assigned to various gods and goddesses became what the Greeks called epithets. One of the most powerful and feared epithets of Aphrodite was *Peitho*. (I'm going to put it on the board, it's a really good word.) Peitho was the goddess of persuasion – it is not persuasion in the sense we might use it today, but instead, was perceived as a deadly weapon, employed to seize the mind and body in a persuasive clutch of passion and suffering. Her capacity to trick and charm is not seen in a good light, in this way. It is considered to be a quite unwelcome tactic, especially if one is in search of more lofty intents.

In Fragment 90 of Sappho's poems, she writes:

> Persuasion is Aphrodite's daughter;
> It is she who beguiles
> Our mortal hearts.[13]

As we will see in the course of the day, Aphrodite's wiles are pretty diverse and manifold.

Several methods of measuring the power and strength of a god or goddess, or any kind of deity in ancient times, are used. For example, how many cults were formed based on the god's or goddess' realms and epithets; looking at the different ways of worshipping; and how

---

[13] Sappho, *Poems and Fragments,* trans. Josephine Balmer, Bloodaxe Books, Newcastle-upon-Tyne, 1992, p. 72.

the people's sacrifice rituals were enacted. All these things are looked at through history to find out how important is this god. If one was propitiating an earth goddess, the Furies, for example, one would kill a black calf and sacrifice it on a low altar, which would allow the sacrificial blood to flow onto the earth; whereas if one were sacrifice to a sky god, like Zeus, the altar would be lofty, the calf white, and the blood would flow onto a dais under the altar, never touching the earth. Then the thigh bones would be burned, so that white smoke would rise up to the heavens. The rituals were very specific, highly structured. If one was not specific, the propitiation would go unrecognized by the particular god or goddess. Someone once said that gods were like dogs – they only answer to their own name.

One thing that is deeply revealing is that there is no indication of cults, sites or rituals for the worship of Ouranos – nothing. This is because he's not personified or anthropomorphized as other gods are. Ouranos is an abstract concept; it's "the heavens". It's not particular and individualized, but is general and collective. Another one is Hades. There's no image of Hades anywhere, no specific cults, or centres of worship. There are many death-cults, but there are no Hades cults. But then, the name itself, Hades, literally means "unseen". He is described as having a mask. But we don't see that.

Aphrodite, however, has many cults, followings, propitiation rites and so forth. She was a highly individual goddess with many functions, and her worship extended throughout the Mediterranean world.[14] Although there are no true parallels to the Greek Goddess of Love, there are predecessors from Asia and the north and Mediterranean regions. However, down from the oral tradition in ancient Greece, it seems that Aphrodite is the oldest of the Greek divinities in the conventional pantheon. The birth of the others came later, in the Golden Age of Kronos, or after, as in the case of Athene, who "sprung full-born from the head of her father, Zeus." Aphrodite, too, was born independent of the conventional union of male and female; she's more associated with her father, Ouranos, than with her

---

[14]Ronnie Gale Dreyer, *Venus: The Evolution of the Goddess and Her Planet*, Aquarian Press, HarperCollins, San Francisco, 1994. For a history of the goddesses associated with the development of the Greek Aphrodite and the astrological Venus, this book is excellent.

sea-mother. In this guise, Aphrodite is actually known as Aphrodite Urania, or Heavenly Aphrodite.

However, there is a later story – that she was born from Zeus and Dione, which is the female form of Dios (god). Homer had heard this tale, as it does emerge in his poems. He has Aphrodite as the daughter of Zeus and Dione. This tale is a more orthodox arrangement than incredible stories of castrations and splits of Heaven and Earth and semen and foam and blood and all of that. She was simply born from the union of a male and a female, who produced a divine goddess whom the ancients call Aphrodite Pandemos. This is a later myth and probably necessary in accord with cultural developmental needs. In fact, her transformation from the sexual goddess of love in the Greek world to Venus Genetrix in the Roman culture – the goddess of fertility and the mother of Aeneas, founder of Rome – is the result of this
myth.

As we'll see, it's significant that this secondary myth unveiled her role as a dual goddess, as she does govern dual images of love and creation. Imbued in all levels of our human experience to date, is the concept of higher and lower, or the sacred and the profane, and as a child of the male and the female, she was therefore very effective in yet another type of translation of erotic experience. So, we have Eros, and we have Venus, who performs two functions.

One, as Urania, is "sacred", and the other, as Pandemos, is "profane". Thus we have the two archetypes of Urania and Pandemos, which satisfy these two levels of experience, Heavenly and Earthly. Pandemos simply means "of the people", "across all the people", "throughout the people" – *pan demos*. This is the dual goddess image – one with a divine visage, even frightening at times, and the other, though still immortal and omnipotent, more human-faced, dedicated to mortal pleasures and human creativity.

The Greeks had a wary respect for Aphrodite. Her powers were generally acknowledged to be equal to those of Zeus – and he was the head of the Olympians. However, she'd been forced, by Zeus – I think out of convention – to marry, which was not her natural

Venus and Jupiter

inclination, as we'll see. The marriage of Aphrodite and Hephaistos – the Roman Vulcan – symbolises a much more earthy side to her nature, the Pandemos side of Aphrodite. Hephaistos was a fully accredited Olympian, a son of Hera. His father is apparently Zeus, himself, but in Hesiod he is a son of Hera only.

Hera was so ashamed of him, she had him cast from heaven, and he was caught, fortunately, by Thetis, who raised him for nine years. He was a brilliant artisan/craftsman, made beautiful shields, just fabulous creations. But he was lame and unhandsome, not Aphrodite's choice of lover. He was not charming or beautiful like Apollo, or cunning like Hermes, or sexy like Ares – he wasn't exciting like that. He was a rustic (not stupid, however), lame man with whom she refused an intimate relationship. She was married to him but there's no evidence of any kind of congress, to put it in those terms. It was a fruitless marriage. Basically, she never bore children by him. Others did, so it wasn't as if he himself was at fault, it was that he was rejected by her.

This recalls the repression of the monsters by Ouranos, and so Aphrodite Urania has inherited the elitist attitude of her father – and this husband is not beautiful, he is ugly, and likely she put him aside and said, "No, I don't want to deal with that. I only want things that are more beautiful and more perfect." Urania definitely was her father's child. She has more of the masculine in her than Pandemos, who bears children, has sex, perspires, and does all the other things that human beings do. Certainly, Aphrodite-Venus Urania wouldn't have any of those attributes at all – completely ideal, very much the goddess, not at all the woman. So, she never bears a child by her husband.

Aphrodite's children

However, Aphrodite had many children from her lovers, both mortal and divine. There was a tragic affair with Adonis, ending in his removal to the underworld for part of each year. There was Anchises, the shepherd with whom she bore the heroic son, Aeneas, which means "sadness", who was the founder of Rome. There is the lesser known son, Lyras, "the lyre". Then there was her beloved, Ares, the

God of War. Their children are Phobos, which means "fear", Demos, which means "panic", Anteros, which means "reciprocal love", and Harmonia, who is the favourite of the children, the ultimate symbol of the union of opposites resulting in harmony.

She also mated with Dionysos, and they had a child whose name is Priapus (some myths have other fathers for Priapus, including Hermes). Now, Priapus was the God of Sex – bestial, animal love. It's the source of the adjective, priapic, which is the male in full erection. The worship of Priapus was a big cult in Rome, though he was a laughable creature. I have a fantastic old mythology book that was written in the sixteen hundreds in England, and it's about the ancient cult of phallic worship of Priapus. It's quite astounding. I bought it in a specialist bookshop just outside Toronto, Canada, and the man who reproduces these old books had to send me the illustrations separately – yes, in a brown paper wrapper – because he couldn't keep them in the shop itself because of vice laws! Seriously! Anyway, Priapus symbolises naked human and animal lust – the more primal, instinctual side of love as well as the procreative aspects of love. He was a fertility god. Hermes was a fertility god as well, but that's about the insemination of the mind.

Also, she had two children with Poseidon. With him she bore Rhodos, and Herophilos, which means "love of great acts". And her relationship with Hermes was fruitful because their union produced Hermaphroditus. This is really important, because when we begin to move into the astrological planet Venus, there is an aspect of Hermaphroditic relationship specific to Venus – Venus retrograde. The marriage of the Sun and Venus at inferior conjunction produces an androgyny which resonates through the Venus retrograde cycle, after the conjunction and before it stations direct. It is akin to the alchemical marriage of the King and Queen and their submersion in the alembic bath, becoming the neuter homunculus – symbolizing the union of opposites. I found the relationship between Hermes and Aphrodite, producing Hermaphroditus, particularly meaningful.

The fact that Aphrodite, among the whole of the Olympian goddesses, was the one who not only ascribed to, but authorised or lured one toward sexuality, caused a lot of distress among her peers.

Her unions with others expanded her persona to include attributes which were not innate, but could only emerge through relationship. Hence, Venus' search for union with the "other" is in part a need for us to develop facets of our own nature which lie dormant until activated, stimulated or even created out of seed-parts of ourselves.

Audience: Does this mean, then, that Venus in the chart might show us where we can find the "meeting of opposites" within ourselves? And why and where we seek the opposite outside ourselves?

Erin: That's exactly right. She is the embodiment of both, isn't she? She is the mother, the maternity figure, because she actually bore children; but she wasn't just a housewife, and the love of males was very important – she is the seductress, the exotic, erotic and enchanting, sometimes frightening and vengeful, face of the feminine. She is both self-contained and powerful, but still needs to find her own femininity in her relationships. It strikes me now that we don't have a strong representation by ratio of the feminine in the horoscope – except the Moon and Venus. Many astrologers now employ the asteroids to enhance the feminine face of the horoscope. We've simply got the Moon and Venus in the classical planetary process of individuation, and they're both considered quite wimpy – but they're not, they're overwhelmingly powerful, complex and polymorphous. There's no doubt that all the attributes of love are attached to the goddess, Aphrodite.[15]

Sappho – Aphrodite's minion

As I said before, the power of a god or goddess rests in his or her minions. The most famous of Aphrodite's mortal minions in the seventh century BCE was Sappho. There are only fragments of her lyric poetry left, and only fragmentary knowledge of her life. The reason why – and it's absolutely horrific – is that her poetry, the entire corpus of her work, was actually extant up to around 1400 CE,

---

[15]See Liz Greene and Howard Sasportas, *The Inner Planets: Building Blocks of Personal Reality* (Seminars in Psychological Astrology, Volume 4), Samuel Weiser, Inc., York Beach, ME, 1993. Good astrology, psychology and mythology of Mercury, Venus and Mars by both authors/speakers.

but was then largely destroyed by the Christian Fathers because of its erotic content. In terms of history, this is really dreadful, because one of the most famous astrologer-magus-historians in England, John Dee, in the late 1500's, was all for reclaiming a lot of the literature that was about to be destroyed because of the split of the Catholic Church. But it was too late for Sappho's poetry. So, every so often there's been a real panic – "Oh my God, we're going to lose this material quickly, let's save it and assemble it!" However, they weren't able to do that with this poetry, and so what we know of her is fragmented.

For all of that, it seems that she was a prominent citizen on the island of Lesbos in the capitol city of Mytilene, and she was very likely the mistress of a girls' school. Her family probably were wealthy and part of the ruling aristocracy, because they appeared to be involved in high-level politics. She was exiled at some point, and her brother was always in trouble – I believe he was sent to jail for political reasons. This might also be apocryphal, but it is said that her brother's slave was Aesop, author of the fables. Remember, it was the slaves and the Hetairai who were better educated than anyone else and the teachers of the children, and Aesop was part of the *oikos* – the extended family – of Sappho.

However, we aren't historians here, but more astrological mythographers, and it really is the poetry of this woman that best describes an aspect of 7th century life and demonstrates the power of Aphrodite. This was still the time of the oral tradition – these poems weren't written, they were recited – we don't even know for certain how they were recited, but it was very likely hat they were not spoken and certainly not read, but were sung. They were very likely accompanied by music, and so there's no real way of appreciating the full fabric of the fragments – they really are just little lines.

However, there is plenty of evidence of her renown and the respect she engendered, because it's proven by other ancient authors' mention of her. For instance, Plato called her the Tenth Muse, and then Solon, who was the great Athenian lawmaker in Greece, after hearing her poetry sung, wanted to learn it immediately, as he said, "So that I may die knowing it." Sappho's virtues were known and

Venus and Jupiter

praised even in her own time, and certainly long afterwards, because there are coins minted with her profile, and statues,. There is a lot of evidence that she was a strong, powerful, respected and extremely well known figure in the 7th century BCE.

Sappho was a devotee of Aphrodite. She was constantly paying homage and propitiating her – holding her in the highest esteem above all others – and there's nothing better a god or goddess likes than to be paid attention to. And that's a theme – propitiation and attention – those functions are essential in love or art. As a person, if you're not paid attention to, if nobody looks at you often enough, or touches you periodically, or is concerned about the way you are and the way you look, you wither and die. It is known that people die from lack of attention. So, there's something about the whole aspect of love and propitiation of love that's tremendously important. There is nothing fearful about Aphrodite in Sappho's work, she loves her best of all the gods. However, she does express *angst* about Eros. I'm going to read one of her little odes:

> Immortal Aphrodite on your patterned throne,
> daughter of Zeus, guile weaver,
> I beg you, Goddess, don't subjugate my heart
> with anguish or with grief, but come here to me now.[16]

There are many such supplications. Here's another one:

> Come to me now. Free me from this aching pain,
> fulfil everything that
> my heart desires to be fulfilled:
> you, yes, you, will be my ally.[17]

If there's some truth to this law of propitiation, like giving attention to and focusing on an object of desire and then in turn receiving *anteros* – a response as a result of those efforts – then I am sure that Aphrodite must have been absolutely mad about Sappho, because the

---

[16]Sappho, *Poems and Fragments, op. cit.,* "Ode to Aphrodite", Fragment 78, p. 66.
[17]Ibid., p. 66.

endless reiteration of names that she has in her poetry indicates that she is certainly fond of Aphrodite. But then again, Aphrodite obviously answered a lot of her prayers! Sappho dreams of her – "In a dream," she says, "I spoke to Aphrodite, the Cyprian Goddess." She pays formal homage: "To you I will sacrifice a white goat." So, she speaks to her in dreams (unconscious), but she also propitiates her (tangible evidence of her love).

There is a crucial difference between Eros and Aphrodite found in Sappho, because there are several fragments which are seemingly dedicated to Eros himself. They are not as adoring – there's something rather dark and frightening about them. For example, Eros, the God of Desire, brings pain, weaves unfulfilling tales for mortals to live out, and he descends from Heaven, his "dark purple cloak" wrapped around him. The "dark purple cloak" sounds rather ominous – it sounds a bit like the paintings of Georgia O'Keefe. I get a very distinct, erotic, swollen, tumescent, engorged image when I think of this Eros coming down stealthily with a dark purple cloak. There are no invocations for Eros here.

There are invocations for Aphrodite, how she'll bring lovers and pretty things, lovely girls and beautiful men. It sounds to me that the tone of the work breathes emphasis that there is a mediating quality to Venus-Aphrodite, which is kinder and more easily assimilated and approached than is Eros, himself, who simply infects or inseminates her with his powers – with a desire or universal longing which simply will never be assuaged. You cannot come to terms with Eros' power. So, you ask Aphrodite to come along and help. In other words, "Look, I'm filled with this incredible desire, where am I going to put it, what do I do? Bring me someone or something that I can focus this through.

In the emotional desert of lack of relationship, for example, someone might say, "Hey, I really would like to have a relationship, it's high time." And yet, there's nobody there and you can't live with that, so you have to ask Aphrodite, and say, "Bring me someone, or at least something, that will fill the gap, so that I can get on with being creative and feeling whole and feeling that I'm not drying up and withering." And so there's got to be a mediator, and I think I'm seeing Aphrodite/Venus in the chart as mediator between this high charge of Eros, which is completely overwhelming and not very well differentiated, and something that you can use in a practical way. I think that's what Sappho was getting at. Eros, alone, brings to mind a tumescent, swollen psyche, like a pregnant woman waiting for term and the birth of the new to occur, which can't come without some form of midwife.

In the myth, we learn that Aphrodite was born out of a violent, bloody separation of Heaven and Earth, and Strife plays a very important role in this. Strife (Eris) was a goddess – she was Ares' sister. There is an interesting play on words in there – Eros and Eris, Love and Strife. There is always that unspoken side of love, that stressful, anxiety-producing side, the stress, the Eris or strife of love. Sappho was pretty clear on this; it's what she hoped to avoid.

Another story that attests to the power of Aphrodite is the Judgement of Paris: At the wedding of Peleus and Thetis, Eris, angry at not being invited, flung a golden apple into the crowd of guests. On the apple was inscribed, "Let the Fairest take it." Hera, Athene and Aphrodite each claimed it. To prevent a quarrel, Zeus asked Paris, son of the king of Troy, to act as the judge. Athene said she would give him success in war if she won, Hera promised royal greatness, but Aphrodite assured him of the most beautiful of all women for his own. He chose Aphrodite to win the golden apple.

From that fateful moment, the inexorable turn of the wheel would eventually lead to the Trojan War. The woman awarded to Paris was Helen of Sparta. That Helen was already married to Menelaos was of no concern to Aphrodite, and when Paris readily agreed, the final act was in place to set the greatest war since the Titans on its path of destruction. Aphrodite was on the side of the Trojans the whole time. In the *Iliad* she plays a powerful role – it seems that the gods and goddesses mercilessly used mortals to live out their latent humanity, and Helen of Troy became a pawn of Aphrodite and as such had no realm of her own but was ridden by the archetype of Venus-Aphrodite, incapable of rendering her own will. The inability of human reason to outwit the powers of Aphrodite comes through really clearly in this one, because the Trojan War was a kind of gemstone of Greek myth set in the most amazing stories and tales which are woven all around this act of betrayal – but Aphrodite started it by transferring her goddess-self into the person of Helen, whom the goddess manipulated mercilessly toward her own end.

If we are seized by passion, love, or gripped by a new creative force, it is like being taken over by a god or goddess – becoming *enthusiasmos* – filled with the divine. For instance, both men and women can be seized by the anima, since the anima is the feminine soul. In strictly Jungian terms this cannot happen to a woman, because Jung called the psychic "inner woman" of a man the anima – a man's contrasexual spirit, if you will, his animating force, his feminine side, his idealised counterpart. However, the way I see it, women have an inner woman, too. A role-model or an image of the ideal woman's way of being is often projected out onto women. Jung would have called this the shadow of a woman, since, again, strictly speaking, the shadow is the same sex interior image, but dark and undeveloped. So, a form of shadow anima can emerge in women and be the source of much strife and conflict, ultimately leading to better understanding of her own feminine complexities – ideally, that is. In a negative sense, it can be very destructive, and the three goddesses, Hera, Athene, and Aphrodite, do exemplify three "types" of the feminine – the wife, the chaste goddess, and the seductress.

Audience: This is so typical a story. There always seem to be "three women" in competition. In this case, one intelligent, another a brave warrioress, and the third a beauty. And beauty wins. This seems to show how our values of femininity are commonly portrayed and valued, they are "only" cosmetic, and the women who have powers of mind and body are undermined. So, is Venus also the planet of feminism?

Erin: Hmmm. I think more is involved with feminism as an ethic than just Venus. Women (or men) who espouse feminism might have the same kind of aspect a non-feminist person has. I think in this case, feminism as an ethic has to be considered first, and the aspects of Venus next. By this I mean, given that a person is feminist, we might look at Venus in their chart to see what kind of feminist they are, why feminism has become an aegis, and if the function of political feminism will be productive in their personal development.

A person with a Venus-Uranus aspect will be a feminist to liberate her ideals, keeping her "chaste", (i.e. vestal, or never giving her soul to a man, yet not necessarily unsexual), while a Venus-Saturn woman might find coldness, sadness, oppression or an impoverishment of feeling and a hard father-figure at the root of her beliefs,. In turn, a Venus-Jupiter feminist would likely find great joy in her (or his) feminine side, and loathe the confines of convention, thus appearing to throw off the institution of marriage in the conventional sense. Do you see what I mean? The aspects of Venus will show the *why* of a situation, rather than its inevitable appearance.

Audience: What about Venus-Mars?

Erin: I will go into the aspects of Venus to the planets later in the day. However, with the feminist theme in mind, the Mars-Venus combination as a symbol is the warrior, the fighter, the hunter. I should think a Venus-Mars type feminist would be a fighter, one who worked toward harmony with a vengeance (remember their child, Harmonia), and was acutely aware of the archetypal differences between the sexes. There may be an underlying feeling of not being able to blend the feelings of sexuality inherent in the passionate aspect, and anger and frustration can breed a lot of energy! Now, I wonder how a Venus-Neptune feminism might work...Ah! The suffering and self-denial of the romantic lover would be a form of Neptunian feminism – a soft feminism that saw the idealistic and romantic side of the feminine as being subjugated and ruined by the harshness of masculine compartmentalisation.

A good example of this is the great poet, Robert Graves. He was thought to be a feminist by early feminists. Indeed, he felt that the White Goddess was his *magnum opus* (though he was a phenomenally prolific writer). He bemoaned the loss of the matriarchal era, the loss or subjugation of the feminine earth-goddess by the masculine sky-gods. Graves had a few highly significant Muses, over many, many years in his life – right through to his last years. He had Venus at 17° Virgo, exactly square to

Neptune at 17° Gemini (which was conjunct Pluto in that generation). Isn't that perfect? And with a Libra Moon! Graves' sole source of inspiration was from the feminine, and although he was very, very masculine, his dependency upon his Muse was almost self-sacrificial, and his loyalty to the long-suppressed goddess culture was undying. But then, Neptune requires a sacrifice, doesn't it? He truly believed that the fall of the goddess culture, the loss of the ancient values of the Minoans, was the source of the strife in the world.

Now, what is interesting about Graves' Venus-Neptune is this: On the mortal or Pandemic level, he did suffer pain through his Muses – they inevitably hurt or abandoned him, or remained strangely elusive. But he also had a wife who enacted the Venus-Neptune for him. His last marriage, of over thirty years, endured all the Muses and the suffering of Graves. His wife sacrificed certain aspects of her own self to preserve the family, and although she did not present as a "long-suffering" type of woman, it is likely that, as long as her husband had his Muse (not all, if any, were sexual – at least for very long), she was happy because he was happy. They had a terribly strong bond, and their marriage was only truly threatened once, and then, it was very late in Graves' life.

On the Urania-ideal level, Graves was divinely inspired, a true poet who translated the beautiful visions of his imagination into well-crafted verse and wrote of myths and also prose. He is an exemplar of the dual goddess influence – from the imaginal realm of Urania through the embodied Pandemos.

Eros, Aphrodite and the astrological Venus

But as time moved on, and nature and culture became increasingly separated through awareness of opposites, a kind of parallel schism in consciousness occurred, provoking a revolution in thought. Late in the 5th century BCE – some might say, out of a split between mind and body – reason was born. The sophists and the Athenian philosopher, Socrates, were enchanted by examining why things were the way they were. It wasn't good enough that things "were". They wanted to know "why" and "what". For example, what was thunder? What was lightning? Well, today we say it's the convection theory – however, till then, it was Zeus – Zeus *was* lightning. Somewhere between saying, "It's Zeus" and the convection theory lies philosophy – which brings us to Plato's idea of the ideal. Now, all of this is pertinent to what we are getting to, because we'll carry this split or schism forward into the Uranian and Pandemic Venus, and attempt to come to terms with the dichotomy that often lies within our own perceptions of love, values and creativity.

Plato wrote the *Symposium,* and it's quite an easy read. It's fun. In the *Symposium,* the ancient Greeks used the terms lover and beloved, with respect to relationships between men, because that's the way it was. While the beloved was the term for the younger male, the lover was the elder, and implicitly, the tutor – he who loved, he who taught. The lover pursued and taught the beloved about truth and beauty and wisdom. Now, today we think that the beloved is the one who is receiving the love, obviously, and the lover is the one who is offering it. These roles are often symbiotic and interchangeable, and they seesaw from one party to the other all the time. It's not fixed, and there's a considerable tension in these two terms, because later we'll talk about the ambivalence of love and the ability to go from Pandemic to Uranian in a matter of seconds. Venus in the chart will highlight how we feel about being the lover and the beloved. Some are more inclined to the giving, teaching, dominant position of the lover, and others more inclined to be the receiver, the passive beloved.

The *Symposium* offers ideas about Eros, Love, Aphrodite and Sophia – Wisdom. In this classic dialogue there emerges a conflict about a division of realms between Eros and Aphrodite. This is a significant theme which we are going to explore more deeply, because the dual goddess image is one of the most significant and important images to be aware of when looking at Venus. She rules both Taurus, which I would probably slot under Pandemos, and Libra, which is very likely to fall into the highly philosophised, rationalised, civilised and polished domain of Aphrodite Urania.

Philosophically, the "highest" or more ideal, level of Eros is personified in the deity Urania, whereas the human level of Eros is personified through Pandemos. Aphrodite Urania's erotic charisma feeds the soul and the mind, and it was the stimulus for the lover of wisdom to pursue truth and beauty and the lofty realms of the perfect ideal – these were the philosophical pursuits. This ideal, heavenly image is compared in the *Symposium* to the other aspect of Venus – Aphrodite Pandemos, or Aphrodite of the people, a more human-faced goddess who was born out of the conventional union between male and female. In other words, it represents and serves the emotional and instinctual aspects of human love, relationships and sexuality.

Now, in fact, it says here in the text, "As we all know, Love and Aphrodite are inseparable. Now, if Aphrodite were uniform, so would Love be; but she is twofold and so, inevitably, Love is twofold too. The duality of Aphrodite is undeniable: one Aphrodite – the one we call Celestial [Urania] – is older and has no mother, though her father is Ouranos [Uranus]; the other, the younger one, is the daughter of Zeus and Dione, and is called Common [Pandemos]. It follows, therefore, that the same distinction of title – Common and Celestial – should be applied to the different Loves who are associates of one or the other Aphrodite. Now, every single god deserves our praise, but we do have to try to distinguish these two Loves' respective domains. The point is that it is in the nature of every action to be, in itself, neither right nor wrong."[18]

Plato goes on to give a pretty culture-biased interpretation of the "two Loves", because it is primarily dedicated to relationships between men. Maybe you're interested in this, I don't know; it's very fascinating because Plato is more prone, I think, to the higher aspiration of homo (same) sexual love than hetero (other) sexual. At least he uses the voices of various individuals to bring out the favour of male-male relationship and the difficulty of male-female relationships. He goes on to say that the higher form of love springs from the heavenly goddess who, firstly, has no share of the female, but only the male, that is, Urania, who was her father's child. Next, she is the elder, and has no violence in her. Consequently, those

---

[18]Plato, *The Symposium*, trans. Robin Waterfield, Oxford University Press, 1994, 180d.

inspired by this love turn to the male because they feel affection for what is stronger and has more mind!

However, in the light of bridging the gap between male and female – masculine and feminine – and staying away from the pro's and con's of personal choice of sex partner, the important thing there is not about whether it's homosexual or heterosexual. The important thing is that this qualification of Uranian and Pandemic has to do with the mind-body split. So, Urania is mental and Pandemos is physical, and in order to have a physical relationship which bears fruit, you have to have a male and a female. So we start to look at something around the ideal in the mind and the physical in the body. It's tough. We're looking at the 5th century BCE, 2500 years ago – pretty serious discussions and concerns here about love.

There's a funny story, too, which I like – by the comedy playwright, Aristophanes. He says there was originally only one gender, a hermaphroditic gaseous ball with four arms and four legs and two heads, which existed simply in a state of perfect harmony, ecstasy and union. However, they were having so much fun that it really annoyed the gods, who thought, "Well, hang on here, that's not what you're supposed to be doing." So the gods cut them in half, which seems rather ruthless. One half was then doomed to spend its entire existence searching for the other half because it felt incomplete and longed to merge with its other half.

Audience: Oooh, I know what that is like! Seriously, this is the foundation for the soul-mates concept, isn't it? The myth explains why we all feel incomplete. It's also the root for Jung's anima-animus work, it seems. I know that many people, clients and friends, spend a great deal of time trying to find their inner opposite on the outside, and find all sorts of faults in their actual partners! The Aquarian Venus or Venus-Uranus type seems more inclined to this kind of split or awareness of opposites, and always seeks a new ideal, or stays away from relationships because they cause a lot of complications. The myth explains that perfectly!

Erin: There are hundreds of "broken heart" myths, and split gender stories, aren't there? Yes, it does help us understand more this deep longing for fused union with another. However, there is only one place where two hearts beat as one, and it was in the womb when we were one with mother. There are so many ways of expressing this split, this irreparable, unhealable, split. It's voiced in so many ways, there are so many myths. First of all there's birth out of Chaos into the world of form via the inseminating force of Eros, and then there's the birth of Aphrodite, who was born out of the split of Heaven and Earth, and then she's split by the myths of her dual origin – so it's all about splitting, being separated from one's opposite or complement, and then filled with the longing to move toward, rejoining, clarifying.

I think that the highest level, the mental level of Eros, is personified in the deity of Aphrodite Urania, whose erotic charisma feeds the soul and is the Muse for the lovers of wisdom and truth, and beauty. The contact with the divine soul, in Plato's mind, was excited by the functions of Eros. You see, we get right back to the origins again. How can you have an amazing thought if it isn't in some way coming from a divine source? Now, Aphrodite is a goddess, yes, but she's not the divine source. She seems to be the one who acts as the mediator. I think Eros is more likely to have his manor in the area of insemination and incubation, but birth and manifestation are Aphrodite or Venus.

There are great arguments about divinity. Is it more divine to love or to be loved? Well, I suppose, when we start talking this afternoon about creativity and relationships, the planet Venus, its aspects to other planets and whether a person might be more, by nature, inclined to the Uranian side or the Pandemic side, we might want to talk a bit about the way Eros moves us. In relationships as well as creative endeavour, we'll run up time and time again to the mortal limits, and in a sense it's like yelling at Kronos for midwiving Aphrodite, and saying "It's your fault that I can't get into the ideal place and can't fuse wholly with my subject or my loved person!" After all, there is a limit to our lives, and I think that's where we have to look at what we expect from relationships, and accept the possibility that some people find it more creative to not be in relationship. Then again, some people find it creative to be in lots of them, whereas others find it creative to be in just one. It's an individual matter, but most people are worried about it. I haven't talked to one person that isn't in some way terribly concerned about the quality of relating in their life.

On one hand, that's probably a good thing, because it means that people examine their relationships – both within and without. But also, it implies to me that there's an awful lot of self-chastising going on, as if people think that they're doing it wrong. Or as if somebody has said that there's a way to do it, and that it would be the way, and if you could do it, then you'd be all right. And that doesn't seem possible if everyone, at some point, not all the time, has a problem in dealing with the high idea of the ultimate, in other words the Uranian side of Venus, and the real, the Pandemic side of Venus. So it strikes me that there can't possibly be the perfect way.

Dual goddess, dual ruler

The process of individuating through relationship is very important, because we identify more facets of ourselves as we interact with others. If you stayed entirely alone in a room, you would not be forced to encounter yourself in a refracted sense; relating would not have its parameters. There would be an undeveloped Venus. It hasbeen found that the main characteristic of autism is its inability to relate – it is not about communication, but about relationship. The contacts in the intra-dimensional points in family horoscopes of an autist cluster around Venus-Saturn harmonics and midpoints. This speaks of a strong barrier in the family system between its individual members, which pops up in the autist as a characteristic, or a "symptom", if you will, of the family's inability to cross the boundaryof its individuals into the collective of the family.[19]

It's in the mirror of relationship that we individuate more rapidly – that we become increasingly more of ourselves. So you could think in a self-orientated way, that relationships are really about one's own self and self development! It's through response to others that we

---

[19]Erin Sullivan, *Dynasty: The Astrology of Family Dynamics,* Arkana, Contemporary Astrology Series, Penguin, London, 1996. See "Tobias - Touched by God", a case history of an autistic boy and his family.

examine our own needs. If you're in a room all by yourself, generally you usually like yourself, you're pretty amused by the inside of your own mind and the way things go and how you feel. But when somebody else comes into the room and you begin relating, you are more likely to say to yourself, "Am I doing this right?" or "How do I look?" or "Do they like me?" That's pretty common. It really is the separation of self from other, and that myth goes on into a story about the sign Libra.

There's an apocryphal tale that the sign of Libra never existed until The Fall occurred – in other words, the expulsion from Eden. The Adam and Eve myth is another timeless story. The mythical pair felt no shame or guilt in their nakedness in the Garden of Eden. They both ate freely from the trees and the fruits and the forest, and it was all very harmonious and peaceful, until Eve was tempted by the serpent (earth-power, feminine symbol) into eating the apple of truth and knowledge – mind, mental, Libran knowledge, the awareness of opposites. It wasn't until they both ate the apple that they saw each other's nakedness, which really meant they recognised their otherness. Their subsequent personal shame and banishment from the Ideal into the Real – from Heavenly Eden into the world of relationships and childbearing and rough work – is a perfect depiction of the Fall from grace that our own selves experience, or we impose on others, when the Ideal of the relationship becomes the Real relationship.

Now, the story goes this way: In the beginning there were ten signs. They went from Aries to Pisces. However, between Leo and Sagittarius, there was a sixth sign, which looked like this:

♏︎

This symbol looks very much like a sign of the Serpent. This sign was separated by the function or symbol of Libra, which then split the Serpent in two:

So we end up with twelve signs rather than ten! We now have Virgo, Libra and Scorpio. Libra divided the nature-sign of the Serpent, the fusion of nature and culture. Saint and sinner, once symbolically fused in the Serpent image, are divided to become opponents. I have to laugh at this. It is as if the Fall created the need for saint and sinner to embody different signs, and Scorpio was assigned the sinner and Virgo assigned the saint – which is absolute nonsense. But this is the nature of splits. The problem with this story is that it meant Venus had to split also, and thus moved from governing only Taurus to assuming the dual rulership of Libra and Taurus. (The biblical Eve had a counterpart as well, and she was Sophia – the Gnostic Eve, the goddess of earthly and heavenly wisdom).

You might think of Taurus/Venus embodying the rough, unmined gem, nestled in the bosom of the earth – a diamond in the core of the earth, in its rough form. It takes a Venusian to see the beauty in nature – someone who has an eye for the perfection that lives inside a rough-looking rock. Since we are the artisans of our own roughness, we have within us the creativity to craft our raw gems into priceless jewels. The work of individuation is akin to finding that shape within, the perfection locked in primitive covering, and chipping away the dross. It is as if we take our Taurus, our instinctual, innate, rough beauty, and slowly, over time and age, try to bring it to the refined and "civilised" condition that society wants. The Taurean aspect of Venus is rough and natural – a valuable thing in itself, but then it is shaped into its Libran potential, becoming an expensive, well set, rare, highly individual gem.

You could think of the process of personal civilisation and individuation in those terms – that the Taurus in your horoscope is the location of the uncut, rough gem, and the Libra function is potentially the beautiful, exalted, civilised aspect of that gem. So, Venus rules Taurus in the primal, instinctual, deeply visceral and unconscious region, and Libra in its more refined, semi-conscious mode. Taurus is the body and Libra the mind – Pandemos and Urania.

As we grow, we are honed under the knife, or the Kronos of civilisation, through infancy, childhood, and adolescence, always testing ourselves against relationship, being hewn and given form and shape. The Libran function shows us where our most idealistic possibilities lie, but our Taurus/Venus is always going to be there to remind us of our intrinsic, instinctual self. We may become over-refined, too civilised, too influenced by received values and wisdom. However, there always lurks the inner Venus, the Taurean, earthy realm.

In the myths we found that Venus/Aphrodite had a lot of contact with the earth through her sisters, the earth-goddesses Erinyes/Furies; through her marriage to Hephaistos; through her desire for the shepherd, Aeneas; through her dual origins as a goddess of mortals, and so forth. The duality is exemplified in the earth sign Taurus – ruling our gut reactions or innate values, and our inherent needs on the sensual level – and in the air sign Libra, ruling our ability to come out of ourselves, to be with others, to compromise our instincts and to be of the civilised, cultivated world.

Our psyche is a mass of chaotic elements, all in the ready for formation and creation – Eros is inside, but we have a surface veneer, upon which many facets are cut. We are polished and express ourselves in increasingly complex ways, in socially acceptable ways which are symbolised by the Libran Venus. The fact that there are these two signs in everybody's horoscope attests to the reality of both. There is the feral face of Venus, the bestial side, the wild, natural side, the earthy side, the pandemic ethic of life which has to do with our fundamental values, needs, emotions, sensations; and there is the Libra side, equally valuable, which has to do with how we perceive ourselves in the mirror of relationship – what we've been taught, how we've been civilised, what's been imposed on us.

Becoming civilised contains a paradox. On one hand, remaining infantile is no good to us as conscious beings. Functioning on instinct alone is not attractive, and results in ostracism or social confinement. On the other hand, we can repress too much of the magical child, the deep inner knowledge of our self-value in the process of becoming socially more aware and functional. Our creative instincts can be shoved back down out of fear or training. Like Ouranos repressed the birth of the Hekatonchires, we too can repress (or have thwarted by childhood training or social dicta) our raw, monstrous side, which is the urge for Pandemic, earthy feeling. If, as children, we are beaten or abused, then our bodies remember this (Taurus), and relate it to our minds (Libra), which in turn create distorted relationships within the world.

We could think of our emerging consciousness as the gem-cutter. The diamond left in its original state is beautiful in its existence. We know that it is as beautiful as it could be. By taking it and shaping it, cutting it and making planes and facets for light to enter and refract outward, to make the diamond show both its inner and refracted light, we've not only exalted the stone, but also have limited it! We've given it a certain shape – one that is going to be more valuable – but its value might only be in accord with the current times. We also might have distorted its nature to the degree that something is lost. One time it's more fashionable to cut it this way, and another to cut it that way. A real gem-cutter cuts the stone in accord with its own need – in other words, what it says inside. The rough-looking thing is there, and there is a shape in there that's going to maximise its brilliance. But it's still according to fashion, the way it's cut.

Libra is the civilised function of Venus. When you look at Venus in a chart, the first thing to do is to look at both Taurus and Libra. Taurus is first in the order of development, it's the roughest, most basic instinctual side of our nature. And then we look at Libra. How have we become polished in accord with our inner needs? Has the imposition of civilisation and social structure been too great, for example? Are we too influenced by what we've been taught? That's usually the biggest problem in relationship – unspoken messages from early childhood shaping and forming us in ways which have poked our instincts back into a hole.

Libra and Taurus – mind and body

Taurus and Libra are quincunx each other in the zodiac. There is a major adjustment needed to bring them into harmony, anyway. Nature and culture are always in a dialogue. They are also of dissociate elements – earth and air – the stress of bringing nature into cultivation is akin to bringing the elements of heaven to earth. We find this in the development of our personality in the form of our desire to be true to ourselves, and finding that we fall short of that mark very often, because it simply won't get us where we want to go. Individuation is the *opus contra natura* – the work against nature – and the Libran refinement brings beauty but it also brings a suppression of nature with it.

Audience: I have Taurus on the IC, Libra ruling the 9th house, and Venus is actually in the 10th house in Scorpio, exactly conjunct Neptune. My Sun is near there in Scorpio, too. Would that mean that I have a deep-seated set of values that are embedded in the family ethic, but that I might try to evade that by imagining myself to be someone else?

Erin: I don't know how you "imagine" yourself to be someone else. Hmmm. How could you do that? By being an actress, or selling a dream? Or travelling away from the homeland and the family to live in another country, thereby fulfilling a great deal of the 4th, 9th, and 10th house (with Neptune) potential? You come from Australia, and have lived in many countries, and are a sailor and photographer by profession. More importantly for the inner world, you might feel as though you had to overcome tremendous obstacles in your home and family origin, fighting for identity in a strange environment.

Audience: I also have Mars at 29° Taurus, retrograde in the 4th house – it's not opposite Venus, but is unaspected

Erin: Oh, yes. This is getting very interesting. Let's see, to put all that into a box of delineation. Starting from Taurus: Although home life is strongly valued, it could be that you felt it was too safe, considering that Mars retrograde in there is waiting for a good revolution to start, or you would like to start one. It implies a level of chaos in the home, picked up by you and introjected (Mars retrograde) until such time in life as you could externalise the feelings of adventure. Also, we look at the 9th house Libra and your need for a sense of benign divinity – this is strong, considering that the ruler is conjunct Neptune. Your need for a relationship with the divine, with God or a god, is very high, and unfortunately, neither the birth mother nor father can fulfill this.

Nor can any man or woman. Hence, your need to seek out the divine image in others, even pursuing a career in creating divine images (Neptune in the 10th) – photography is an excellent art and craft for you. The problem is, you could be the recipient of a lot of Neptunian projections, where other people see in you something of themselves. This might make you afraid of getting too close, or you might try to become what they want. The drive (Mars retrograde) to "go" is likely to have been partly frustrated, as well as fuelled by the undercurrents of animosity, rage, or Eros felt in the early home environment.

The fact that it is unaspected, and in the latest degree of your horoscope, means that any transit in the chart will always terminate with Mars. This effectively says, "Now that the work is done, it's time to go." Perhaps you felt – unconsciously – the need to live out the unspoken frustrations of the parents (4th house) and their unlived adventurousness. The restlessness which counters your need for security is likely a point of work for you, a place for self-development. You have to stop reacting to the family, and become more proactive – that is, be yourself, not them. Have you ever married or had a long-term relationship?

Audience: No. I have always had short, intense and painful relationships. I want too much, or am afraid of being smothered. Or I would have to sacrifice something of myself. In fact, it's confusing to me, because I lose my identity when I am in love, and have to be cut away from the person. Besides, I came from a family of eight children, and I wanted to be alone, I thought. Or I used to. But now I want to be with someone, but I am used to being alone. Maybe transiting Saturn in Pisces will help with bringing my fantasy of the divine relationship into something real!

Erin: Precisely. Isn't that what Saturn's job is all about? About creating an horizon of awareness and bringing us to our limits, so we can make choices? The trines of transiting Saturn to the Venus-Neptune could very well offer the container you seek – if you are willing to bring your standards of divinity into reality and accept the rough with the smooth. Too, the feminine side of you is mirrored in a shape-shifting surface – it would seem that your mother (Venus ruling 4th in 10th, with Neptune) didn't have much of a shape to you, with all those kids! It would have been difficult to bond with her, and likely her with you. What "number" were you?

Audience: Fifth of eight.

Erin: Oh, dear. She didn't have much opportunity to lavish upon you the affection you needed, did she? As an infant, you may not have known she would be back to you, after she left you. Very unsettling and insecure. This is reflected in how you described your relationships – desperate romance, longing to fuse, then a terrible, wrenching separation, followed by the void. This is something you can work on very creatively and positively, with the Saturn in Pisces transit! Often people meet someone very sane and equal, when Saturn makes a nice, boring trine to their Venus! Good luck on bringing the Ideal to the Real!

There is some preordination and limit to who we can become. We have a set of values at birth, which always remain at the base of our nature. Infants exude their personality from the minute of their birth. Thus, we are bound to our potential. For instance, if you are five feet six inches tall, and have blue eyes, you are not going to change that. There's *nothing* that's going to change that. You can wear green contact lenses and put on high heels and appear taller, but otherwise, just like the context of physical limits, our value system has a preordained shape. It is the *prima materia* – the basics of your Self.

The fact is, we are not perfectly perceived or understood when we are being raised. We are often shaped and moulded against our wishes – the natural stress and adjustment of the quincunx between Taurus and Libra exemplifies that problem. If, when being brought up, the values of your parents' generational ethos are in direct conflict with your own generational ethos, then it gives something for the ego to run up against, and creates a big question within one's own self, about values. This split between one's inner values and what is imposed in the family can be pathological, wherein the reality-frame becomes so distorted that there's hopelessness at a certain point in life. That's where a person seeks help, or falls apart, or in some way dramatises or externalises the discomfort with Taurus – I am who I am and that's the way it is socially – and Libra – this is how I'm supposed to be and don't I look nice? We are stressed, we grow.

It's complex when you get into the deeper levels of Venus. It's not all about loving relationships. Not only do we look at those houses which Venus rules, we also look at Venus in relationship to other planets. I'm winding up now to take our lunch break, and when we come back, we are going to do the aspects. Think of this: When Venus is in a chart, it's "looking" at other planets – what does it see? We want to look at what it sees first, and then next. This might be a little exercise at lunch – find your contacts to Venus and list them. It would be the planet in closest aspect which Venus sees first.

Let's say you've got Venus conjunct Jupiter within ten minutes, but Venus is just coming up to Jupiter. The first planet that Venus "sees" when it looks out – *aspectus,* meaning to look at or regard – is Jupiter. But then it also might be 2 1/2° from forming a square to Saturn. So, first it looks out to Jupiter – yes, everything's OK, it's fantastic. Then, it catches sight of Saturn out of the corner of its eye, and, "Oh no, it's all too much work. I didn't expect that at first."

So you get a mixed message if you've got a Venus-Jupiter conjunction in a square to Saturn. But always, because pure astrology is true, you look at what's happening first. Like so: I've got Venus coming to conjoin Jupiter, so that means, fundamentally and basically, I think everything is great. I've got an open attitude, I feel good. I can work anywhere, I can talk to anybody, I have a really broad horizon. But no sooner than that assumption is felt, which is highly optimistic and idealistic (Jupiter-Venus), then I am confronted by the realities of life (Saturn square). The Saturn square is a particularly hard reality-shaper! In other words, what follows the initial Jupiter-Venus statement, "Yes, it is all possible," is, "No, you're not going to be able to go anywhere, talk to everyone. There's a lot of hard work going on here. Relationship and creativity mean work, they are not always about having fun."

So there's a conflict, and when we look at the various complexities, you'll see that, on one hand, there you are with your basic self, your Taurus house and your instinctual, natural side, and then with your Libra house, the place where you're most likely to be influenced by the civilisation process and socialisation of primal gut reactions. There are your basic instincts of the planet Venus and its relationship to all the planets from the Sun right out to Pluto to consider. This dialogue between Venus and the other planets can clarify why you might be more inclined toward removing yourself to the ideal, or why you might find the ideal, imaginal realm threatening.

For example, a person whose Venus is in Aquarius retrograde would probably feel more comfortable in Plato's Academy than they would in bed with someone. It makes a lot more sense. It would be very healthy, much, much, much more natural to them, to live in the ideal world of perfect forms. This doesn't mean that they *can't* have a relationship – it's just *how* they have a relationship. It's very likely, if Venus is retrograde in Aquarius, that they did not enjoy overt displays of affection and might even have rejected parental overtures of kissy-kissy stuff – they'd hate it – horrible! So this person might pull away and say, "Oh, my parents really suppressed my own nature, they smothered me with love." And the parents might then turn round and say, "Well, we don't know what's wrong with our son, because he's so repressed. He doesn't have any feelings, he's not in touch with his feelings."

If he was emotionally demonstrative and touchy-feely, then as an astrologer I would wonder why. You might say, "There's something wrong with this person, there's something not real here. Why is he so effusive and overly friendly? It doesn't seem quite right." Some people are just like this. If they are born with a horoscope that looks like that – emotionally cool and not inclined to fussiness – then it must be OK. That's my assumption. If it isn't a problem, then it isn't a problem. When it becomes one, then we look at it, and tackle what it represents. In astrology we can analyse things like that very well – but the value of astrology lies in validating an individual's uniqueness, and possibly even being able to assess if they really do have a problem, or whether others have a problem with them.

Anyway, let's take our lunch break now. Remember your homework, and then, after lunch, I'll talk about Venus within – projection – and, lastly, aspects of Venus.

The projection of the ideal

It's fascinating how the subconscious acts as a kind of compensatory device. The first thing I did when I left here was walk across the road, and I went into that rose-garden lunch place and immediately walked straight into the men's washroom, which I thought was kind of funny. I misread the symbol – my brain transposed it. After talking so much about Venus, I forgot that the girls' symbol has a skirt on and one leg, and the boys' symbol has two legs. I saw these funny sinks and I thought, "Oh, I think I'm in the wrong room." Fortunately, nobody noticed, so I was saved embarrassment and was allowed to think of it as being profound. So, I didn't get too caught up in Venus and got to take a peek at the men's room.

Audience: What do you think that says about you – you must meet your opposite?

Erin: Yes – just because I understand the game doesn't mean I am exempt from playing it.

I must read this treatise on projection that was written by a Roman poet, Lucretius, almost two thousand years ago. It's found in *De rerum natura* – "On the Nature of Things". When I was studying this material, I was absolutely dumbfounded. First of all, the entire poem is about nature and the way things are. It goes on and on about all sorts of amazing things (including atomic theory). When we speak of Love and Eros and Aphrodite in Greek times, it really had a lot of power to it. It's very alive, extreme, dynamic and resonant, but by the time we get to Rome, Venus had become pretty much of an agrarian goddess, or the goddess of sex. She looks after fields and streams and ensures that seeds take root and sprout, or she lures people into the vicissitudes of love.

The Romans still followed the rules of pagan worship, even though they may have had no real "feeling" for the ancient deities. However, they didn't take any chances, so Lucretius opens his poem with the requisite dedication to Venus on the first page of Book One:

> Creatress, mother of the Roman Line,
> Dear Venus, joy of earth and joy of heaven...

And so on. However, his real feelings about love, and women in particular, are shown in Book Six. This is a very a famous diatribe against women. The first thing that I am going to read to you is about passionate love. He writes in here:

> Avoiding passionate love, you need not miss
> All the rewards of Venus; you might gain
> Easing and comfort without penalty.
> Surely, delight comes in a purer form
> To sensible men than to your love-struck wretches
> Who, on the verge of consummation
> Can't make up their minds, thrash about uncertain
> Which should they pleasure first – their hands? their eyes?
> So they bear down with all their weight and squeeze,
> Tight as they can, the body they have sought,
> They make it hurt, take hold of lips with teeth,
> Kiss with insistent fierceness. Such delight
> Is never pure, for in its impulse lies
> The appetite for pain, the urge to hurt,
> The germinal seeds of madness. Even so,
> In the very midst of love, ever so lightly,
> Venus abates the punishment and blends
> A sweetness with the sharpness of the bite.
> There is the hope, always, that the fire may die,
> Extinguished by the body which aroused
> Its ardor in the first place. What could be
> More contrary to nature?[20]

---

[20]Lucretius, *De rerum natura*, trans. Rolfe Humphries, Indiana University Press, 1969, Book IV, Lines 1077-89.

Venus and Jupiter

Really, he's saying it doesn't matter how you pursue it, love is never going to fulfill you – that no matter what area you seek to find love, it will never feel full and complete. He then goes on to say, "Venus plays tricks on lovers with her game of images which never satisfy... All in vain, for they can gather nothing. They cannot effect real penetration, be absorbed body and body utterly. They seem to want to do just this, God knows, they try. Cling to each other, lashed in Venus' chains." It talks about how love is going to die out and blaze again, over and over, a merry-go-round of wasted energy.

But this is the passage that really got me, and this has to do with projection. This was written two thousand years ago, remember – this isn't the 1900's, this isn't out of Jung, but it may well have been the origins, the concept, of projection. It's really a cry against the dangers of romantic love. He goes on to say:

> It's easier to avoid the snares of love
> Than to escape once you are in that net
> Whose cords are not so strong: but even so,
> Enmeshed entangled you can still get out
> Unless, poor fool, you stand in your own way,
> Forgetting, for example, all those faults
> Your little darling has in body or mind.
> Desire is blind, desire is ignorant
> And men can never stop this foolishness
> But keep on praising an attractive charm
> Which simply isn't there. We often see
> The crookedest and ugliest women held
> In high esteem, somebody's precious pet;
> And some men laugh at others, urging them
> To placate Venus, have her intervene,
> Ease the affliction of so foul a mess,
> And yet these wretches never understand
> Their own calamitous case. A black wench
> Is a nut brown maid, and some untidy slob
> Praised for a sweet disorder in the dress.
> Some idiot with a pallid, washed-out stare
> Is called grey-eyed Minerva, olive groved.

> The lumbering lummox is a wood nymph wild,
> The sawed-off runt, a doll. The over-grown
> Hydrocephalic is divinely tall
> And walks the night in beauty – (a good thing, too;
> Keep her locked up by day.) That speech defect
> Turns out to be the thweetest little lithp,
> The one too dumb to say a single word
> Is shy and modest, while the gabby gawk
> Who never stops talking, flings herself around
> All over the place – who can this Sylvia be
> Except the life of the party. Miss Flat Chest
> Is slender-slim as willow-wands or briony...[21]

Anyway, do you get the point? Phew.

Audience: He sounds like a cynic.

Erin: Philosophically, he was not a Cynic, but an Epicurean! But yes, the Romans were terribly jaded. However, they were the ones who instituted marriage to one person – and divorce before taking another wife. Common law originated in Rome. Anyway, there were many authors who did this kind of thing, poking fun at love. Ovid, the sensitive author of the *Metamorphoses* – the Roman rendition of the Greek myths of transformation – wrote something called *Ars Amatoria* (The Art of Love), which was a parody of love and its various activities. Quite amusing – it should be read. However, amusement aside, the deeper meaning of a culture which produces a literature of this nature shows a loss of innocence and a breakdown inthe balance of masculine and feminine in culture. Western civilisation had reached a point of no return, wherein the gulf between the ancient worship of the mother goddess and the exaltation of the masculine sky-gods had become a vast chasm. A culture that makes mockery of love and imagination is a culture bereft of soul – rather like ours appears to have become.

Anyway, this piece is pretty straightforward in its intent – to discourage men from falling into the trap of romantic love. It is

---

[21] Ibid., lines 1146-67.

rather crude, but then, the Romans were less aesthetic than the Greeks, and anyway, more important than its style is its content. It is a dissertation on psychological projection. We have many names for it, but basically, projection is seeing your own divinity in someone else – your own image of beauty reflected against someone else. So, we live in a hard world as Venus' minions. And, too, love receives so much hysteria because it's fashionable in some eras, and not fashionable in others; and sometimes romantic love is wonderful and other times it's stupid. It's a real problem. So when we look at the horoscope, sometimes it's a little clearer, because at least we are talking about individuals.

There is always projection in any relationship; that's how it gets started. The hook is there in one person and not another, because there is obviously a personally recognisable aspect of the "other" which is familiar to oneself. What mirrors your own needs and your own love inside in someone else creates the basis for a meeting. Projections do fall away, or are withdrawn,, and the more slowly a projection is dropped or removed, the more likely is the relationship to have strength and last. If projections are shattered immediately, then the relationship breaks, because that is what happens. If the projections are withdrawn slowly while being simultaneously replaced with the real attributes of an individual, and it turns out that the reality is actually just as nice or maybe even better, then obviously you've got a really good relationship.

So, there is nothing wrong with projection. It's instinctive and natural, and the mystery of it is that you don't know that it's happening until it is gone. So that's the way it goes. The unconscious is exactly that. Getting in touch with your unconscious is absurd. It gets in touch with you, like me walking into the men's room at the lunch break. It's the same with relationship. It's usually not until you see what has happened in retrospect, that you know. We can look back through history, or look back through our own lives, and add up the patterns that we might have created ourselves. And it seems that if we want to look at creativity specifically, then that too is something that has to be treated very gently. If you have a creative impulse, and you wish to bring that to fruition, to something real, then you have to be very sensitive, very gentle, and recognise that it too has a life of its own and that it will leave if you don't treat it properly. If you don't respect it, for example, or if you don't incubate it, then it will abort or wither.

Incubation of the creative seed

If you have a very strong creative impulse, it's actually best to leave it for a while, and not talk too much about it. This is the secrecy of the artist or the writer, they are not being coy. It's a deep instinctual awareness, and if you expose it too quickly, it's likely to die, because it can't stand the light of examination until it has in fact got some kind of stability to it. So if you do know someone who is creative and actually produces their inner vision, whether it's writing or artistic creations like paintings, or whatever, it's absolutely necessary to be secretive about it. And also, it's necessary to be secret about new feelings about your own self – if something is born within the self, then you shouldn't blather on to friends, or in groups and that kind of thing, about this new self-discovery. It is reasonably healthy to keep it inside until you fully bring it to consciousness by the internal process of incubation and gestation.

The trick is to keep the erotic seed *sub rosa, in camera* – lovely Latin terms for secret, hidden – it is to keep the light (of reason) out of the picture until it has fully matured. If you expose your film in the camera before it is treated and developed in a darkroom, then you ruin it. Likewise, a project, idea, relationship too quickly exposed or developed will often have tragic consequences. When two people meet and fall in love, their instinct is to withdraw from others, hide away, incubating – the popular term in the eighties was "cocooning". Too true. However, at appropriate stages in the development of relationship, one steps out a bit more, a bit more, until it can stand the glare of the crowd, or the test of social interaction. Love needs this sacred, secret period of intimate symbiosis to fully germinate the seed – if it is broken too soon, often the relationship comes under stress or becomes too mundane too quickly. And, it can die. The individuals each must be aware of the sacredness of the union.

Dreams, too, are in this secret place. They should only be revealed in the safe circumstances of a good analytic situation, or with another whom you trust, who knows you intimately and has little in the way of projectile expectation. It does not serve to expose the deep symbolic part of yourself to the brightness of day too soon, not because something horrible is going to happen – though it could – or that it's against the law or isn't cool, but simply because you expose it too quickly. It's like a premature birth, it becomes too vulnerable to its environment. There are some people who tend towards this excitation and premature delivery, and there's a caution around that. This process of secret development is a natural process of insemination, incubation and gestation, and right time of giving birth; and that's an essential aspect of creativity.

It also has to do with love and relationship. There's a shaky period in any developing relationship after its inception, and then it mysteriously grows and then reaches a level where it can pretty well withstand anything. But this shifts all the time, and it requires consciousness on the part of both people. However, it's in that shaky period where people are instinctively afraid of exposing themselves. After the strengthening of the cocooning part, projections begin to fall and be withdrawn; whereas, in the beginning, it feels as if you can tell the new partner anything and everything – it will all be OK. Often this time is followed by a period where people feel that they'd better not tell their beloved anything, because if they find out what they are really like, they are going to leave! So there's this mysterious part where everyone's a little nervous about behaving normally. Around the new person you get very quiet and kind of withdrawn, and the real, solid, alive, and tangible birth – the creation itself, whether it's a relationship or a project – should be able to withstand a lot after that phase has been undergone.

These phases and stages of both love and creation are parallel, and Venus in the chart shows our attitude toward it – for example, if there's a tendency to be afraid of love or insecure about creativity, if it's too hasty, dashed off, not enough solidity, not enough Saturn or earth and so on. There are two questions to keep in mind: How does one approach creativity? It doesn't matter whether it's the creation of ideas or things. And how does relationship aid self-development or the process of individuation?

Aspects of love and creation: Venus to the planets

There are far too many ways to approach love and to experience it than can be listed. It is this very complexity that makes love and creation a difficult subject, it is so deeply personal and is experienced by each of us uniquely. Indeed, as we now know, even the two people in relationship – lover and beloved – love differently, which presents a dilemma with its own inherent problems.

It seems we love each other as much for our differences and flaws as we do for the harmonies and affinities. The fundamental basis for the creative urge and love may never really have altered one bit in the long course of human life, and the experience that man might have as differing from what woman might have may also never really have changed. What does change, however, is the prescribed boundaries within which Love is defined, in social, cultural and religious expression. In different times in history, as well, Love is perceived and given dimensions and aspects of expression which we might call "collective" or social, which say nothing about how I or you might really, secretly and deeply, feel about loving and being loved.

It would seem that all aspects of love (or some of them) have been highlighted and enhanced, given greater latitude for "popular" expression, in different periods in Western culture. Sometimes love has been exalted, and at other times, scorned as being foolish – love may be both exalted and foolish, but the heart of romance never skips a beat, cultural, social or psychological popularity aside. There are infinite ways of loving and being loved, and there is no right or wrong way.[22]

---

[22] See Ethel Spector Person, *Love and Fateful Encounters,* Bloomsbury, 1989.

Astrologically, the whole horoscope is the aspect of love for each of us, but the planet Venus plays a great role in our capacity to give and receive love, to experience and reflect back our experience of another. In fact, Venus is about both sacred love and profane love – Aphrodite Urania the celestial, Platonic love, combined with Aphrodite Pandemos, earthy, human love. These two aspects of Venus do not always harmonise within us. Love is not about someone else, it is about ourselves and how we feel in ourselves about loving.

It seems we are born with a predisposition toward the experience of love – how we are received by our mother at birth, how we are touched and nurtured, how our environment strikes us, are all imprinted in our cells and body memories. Those actual experiences are the reality factor (the earthy, Pandemic Venus experience). How we feel about it all is the Uranian, Celestial factor. Whether the two are sympathetic or not determines a great deal of our habits in love and loving.

We explored the fact that Venus rules two signs, Taurus (earth) and Libra (air), and we saw it was deeply meaningful – there is the sensory and sensual aspect of Venus and the social, relative type of experience. Sometimes we might find that the two argue within us. A refined, idealistic and socially acceptable "type" of love which receives approval from society (family, etc.) might be totally repellent because we are more attracted to and attract people who are outside our social milieu, or indeed, outside our primary relationship. This is not an uncommon experience, and the vast majority of people I have spoken to have, indeed, loved an "inappropriate" person, met the "right" person at the "wrong" time, had a "horrible" relationship, and have also had an experience of rejection by someone with whom they themselves have experienced a loving transformation. Rare is the person who has not experienced a type of unrequited love. Clearly, there is no answer to some of these dilemmas. These are simply aspects of love.

More often than not, our clients will (boldly, or shamefacedly) ask us about love and relationships. Sometimes they are kind enough to ask only about the general "conditions" around their Venus, 7th house and Moon, but others ask the impossible – when will I fall in love? And with whom am I best suited? These questions might be better put as, "Why do I fall in love, and in whom do I see my own divinity?" This is where Venus enters in all her splendour! Somewhere along the line, the natal Venus will have experienced love, and in the memory of the experience, repeated patterns will be established. By the time one reaches the Saturn return, all aspects of Venus have been polished by Saturn, shaping, forming and defining the boundaries and experiences of love.

It would do to look back in the ephemeris to the times in which experiences might have happened that would be involved with Venus. For instance, when progressed Venus conjoined the natal Sun or vice versa, when Saturn made exact aspects to Venus in the course of the life, when other major transits "hit" Venus, and so on. You can create a "Venus memory line", and track your Venusian developments from the moment of your birth. Therefore it is important to rephrase the question of, "When will I fall in love?" and ask, "Why would I, and under which conditions have I, fallen in love?" We fall in love at different times and for different reasons – sometimes those motives surprise us, sometimes they are downright pathological, and we wonder at our psychological well-being! Please don't tell me, anyone, that you have never had a sick relationship – unless, of course, you have never had a relationship! Even when we have had such a relationship, in the face of various types – dependency, co-dependency, unrequited, abusive – we, the lover, must see our own face mirrored in the beloved.

We fall into different kinds of love at different times in our lives. Age makes a difference, as do time and circumstance. But astrologically, the transits of the chart define why we fell in love, and what kind of love it is, and what dimension or aspect of love we need to have exposed and explored within ourselves. It's not all about Venus, by any means, its about the quality of the time and the aspect of love. If we fall in love when transiting Saturn is square our Sun, then we are in love to learn a rather hard lesson, perhaps about not getting our ego soothed and our needs met in a passionate way. When transiting Neptune is conjunct Mars, we may find ourself in a triangle or a relationship with someone who simply cannot tell the truth, which

Venus and Jupiter

means we live with a lie in ourselves. Or we fall in love when Pluto transits opposite the Moon, and our inner mother stands before us forbidding the love we think we want so desperately, and emotions surface which we have never experienced before. We are stripped bare and, like the poet says, "lie wailing for the demon lover". Or we might fall in love with ourselves and feel whole and rich, or we might have a flash when Jupiter trines the Moon, thinking, "This is it, my salvation has arrived," until Uranus comes along six months later to throw, yet again, another light on the aspect of Venus.

Knowing we learn more about ourselves in relationship than we do when alone, not all the lessons are wonderful. We learn from our loves, both wonderful and terrible things! For love to endure, all aspects of it must come forward, not all of them particularly charming or courtly, many of them earthy and primitive.

As I said, the word itself, "aspect" derives from the Latin *aspectus,* and means, "looking at, being perceived, having a certain countenance". Therefore, when an aspect occurs between two planets, they could be considered as looking at each other, regarding each other, and experiencing each other. What does Venus see when she looks at Saturn or Jupiter or Uranus and, in turn, how do they perceive and reflect on Venus? Think of that for a minute – personify Venus and the other planets and feel how your own Venus sees the others, and how they might see Venus. This might be as simple as having a Venus-Saturn conjunction, or it may be as complex as Venus sitting at the midpoint of Saturn-Uranus. Or, Venus in Cancer would have the flavour of Moon-Venus.

To the degree that you are aware of your own Venus and its interaction, its dialogue with the rest of your chart, ruminate on it for a bit. You may find that, within yourself, you notice certain motifs which seem immutable. When you see a painting, you see it with the same values as you experience a sunset. These values are intrinsically woven into our ways of loving and perceiving beauty. No one sees or projects and receives "aspects" of a painting, a sunset or a beloved in the same way.

Venus and Mercury

I thought I would talk about Venus and Mercury first. Because of their mutual proximity to the Sun, you can have a conjunction, a sextile, a semisquare, a square, or a quintile. Venus can be 48° from the Sun, and Mercury can be 28° from the Sun, so you can get the 72° aspect between them. It is a rhythmic but rare aspect. I've not seen lots of the possible combinations of Mercury-Venus conjunctions because they are too multiple and their pattern is quite different from other planets. It's made very clear in the *Retrograde Planets* book, but Mercury and Venus form very different patterns with respect to the Sun and Earth than the superior planets. You don't get a cyclic conjunction of Venus and Mercury in the same way as you get Sun-Uranus conjunctions or Sun-Saturn conjunctions. Because we perceive them from Earth, looking inward to the Sun, there are two types of conjunctions that the inner planets have with the Sun, whereas with the outer planets, there is only one type of conjunction that can occur between the planet and the Sun. It's a bit too technical to explain right now. However, it's easily seen if you understand about retrogression and solar system movement.

I want to go into the conjunction of Mercury and Venus in a bit more depth than the other aspects, because it is filled with many implicate possibilities. By conjunct, I mean within four degrees of each other, no more – the closer they are together, the more intriguing the possibilities. You can have four kinds of Venus-Mercury conjunctions. Mercury can be retrograde and Venus direct; Venus can be retrograde with Mercury direct; both can be direct and both can be retrograde. This astronomical dance produces very subtle differentiations on the theme of androgyny. Androgyny is not about cross-dressing, but about balance or harmony between masculine and feminine values, mind-set and creative urge. When we think of the conjunction Aphrodite had with Hermes, which produced the sweet, innocent, but lonely Hermaphroditus, there is a cleanness of mind that can be present.

However, remember that, because they are both inner planets, they can be in opposition to each other heliocentrically, and yet appear in the same zodiacal longitude from our Earth perspective. If one or the other, Venus or Mercury, is retrograde and the other is direct, then the one that is direct is in the superior place (on the other side of the Sun from Earth) and the retrograde planet is the one which is between the Sun and Earth. There is an interior conflict which sets up a dialogue between the person's values and their own attitude toward those personal values. It produces a real thinker, someone who is in the business of sorting out values or ideas.

If both are direct, thus superior, then the dialogue is less of a conflict, and more externalized, but the weighing and balancing of values and thoughts is consistent.

If both are retrograde, then there is a propensity to introspect and churn values, relationships, relativity of philosophy and thoughts in the mind, over and over. This can be a very productive, obsessional thinker. But it can also result in over-think, in analysing their personal relationships and their creative impetus to death. Relationships are never easy and always an issue – something that becomes a project. The creative life can be very rich, filled with versatile ways of demonstrating inner visions. Inner planets retrograde are always between us and the Sun, so have an instinctive pull away from nature – more Uranian, if you will, because most of the life experience takes place in the head. When Mercury and Venus are conjunct and one of them is retrograde, the direct planet is the one which "carries" the inner experience out into the world of relating.

Also, if just one is retrograde, then the potential for projection is very high. It is difficult for the person to separate their own values (if it is Venus which is retrograde) from their partner or society; or, if it is Mercury, then the person might feel that everyone is thinking what he or she is thinking. This can lead to inflation, megalomania or paranoia – all are simply aggrandized conditions of normal thinking/feeling patterns.

If Venus is retrograde and Mercury direct, and they are conjunct in zodiacal longitude, they are then in exact opposition to each other heliocentrically. We see them from earth as being together, but in fact they are diametrically opposed – the astronomical position belies what we perceive from the Self. Thus, the inner ideals – which are very high and celestially motivated – are more easily carried out by Mercury into the world via creative outlets. However, often a conflict will arise between one's inner beliefs and ethics and the social form.

If Venus is direct and Mercury is retrograde when they are conjunct, the reverse manifestation is more likely – that is, the inner perceptions, ideas and beliefs which run against the status quo can be harmonised by Venus' more socially orientated position. Thus, we might find a person who is able to express unorthodox ideas in a palatable way because their socialisation is good, thus creating a revolution in ideas but gaining acceptance for those ideas. There is an interior argument about what society has imposed and what the individual really thinks.

At best, there's something about a Venus-Mercury conjunction that seems to talk about the ability to quite reasonably and rationally see what one's values are, and, if not actually doing that, to spend an awful lot of time making valiant attempts to understand the mysteries of love and life – making attempts to discuss, to talk, to separate, to understand, to communicate about feelings and relationships and communication/creativity. None of these things say whether it's a successful quest or not, but the ultimate role, through the process of Mercury-Venus to creativity, has to do more with lists, understanding things rationally, being logical, formulating, which can be quite annoying to other types of people, and doing a lot of very real serious thinking. It's also an incredibly playful aspect, aside from what sounds like a terribly organised setup. It's very playful because Hermes is the boy, the eternal youth. He's a very good symbol for the *puer aeternus,* in Jungian terminology – a very good symbol. He's perfect. He never grows up. He is so favoured by the gods that he gets to do the journey to the underworld and return! He goes to Hades and back frequently. He's like a little tourist guide to the netherworld – or the unconscious, if you will.

Therefore, Mercury is a complex and deep figure. As Psychopompos, he is the soul-guide, bringing unconscious contents to consciousness and returning thoughts and perceptions to the unconscious for deeper processing. If he is connected to Venus, then

Venus and Jupiter

body and soul are intertwined – if one expects body and soul to be intertwined in love and creativity at all times, then there will be both small and large disappointments. When you have Mercury and Venus coupled together, because the conjunction, of course, is the seed of all other aspects, there is a deep connection between the conscious and the unconscious mind. This is inevitably creative in its essence, but will take other aspects to describe how and in what ways creativity and relationship are manifest.

Does anybody here have a Mercury-Venus conjunction?

Audience: Yes, I have Mercury and Venus at 11° and 12° Aries.

Erin: You do? They are both direct? Do you find that you are not particularly perturbed about friends being male or female? I'm not saying that you're perfectly balanced, but it is a good balance. I think it's more objective, perhaps. It's objectivity that's added to relationships, and a genuine curiosity.

Anything with Mercury adds a note of curiosity. "I wonder what makes this person tick?" It doesn't have much to do with feelings – in fact, it is a sign of objectifying feelings. Interestingly, at lunch Alexandra said, "Isn't it funny that there aren't any epithets associated with Venus that have to do with emotions or feelings." I'd never thought of that, and indeed, it is true. Venus is not a feeling function. It's sensation, like earthy Taurus, or thinking, like airy Libra. But I think Mercury-Venus tilts the balance towards the Ideal and away from the Real. Mercury and Venus are very tightly associated towards Urania, which has a problem with the irrational. So it's perhaps more of a Venus Urania than Venus Pandemos. It might be harder to get in touch with Venus than Mercury.

Audience: Yes, I do find that my mind is watching all the time. Even in making love, I might find myself suddenly thinking something or watching my own responses! This is a consistent thing, and it is a natural characteristic – by the way, it doesn't deter me from
the fun or pleasure, and it doesn't mean that I don't lose myself, but I am frequently disturbed by my inner eye.

Erin: We see this kind of split in everything, in all the different planets. However that is a strong characteristic of Venus and Mercury. But it's interesting to see that there is just one Mercury-Venus conjunction in a room of people this size. It happens often enough that there ought to be lots and lots. I would read any contact between them as a meeting of mind and values, and a matter of thinking everything through.

Audience: Would it be like having Venus in Gemini or Virgo?

Erin: Yes and no. First, I would think more in terms of Venus than Mercury. However, Venus in those signs is disposited by Mercury, therefore there is a relationship that it shares with the quality of the sign. Well, if you had Venus in Gemini, you would find a Urania-type attraction to clean air, where there is a feeling of "Don't let's get too murky and too emotional!" – a desire to keep a lot of breathing space in relationship, and clarity and vision. It has nothing to do with lack of feeling or passion, but there is always the objective side that alerts them to problems, flaws, lack of perfection, and so on.

But Venus in Virgo is actually very earthy, and shows its feeling through practical means, like doing something for someone, giving something to them, or making their emotions tangible. It's still analytical, it isn't terribly emotionally open or demonstrative in a tactile way. Venus in Virgo is highly sensitive to emotion and undercurrent, though. (Remember the Libra story, and how it split the sign of the serpent?) Well, Virgo is the "other half" of Scorpio, and thus it has a deeply feeling and sensual side to it – it has more capacity to touch emotional zones than Venus in Gemini, but it's still terribly rational and a bit slow to act. The senses are alert, but there's a kind of analytical, intellectual process going on with Venus in Virgo.

Audience: Isn't Venus in earth signs more inhibited?

Erin: I think the kind of reservation and inhibition to which you refer is more a product of another aspect, rather than Venus in Virgo, Capricorn or Taurus, though all of them feel rather solid and unimaginative. Deeply cautious, and slow to burn, would be earth's *modus operandi.* I think there is a lot of reserve if Venus is in an earth sign, but it's more that they are right where they are at the time. By that I mean it isn't fiery and future-orientated, racing into the relationship or idea with all barrels blazing, or watery and high-risk emotionally based, or airy and cool-feeling. Because earth is fundamentally shy of dramatics, I think that fear of exposure is right for them, but it might feel repressed or arrested to someone with more adventurousness or neediness in their nature. But when moved, you won't find anything more sensual than Venus in earth signs. But they have to be safe, that's true.

So, what other associations do we have with Hermes and Aphrodite? It's funny, because, when Ares and Aphrodite were caught *in flagrante delicto* and all the other gods were sitting round laughing and mocking them, they all said, "Oh boy, I wouldn't want to be in *his* position." All, that is, except Hermes, who said, "Oh, I would." He was very quick to say, "Oh, that's not too bad." So, Mercury will try anything. That's the other side of the Mercurial Venus. They're are willing to think about and be objective about anything that has to do with relating, and also very open and very creatively versatile. There should be more possibility for experimentation in ideas and projects. Sometimes it's jumpy. Sometimes there are too many things going on for that same reason, and they get bored quickly and move on.

Audience: When I had a Saturn transit to Venus, I changed my style – this seems superficial, but it went core-deep. Everything, literally everything in my closet was unwearable, because I could not relate to it. I wore the same three things for almost six months. I couldn't afford to get a new wardrobe of clothes, so it took a long time. My insides had changed so much that I couldn't even look at myself in certain things. For six months I wore black – and I couldn't find a "style" for almost two years. That was about five years ago.

Erin: Yes, that would fall into a Venus category. It may seem superficial, but what we put on our bodies, or clothe and house our bodies in, is a statement, a tribal statement. It talks about where we come from, what side of the tracks, and the outer things we are at one with. Hair is also very good for that, too – Mohawk style, pixi-cut or pouffed coif? Ears are very good these days for telling what tribe someone is from, for instance – how many rings you have in your ears. It's pretty good for demonstrating tribal statements. And that's all part of Venus, too, isn't it? We can explore all the emotional, philosophical and archetypal levels, serious psychological stuff, and then, there it is. It's all about clothes, when you get right down to it – going shopping!

Seriously, though, transits to Venus always manifest in an evaluation of needs, values and relationships, and can precipitate an abrupt break from past affinities on all levels – friends, lovers, appearances, beliefs and so forth. It is as if a seed of change is planted, and its maturity flourishes with the major transit. Your wearing black is fitting, since Saturn likely killed off something deep inside you, and you went into mourning, purging the old self from its now outmoded way of being. This will always be reflected in our persona.

Audience: Oh, right, I forgot to say that I left my marriage in that year, as well.

Erin: Oh, right, glad you mentioned it. Amazing, isn't it – there are likely many, many things that died in that cycle, and your inner resources were low and in reserve while you underwent a massive emotional and creative overhaul.

Venus and the Moon

This is the subject of a seminar of its own. These are the only two real female images in the horoscope. They can make any aspect, from conjunction right on through the whole evolution of aspects, and they are in some way in collusion at all times, because, in a sense, they are isolated by gender. There is a tendency for them to be either overemphasised, de-emphasised, or in some way undernourished or perhaps overfed. You have to really look at them very closely to understand how it is that both men and women would be able to use the feminine symbols to their comfort. The Moon-Venus polarity for women is just as demanding on the self-developmental level as it is for men. It would be like saying men are happier with Mars – it isn't true. They are not. But the Moon and Venus have to do with specific images of the feminine – the natural split in the feminine mystique – or, at least, the split between two types of feminine symbol. It's like two goddesses viewing each other with a decidedly wary eye.

We must remember that, from Earth, our view of Venus produces her in phases as well as the Moon. Venus, when furthest from the Sun, just before and just after its stations (both retrograde and direct), is in a crescent shape. Its distance from the Sun results in magnification of solar reflected rays, and on a clear night, during a new moon, and at its points of greatest elongation, Venus can be bright enough to cast a shadow. Venus is many-faceted, not only by her dual rulership over celestial and earthy matters, her dual rulership of signs, but also because she is a shape-shifter and has many aspects to her presence in the heavens.

The images of Moon and Venus are antithetical, but they are also necessary polarities to the whole feminine encounter, and I think the synthesis of both is necessary to keep the feminine function in working order. Moon-Venus oppositions and squares – and this is evident by sign alone, the aspect does not have to be exact – show a split between two aspects of the feminine. This split can pose a problem with the integration of the maternal function and instinctual, intuitive nature (Moon) and the exotic, independent, siren aspect of woman (Venus). Sometimes it is a result of the mother herself being in conflict about her own femininity, and she has hidden one aspect of herself (either the Moon or Venus) in favour of the other. But it can also be that one's mother was a deeply intuitive woman, and her knowledge of you was felt as invasive and needed to be countered by keeping your feelings a secret from her.

It is entirely possible that one's mother can also be a seductress and sexual creature (how else did you get here?), whether or not it is considered in good taste. The confusion between the two can rend a great tear between what one needs for sexual release and pleasure, and what one needs in order to be nurtured and coddled. That the same person might be able to do both is a difficult thing for the Moon-Venus split person to accept, and very often they don't accept it, but find two outlets, a "wife" and a "lover". This applies for both men and women.

In the most extreme examples, we all know of men who have ideal wives whose sole job, it appears, is to keep the hearth-fire burning and the children well-nourished, while his is to support the family financially and make regular appearances as Father. The saddest part, for the man who finds his Moon-Venus split irreconcilable, occurs when he turns his sexual desires toward other women, who inadvertently act out the siren-anima for him, becoming his mistress, but never his wife. He feels incapable of experiencing both tenderness and erotic passion in one woman and for one woman.

In the case of a woman, once married, she might find herself oddly embarrassed to express her sexuality and seductiveness, and becomes her husband's mother or sister, all the while wondering what happened to her once uninhibited unbridled passion. Perhaps, to her dismay, she finds it exists only outside of her role of wife (and/or mother), and she herself must take a lover. The incest taboo enters at this point, where the relationship has become so familial that sex is sublimated in favour of a more platonic relationship – one acceptable within the social taboos of the family dynamic.

Anima-split women will be uncomfortable in one or the other role, if it is carried out for too long. If Venus wins out, she may be a seductress but fears mothering – it will render her potency as a vamp ineffective. That it is possible to experience femininity and maternity is quite beside the point; it remains a valid perception for the Moon-Venus split person that there is only an uncomfortable marriage between earth-mother and goddess-lover.

Another extreme possibility is the professional mother, who can only relate to her function as a nurturer and controller of the family (whether that is the corporation or the kids), while denigrating her more cosmetic self, the side that longs to express her wild or independent nature.

That the classical horoscope contains only two clearly feminine symbol planets, the Moon and Venus, itself speaks of an inherent imbalance of priorities. But when those two are also sharply placed against each other, it becomes important for the person to make attempts to be more in touch with both the seductive and nurturing sides. Moon-Venus is largely a maternal legacy, and will very likely run down through the family line – it is one of the strongest of dynastic aspects I've seen with respect to matrilineal inheritance. As an aside, I feel that both Neptune and Pluto have strongly feminine characteristics, which speaks of an emerging feminine in the collective which is affected by and affects simultaneously the individual's response to the feminine archetype. Uranus is distinctly masculine, while Neptune has a domain in the earth – Poseidon rules the underground streams – and Pluto is the mother of the dead, and has married the earth-mother's daughter. Pluto also has characteristics of an avenging goddess, global, consuming, obsessive rage, as well as the fertility associated with the liberation of Persephone each spring, bringing renewed fruitfulness to the earth.

When they are in trine or sextile, the duality is more clearly seen, though obviously by dint of nature it still exists as a dichotomy. In other words, by the very existence of a Moon and a Venus, there is a polarity, but it is not necessarily pathological. In fact, it's only a problem if it is a problem, isn't it? It is quite natural and healthy to separate the two functions, being aware that each has its zenith and useful nature, but to divorce them, or to deny one or the other, is to produce an unhealthy complex. Mothering and seducing are not polarities or warring forces, but are the two sides of the same woman, and each can be employed more easily at the right time and place. It becomes more possible that woman can be mother and lover. And, in turn, men are then freed to be feeling, loving, and needy as well as providers and protectors.

So you have the Moon, which is really about maternity and femininity through maternity, nurture and nurturing, and you have the feminine through the aspect of its being a kind of exotic, more eroticized form of femininity – that which deals specifically with the crafting or the creating of art, or ideas, or relationships. Now, the Moon attracts you instinctively to something, whereas Venus likely has the potential for a little more objectivity to it. Venus has more facets; it can warn you of the danger ahead in a relationship by gut reaction, the ability to see more objectively what you are getting into, or what it is that you are desiring and what it is that you want to do with it. But the Moon is pure need.

The Moon is at home in water signs, feeling, moving, responding and can be deeply intuitive and attached to family (mother to child and vice versa) by a kind of psychic umbilicus; while if in earth signs, the Moon can have slow reactions to emotion – both their own feelings and in receiving other people's feelings. But they respond in their bones and bodies very strongly. They can appear very complacent and accepting of life's offerings, bad or good. Air Moons can think about feelings, but it is often after the fact, and they may find their rationalising ability gets in the way of their gut instinct, They can carry a bad relationship longer than necessary, because of a distrust of their own feelings. Fire Moons are impulsive and headstrong, with a gut feeling for the future potential of a relationship – they always know when the relationship will start, what it is good for in the long run, and significantly, when it is over, having run its creative course.

Therefore, if you have a sharp angular relationship between Moon and Venus – let's say there is an opposition of the Moon to Venus – the reconciliation of the lover, Venus, and the mother, Moon, is often uncomfortable. Problems can arise when one is confronted with either the seductive aspect of femininity, or the more functional aspect of nurturing and nourishment and maternity. That doesn't mean that everybody with a Moon-Venus opposition runs around going from one side to the other in their attractions – or going for really nasty relationships, which are exciting and scary but you wouldn't want to bring him home. It's not always that dramatic, but it is a real internal dichotomy that is posed between the socialised image of the feminine, which is Venus, because it changes form, and the archaic, age-old, changeless face of the Moon, reflecting basic, fundamental, emotional needs. The Moon is about feelings. Venus is not really about feelings at all.

Sometimes it feels more like a detachment from feelings, where Venus "watches" the Moon. Another manifestation is disliking one's own taste in things, not trusting how the instinctive reactions lead you into situations or relationships. Someone once described their Moon-Venus square as a feeling of distance or separation from feelings in a relationship, which was disturbing to him. Because relationships are about two people, it is more likely that resolution of conflict takes place in that context. Conflict would be more easily integrated if a person with a Moon-Venus "problem" actually had a relationship with someone whose Venus touched or "softened" the other person's Venus or Moon, and contacts between them enhanced feelings of safety and receptivity without reprisal. Integration of hard aspects is usually a social activity because the mirror of relationship throws us back to ourselves. Also, being aware of a split helps the inner dialogue to become more active and consciously workable.

Now, what do you suppose might be a remedy to that kind of circumstance? What would you call a Moon-Venus healing experience? Any ideas? If that's how it manifests, what is a person to do? Because we've all got the Moon and Venus within us, we all have in us the tendency to do that very thing in greater or lesser degree. So it exists. But when you have Moon-Venus in hard aspect, opposite or square, you've got a problem with the inner comfort of it.

Audience: Both my two brothers and myself have Moon square Venus! And, we all feel that our mother hid her seductress from the family – we never knew her to indulge in herself at all, and we all feel quite guilty when we treat ourselves, do something "unnecessary", or waste time! Do you think that has anything to do with the aspect?

Erin: I do. That is one attitude of Moon-Venus – the ability to be frivolous and enjoy life for its simple things, to play. Now, this moves us into a place where training and received values are playing a strong role. The very fact that you used the words "unnecessary" and "wasting time" makes me ask if there is a voice inside saying that what you need is unnecessary or time-wasting. It may be that your mother herself felt so tied to you, her children, that she couldn't free herself. Partly, it is a value judgement, this business about things unnecessary. For instance, the source of the word ludicrous is *ludere* – to play – or *ludio,* I play. So, playing is ludicrous? You are experiencing a form of Moon-Venus split because the Moon is about nurture and it is very necessary to nurture oneself through play.

Creativity is about being able to play and contact the magical child, reconnecting with the imaginal realm, the enchanted world. Aphrodite can be very serious as well. If you are propitiating the Moon too much – that is, doing habitual things taught by mother or society – she might become jealous, giving you a feeling of guilt (Moon). We become disenchanted when the Moon dominates by habituation and Venus is countered by not being allowed out to play. Listen to the dialogue between your lunar instincts to be secure and loved, and your Venusian duality between the ideal way of experiencing your own form of creative release and the practical ways of acting that creativity out.

The most significant thing that you've just said is that it runs through the family. That's the first place to start. Start looking back. In *Dynasty,* that is exactly what I'm saying – there are strong planetary combinations that run in families along various thematic lines, and the Moon-Venus is one of the regular signatures found consistent in family groups. You (and your brothers) are running up against a family aspect; it's inherited, it's one of the strongest ones, it is bred in the bone. So it wouldn't hurt to examine very carefully how this is manifested in each of you, and how you might "open up the square", that is, release some of the desire unfulfilled because of duty, playfulness unlived because of inhibition, and sensuality unexpressed because of guilt.

Audience: Are the needs of the Moon more simple than those of Venus?

Erin: Not really, needs are always complex and layered and woven into each other. That is why they are difficult, if not impossible, to meet fully. The lunar need is very basic but not simple. It doesn't have to be all fancy and tarted up. It needs lovely basic little things, like a tidy garden, or something that's very pretty and very simple and very nurturing and a very simple side of the relationship where you just make dinner with somebody or where you really do sink into something that's secure, that's safe, that's contained.

On the other hand, there is a side of our Venus that really likes being scared, that is excited by challenge and something new, untried, untasted, unfelt, unlived – that challenges us to explore new aesthetic and creative potentials. There is a bit of all of us that likes walking on the edge of the creative life, of the emotional life. The Moon doesn't want that at all. It likes to be really safe in a nice warm dark place where all things breed. Now, some of the things that breed are not in harmony with the civilised aspect of our own selves – we might disapprove of ourselves. That is OK, that is part of individuation – discovering the aspects of the self that do not work and need revision – but we must be careful that it is really our basic instincts that are telling us this, and not our parents, teachers, police, and so forth.

Audience: But, what about men? They've got Moon and Venus in their chart, too. What do they do with that split?

Erin: Same thing – planets are not gender-biased in themselves, they deal with human nature. But obviously, a man will cope with his Moon-Venus within the sphere of his limits as a man. I mean, within his definition as a man – as women do with their own limits – fewer, of course. It still boils down to the pleasure principle: How much feeling can be coped with? How much real benefit and love and good life can be managed? Most people judge themselves and others from distinct personal biases – in the same way, we can be very unpleasurable to ourselves. Clearly the Moon-Venus aspect will help understand where to begin to get to the bottom of the most basic instincts on feelings and moods.

Because men are still required, by and large, and still desire, to do most of the providing of shelter, money and goods in a family, a man might not be able to live out his dreams – his Ideal may not be met in his real world. His business urge or success urge might conflict with his desire to be an artist or a softer person. This is a male thing, wanting to be lunar in a masculine way. Often a man can best show his love and caring by providing shelter, food and substantial things, ignoring his Venusian needs – his own frivolous and aesthetic side – and not developing his taste, for instance, leaving his wife or partner to look after the decorating of the home, or preparation of the food, or playing with and disciplining the children. He may long for the freedom to explore his artistic, his musical, his instinctive or his intellectual side but may not because of the nature of cultural bias and his own masculine drive.

If the Moon and Venus are in the 12th house, for example, then there will be a likelihood that someone else will carry the feminine side of that individual. The 12th house holds planets longer in the unconscious – that is, they are born into consciousness later than in other houses. For a man, it is likely to be his lover – whether that is a male or a female lover is quite beside the point. His feminine side will be shadowed and unfamiliar and thus more easily assumed and carried by a loved one. For a woman, she might have a very hard time with her own femininity – it may embarrass her, she may not have "given birth" to her needs because they have been shadowed and mystifying. The 12th house Moon-Venus can manifest in an inability to love actual individuals, but love and projection of the divine fall onto a guru figure, a spiritual carrier of one's own emotional value and feeling-tone.

I know a man who has a Moon-Venus conjunction in the 12th house in Virgo, and he has never connected to his feminine self except as a "mother" – he has withheld a great deal of himself through serving others. Always looking after others keeps him in control of them. He has a history of many sequential, short-term affairs – all during the last seven years of a thirteen-year marriage, in which neither his needs nor his wife's were met. They each kept up appearances, each having affairs with others. This behaviour pattern often keeps a potentially loving relationship at bay, avoiding the responsibility of the ebb and flow of long-term relationships. By having a marriage which one cannot leave, one is free to have affairs with others and leave them, thus cheating everyone out of true intimacy.

Fundamentally, this man is incapable of love on the personal level, so uses women for his own physical and emotional needs; but his true love is a cult figure, a guru! His personal humanity is lost to the collective, and his Moon-Venus (in the 12th) is projected onto a "divine" figure as a way of escaping personal responsibility in partnerships. When finished with them, get rid of them! Part of the 12th house is sacrificial – to sacrifice personal happiness and emotional gratification is not only inherent, but is also learned.

Something about the mother was slippery, evasive, ambivalent and long-suffering. She was also overbearing and invasive – Moon problems in men are often manifest as fears of being devoured, swallowed, watched, invaded psychically. So, the man in question had this as a training ground.

Audience: Funny, I knew someone like that – I wonder if it is the same person? Anyway, this man seemed to assuage some feeling of guilt by giving, giving, giving on the material level, but there was a blank spot somewhere, a dead place. Obviously he has true feelings, but they were never conveyed, and when they were it was too late to do anything about them. He hates intimacy, in fact, rarely makes eye contact, and when he does, his eyes flick from place to place. I felt very unnecessary to him, it was very sad having to do all the feeling and outreaching. He, too, had a guru, and meditated all the time, but never seemed to become conscious in the way we are talking about. It was very sad.

Erin: The overvaluing of the Libran side of Venus at the expense of the Moon – that is, attending to the surface appearances of generosity, friendliness and social acceptance and not being connected to the deeper, more feeling function – means that perhaps your friend wanted everyone to like/love him, but he was unwilling to go the extra mile by giving himself. Certainly the Moon-Venus in Virgo in the 12th house man I mentioned found he could not give of himself, only of things. An overvalued Venus results in a situation like this: It really matters what you look like, and if you don't feel well, don't tell anybody. Just keep it together, because it's not going to be nice if you aren't nice to everyone. Being nice is very important, isn't it? I'm glad you see that. I'm glad you appreciate the value of being nice. Now, how do you *feel?* You can play these inner games with the planets. That's what they are doing, they're talking to each other, and you can do the same thing. Venus is looking at the Moon, and it's in a square, and it's saying, "Oh, this is really uncomfortable. What's all that emotion going on over there?" And the Moon is saying, "Oh my, that's very pretty and decorative, but it's cold as hell."

This is an interesting correlation, because the planet Venus is like the biblical Hell, if we were to describe it in meteorological terms. It is 900° fahrenheit. It has an atmosphere nine hundred times ours – it's heavy, it's dense, it's wet, and if you had eyes to see on the planet Venus they would have to have millions of facets because, due to the greenhouse effect in its atmosphere, everything is refracted. Light is trapped inside and it refracts. It would be like living inside a prism – a multiple rainbow. Sounds interesting. Not very comfortable, though.

And one of my favourite descriptions of being in love is the meteorological code for the thunderhead, "Cloud Nine", which means that within minutes there will be a huge, crashing storm. It's one of those beautiful cumulo-nimbus that look so beautiful, they're pure white, hugely billowing and often painted by artists who love sky. But they have highly charged electrical interior – very dangerous. If aeroplanes enter them, they usually crash. Cumulo-nimbus, Cloud Nine. So, when you're on Cloud Nine, that's what you're doing!

OK, back to Moon-Venus and the family. For example, mother can both be a seductress and a sexual creature. After all, how else did you get there? Even if it isn't in good taste, that's the first thing you have to realise! It's very difficult to imagine this, and one hopes that you don't do it too often, but the fact is that it happens and it must be there. But it's as hard to reconcile mother as lover, as it is to imagine it in your mind. Imagine how deep it is if mother says, "I'd better not let the children know what goes on and what I'm really like." And, for boys to see this, well, it gives them a very strange and lopsided view of their own feminine, and they don't get to appreciate aspects of their feminine which have to do with the more adventurous, more exotic, perhaps risky side of life and love. Instead, it might become projected outward, or they may be wanting to see it and be attracted to things that are dangerous to them emotionally.

Or, they become more nurturing. They become over-nurturing and they lose sight of their dangerous streak, and they become too female in their responses to things, too withdrawn and too emotional, and far too irrational in a very negative sense, in that there's no spark, no courage. The other male escape is to block feeling and not have it emerge, thus finding women to carry the feelings for them. If we were all Moon, it would be awful. We would be completely witless, without any shape, and all feelings and masses, rather than adventure and change and challenge, which is very much Venus.

Audience: What about the trine? Would the natural split between the Moon and Venus be easier to work with or integrate if they are in a trine?

Erin: I think any contact is a contact. I think that when you have the trine, there is an easier flow of feeling between the nurturing needs and the sensual or philosophical needs. I think this has to do with trines following squares and oppositions, that in the trine aspect is the release of tension from its previous aspect. The polarities that Venus and the Moon demonstrate are naturally different, but I should think that you would slip more easily from one side to the other if you had the trine or sextile. Venus trine the Moon strikes me as somebody who can slip back and forth more quickly between the ideals of the imagination and the reality of the situation. They're not as locked or polarised into one or the other's image. So it might even be more confusing at times, to have the trine. It's a creative angle. There is a flow from Eros, to Aphrodite and the Moon. – raw generative power is not as stressfully gestated and delivered.

How is a boy to learn how to please females if he doesn't first learn it there at home? Mother's the only woman that he's going to come in contact with for quite some time. If there are strong Moon-Venus contacts of any type at all in a boy's chart, or a man's chart if we're talking about an adult and his child within, then that boy's more susceptible to being seduced by the mother – not in the formal, biblical sense, but certainly more enchanted by her. The son can be in love with his mother to the degree that it makes it impossible to love another woman.

Andrew Harvey wrote a book about an Indian woman who lives in Germany, Mother Meera. She is currently [1994] a popular receiver for the projected divine mother. In an interview, Mr. Harvey says that he was so in love with his own mother that he would never get over it, and that he is obviously transmitting this mother-love and translated it over to this woman – who is now the recipient of his great passion. And it makes sense. The Mother Meera phenomenon [in the early 1990's] seems to want to balance out the overabundance of male guru figures![23]

Audience: Do you think the trines would make it easier to receive the mother's love? Or would she have been more loving toward the Moon-Venus trine child?

Erin: I always assume that parents love their children – whether or not they love them in the way the child needs is another thing. With the square, the person might feel she was a bit iffy about loving – ambivalent – or she was too connected to the child for his or her taste, so the Moon-Venus split becomes operative as an emotional survival technique. With the opposition, she really did love you, but she did go back and forth – she may literally have had to go away for business, or travel, or play two distinct roles, being both mother and father.

Remember, it's *your* chart. The horoscope is the eyes of the individual who wears the chart. Let's say I had a Moon-Venus opposition. I might see my mother on one hand being incredibly interesting, and dashing, and quite amazing and out doing all these fantastic things, and probably being a bit overburdening to compensate for it later. Or she might be one or the other, never demonstrating her executive abilities, or burying her executive abilities in the family bosom. So it can flip back and forth. And for both men and women, that causes conflict, but it's not bizarre until it gets into the complex zone.

Audience: There is a great deal of media focus on the sex lives of government officials and public people – it is if there was a Moon-Venus split in the Houses of Parliament.

---

[23] At the time of editing this transcript (1996), Andrew Harvey has publicly denounced Mother Meera, and left her fold - withdrawn the projections - and founded his own personal quest. It seems that the divine mother disapproves of homosexual love. So much for being enlightened.

Erin: Well, there is. The lunar representative in the House of Commons is the lady Speaker of the House, who keeps the bad little boys in line as they hurl epithets and inanities at each other, playing with power when they really are overgrown schoolboys with no sense of essential global or local issues. They are certainly not the protectors of the future, the children, nor are they respecters of the elderly.

I think the revelations in the media, focusing on the sexual peccadillos of public servants – be they royalty, ministers of parliament, senators, or the president of the United States – is a new form of witch hunt. On the one hand, it illustrates the Moon-Venus split beautifully in the individuals who have been "exposed", but on the other had it shows how – generally – the Western cultural ethos has not found a comfortable way of expressing Moon-Venus in the collective. Too much prurience makes me suspicious. We are far away from the conscious, acknowledged polarity of the wife and the Hetaira, and find it very painful and sad.

It is very like the Moon-Venus in the 12th house man, only writ large: This is a collective inability to integrate values, needs, sensuality and sexuality. It strikes me that political life makes a lot of this happen. It's unfortunate that it appears the world can't be run without men splitting off their emotions and feelings, that we can't be more responsible in lunar ways and in Venusian ways so that it can be both healthy and beautiful. It's unfortunate that it is, by and large, men who are forced into it, partly by nature and culture and inclination and the way it's set up; they are so overworked and so pressured by democracy that they have to split off their feelings. And, they're supported by the women, too.

It wouldn't be happening if there weren't women to support that myth. It's not how awful they are, the men. I have some sympathy there. If I want to put myself on the other side, I wonder if it's about the Madonna-Magdalene split in the woman herself, who will spend a life of dedication to a man who finds it impossible to synthesise or agree internally what he wants in the emotional and physical sphere. So, I think that the woman would also be having this split, so maybe Moon-Venus problem types attract each other and feed each other. It would be like a mirror, wouldn't it? It would make sense. It would make perfect sense that whatever we are experiencing consciously in our own mind would probably be experienced unconsciously in the other, and vice versa, so we would be trading emotions and feelings. One carries what the other one has got, unconsciously.

The image of woman, of the feminine, has lost its place in the world of power in the last three thousand years or so. The Sophia, the wise woman, has no status in our society. The split I am talking about is a cultural, collective, global problem. It is not confined to individuals, and it is not all about neurosis and Freudian mother or Oedipal complexes. It is something to be angry about, because both men and women as individuals have lost something terribly valuable in their own collective unconscious. The trusting of the mother – Ge, Gaia, Earth or however you perceive the Great Mother – has gone. Men and women have suffered, and continue to do so, because it isn't encouraged to trust the feminine side. The Cartesian split, scientific method, logical positivism, and the Inquisition put all that to death in a swoop. Granted, there is the nasty, dark, avenging mother in the mythic realm, too, but she is not properly propitiated, either! She's likely mad as hell right now, and reclaiming earth for herself, since humanity has done such a botched job of managing it.

Mothering and seducing are really one – they are two sides of the same experience, two sides of the same woman, or the dual aspect of the feminine function. And they each can be employed in the right time and place. It's a dance. It's complicated, it means not always being comfortable, it means not necessarily thinking in terms of synthesising, but actually wholly living this split. Maybe there's something about splits that is necessary; we want to compartmentalise. You might want to be Moon one day, for an hour, and Venus for the rest of the twenty-three hours, or the next day. There's no reason why you can't accommodate all of it, by playing out or being all of it. All of this business of wholeness and integration is a bit problematic,. If people have been psychologised, they have heard about becoming "whole" and integrated, but frankly, most people find it virtually impossible to achieve this Ideal state – and, as a result, highly disturbed that they aren't whole!

But I feel that looking at horoscopes shows us there might be some validity to being split off, or compartmentalised, or living out segments of the life at certain times because we can only be so many things at once. We can't be all and everything to everyone at all times. And so, how can you be all of yourself at all times? All wonderfully harmonious – you can "up there" in Urania land, definitely, absolutely, but "down here" in Pandemos' realm, all is not whole. But the fact is that there are two of you in there – a Moon and a Venus – and they both want out. Much is being done on a consciousness level these days, to reclaim the lost earth and feminine goddess archetype – and I hope it has some effect!

Mars and Venus

Let's move to Mars and Venus now. I should think, if they're looking at each other, they find each other pretty attractive. I think it's a compelling attraction, Mars and Venus, in any aspect – and with the understanding of aspects and conjunctions on the round, use your own head. Earlier, I mentioned their favoured child, Harmonia. I think what's happening, when Mars and Venus look at each other, is that each views the other as the archetype of male and female. In other words, it could be highly social, very dynamic. It's quite an extroverted contact, Mars and Venus. Whether it's a conjunction or an opposition, a square, a sextile, a trine, it really talks about needing a lot of contact with other people.

Creativity is gorged on, relationships are to be devoured, the hunt is important, everything has got to be huge and big and really intense and exciting; and the more dramatic and dangerous it is, the better it is. The more challenge there is, the better – whether it's creation or whether it's relationship. That is the need in the Venus-Mars type person, where that is the dominant relationship. Aphrodite and Aries were the ones that were caught *in flagrante delicto*.

This story appears in the *Odyssey*. What happened was that Aphrodite was married to Hephaistos, who used to go out of town quite a lot, probably out measuring heroes for shields and showing his goblets, amulets, and other wares. One time when she thought he was away, she invited Ares over. But Hephaistos already suspected that Ares was going to show up while he was gone, so he had prepared ahead of time. Although he was lame, he was no fool, his mind was OK. Hephaistos made a beautiful golden net, and when the lovers came together, he threw this net over them and then called all the other gods, and said, "Come on, see what's happening – come and mock them!"

And so all the gods gathered round. Being caught in a golden net *in flagrante delicto* to the amusement of the Greek gods, unable to control their passion for each other, portrays the combination of Aphrodite and Ares as being willing to throw all caution to the wind to consummate their passion. Likewise, a strong Mars-Venus aspect in the natal horoscope can lend this willfulness to passion and pleasure. You are willing to overcome anything to build your creative world or to have the relationship you want.

The Mars-Venus type of creative nature wears better as you get older, because it's one of those passionate exercises in numbers and endurance which can be attractive in or to a young person, but wears thin after about forty years. It really becomes absurd after a certain age. The drive moderates itself, it becomes mellow with age. I'm sorry, that does sound terribly "ageist". Biology eventually wins out in the end, and people who are engaged in the hunt can slow down to a slow burn rather than a raging bonfire. In this case the beloved and the lover are often interchangeable. The Mars-Venus person really does love the hunt, but they can settle down and eventually learn how to create excitement and passion in their relationships – not just passion, but compassion.

Mars and Venus certainly view each other with compelling attraction, each seeing in the other the archetype of male and female – the ultimate lovers are Aphrodite and Ares. Those with strong contacts between Mars and Venus are, in themselves, deeply passionate people and frequently seek out their opposite in relationships. It is the signature of the man's man and the woman's woman. This can clearly cause problems, for in meeting one's opposite, one must then develop compassion to moderate the passion. The hunt is important –

the beloved and the lover often argue and engage in war, which stimulates the love to higher and higher levels.

Along with this configuration comes burn-out, where lasting relationships must be based on something more, deeper, than passion and sexuality. Frequently love demands a sacrifice or compromise – with age and maturity, Mars-Venus people learn to love on a more constant, less tempestuous level. The gut level sexual responses are likely very high and true; deep, abiding loving can curtail the desire to run away after the first flush of passion is spent. Indeed, passion means "suffering" and much suffering and loving goes on in the heart of the Mars-Venus person.

Creativity is a flurry, there is an intensity to Mars-Venus creativity that can burn and burn and burn. There is no end to the possibilities of things to do, projects to create, and people to try them out on. Depending on the personality type, this can mean a person who finds endless ways of perpetrating their Eros, their creative essence. Because of the conjunction-opposition flavour to the combination, self-seeding, innovation and independence in the creative sphere are needed. They tend to be singular as opposed to group-orientated in their chosen type of work and creative projects. They are always on to the next idea or project as they finish one up. The harmony that can result from Mars and Venus means there is potential to create many variations on the same theme, all ideas stemming from one source.

A Mars-Venus connection, like the opposition, could be a polarisation between masculine and feminine. There is an inner tension between aggression and passivity, or receptivity and creativity. If there is a polarity conflict, then the resolution lies in recognizing that there is always tension or strife in all relationships, but that there is something of a predisposition to be more attracted by and involved in strife-filled relationships. Remember, it was Ares' sister, Eris – Strife – who tossed the golden apple into the wedding and started the Trojan War (which was all about love), and so there will always be a kind of erotic, strife-ridden, exciting atmosphere around Mars and Venus looking at each other. And, obviously, if there are angular polarities like oppositions or squares, then there's going to be more tension between animal instinct and refined expression of those natural primal desires.

But, you know, I think that we are still talking about an intensely passionate inner experience. It may come out socialised, but I think on the inner level there's an anger about life and its difficulties. Venus-Taurus and Venus-Libra are fundamentally passive and desirous of pleasure and pleasing, whereas Mars is about getting one's way. But, and this is a big "but", the Libra function, which operates as the sign polarity to Mars-Aries, is cardinal by mode. Therefore, there is a cardinality to having Mars and Venus in aspect – both want their way, one by aggression and one by coercion.

Both Venus and Mars are territorial. The old books say Libra is the sign of the General, that is, it represents a function of war, but is distant from the front line. Libra (Venus) is in the watchtower, with the models of soldiers and a map of the battle front, and gives the orders, whereas Mars/Ares is down on the field, fighting it out. Their common modality – cardinal – can lead to an inner conflict between desire and method. How to act out desires comes up a lot. For instance, during the break you asked about having Mars and Venus conjunct in Taurus, with Libra rising. There could be a conflict around your stubborn adherence to emotional security, but with Libra rising, the desire to please your partner or friends, or your own embarrassment about anger, could cause you to compromise your own assertiveness and aggression. This can result in what psychology calls "passive aggression", or anger which is rerouted rather than dealt with in a straightforward way.

Audience: Oh, yes, I do boil inside, but am afraid to claim my own needs, for fear that I will be abandoned.

Jupiter and Venus

If you think in terms again of these as individuals or entities having a relationship with each other, Venus and Jupiter have a soul connection. They each see the other in a pretty exalted way – there's an awful lot of projection going on about how beautiful the thing is, whatever it is that is being felt, experienced or done. So somebody who has a strong Venus-Jupiter contact has an inner dialogue about aesthetics, about how beautiful life ought to be, if it isn't really beautiful. Venus-Jupiter is deeply aware of the disappointments that can happen between people whose fundamental beliefs, ethics or philosophy are not harmonious. They are inherently aware of the nature of creativity, even if not practising artists, writers and so forth. Socially, things must be graceful. Someone with a Jupiter-Venus sextile once said to me that the thing they most feared was a sordid life – I think this speaks for many of the Jupiter-Venus contacts.

Now, whether that harmony of inner vision can be made real or not remains to be seen by looking at the other aspects in the chart, and the personal experience. It's terribly philosophical, idealistic and ardent; there is a tremendous desire to move beyond all boundaries and to experience all possible ways of loving and creation. Anything is possible. Now, obviously there are going to be extremes here. If you have a Venus-Jupiter opposition, here's somebody who may take this one a bit too far, who may be so ebullient and so gregarious, and so open to new experiences, that they always fall short of the mark or take on far too much, expectations far exceeding reality. It all gets too exciting, and it's too much, and, of course, it can't be fulfilled. If it's a project that's going to be done, like a building, they decide to build the Taj Mahal, rather than a little cottage. That kind of thing is very Venus-Jupiter, *in extremis*.

Venus-Jupiter people like to see the beauty and the wisdom and the love – they love to fall in love in order to experience higher or altered states of being. Venus is closer to Urania in its relationship with Jupiter, if it is the religious, idealistic type of person. However, the Pandemic side of Venus can unite with the Dionysian side of Jupiter, and supreme indulgence of the senses and the psyche can be the result. It is an indication of extremes. Similarly, in the creative sphere, they love the altered state that comes with accomplishment of something beautiful – they believe that their contribution to the beauty of the world is significant, no matter how small,.

They are not so crazy about being loved in the sense of being contained, or constrained by it – because there's a loss of mobility. This is not about being unfaithful, it's about being free – there's a big difference. And I think, basically, what the Jupiter-Venus type of person loves about love is the feelings that it produces, the sensory alterations, the feeling of an altered state of being in the world. I'm not confusing this with Neptune, but there is a strong attraction to mind-altering experiences – the experience of love and creativity is supposed to change your perception, and that's the whole point of it. If it doesn't, then they won't be there – they don't want to be in love. They only love it if it's going to be intense and physical.

I mean physical in the sense that the physical body is coursing with new energy, with life, new blood. It's very, very sanguine, it wants to feel something extremely sensual. And love is like a drug, it's the ultimate narcotic in this case, and the best stimulant. And the wonderful thing is that you can find it on any street corner in any part of the world – that's the beauty of this one. So Jupiter-Venus will cross borders to marry, they will fall in love with somebody in another culture and go there – they cross religious, social or colour bars. There is nothing that would stop them in the pursuit of happiness, love and creativity. Therefore I see the two planets as being intensely harmonious – and equally powerful.

But it's another one that needs to mature with age, because ultimately I think that the problem lies in being so idealistic. Clearly there's going to be a disillusionment at some point. Now, disillusionment could simply mean that – dis-illusioned that is, a subtle withdrawal of projection which allows for a more realistic state to enter. If there is a good relationship, then the Jupiter person will go anywhere, they're going to be in that relationship. But they are going to have a much more mellow way of experiencing it. Aspects are played out differently when is one much younger, for instance, teens or early twenties, than, say, in your sixties. Hopefully, one finds new ways of developing the potential. One hopes that chronological age has something to do with greater and greater wisdom and less and less need for experience – especially with Jupiter-Venus. It is the signature of a philosopher, a person with high ideals, which means that a Jupiter-Venus person is capable of love without it being consummated physically, and deep love, passionate love, erotic love with consummation, doesn't have to be physical. There's a lot of commitment to the ideals that are established in the fundamental stages of a relationship.

Jupiter and Venus both are concerned with appearances, so therefore there is a kind of social thing goes on here with Jupiter and Venus – a Jupiter-Venus person does like to be considered one of the "beautiful people". And, because those two planets support grandiosity and great and wondrous things, there obviously is a taste for the exotic and the expensive. If the money isn't there, it's still going to be beautiful. It doesn't matter if it's inexpensive, as long as it brings beauty and, in some way, harmony, to the observer.

Venus-Jupiter people fall out of love for some ideological or philosophical reason. The other person, the beloved, suddenly becomes tarnished or sordid – they lack the spirituality or the ideals that were projected upon them Or, perhaps, they've become satiated, because that's also possible when there's such hunger that one eats too much at times, and takes on too much, and then bores of it or becomes literally full. And so the Venus-Jupiter person isn't being fickle, or going against someone else, or going behind one's back, but it's really about being so intense that it's difficult for them to moderate their experience of feeling. You can almost be gorged on the excesses of the idea, the feeling, the project, the person. And sometimes it means that there will be a burn-out sort of experience. They'll find that they'll go into these idealistic, monastic-like retreats in order to feel that they are pure and free of it all, of all the passion and the seduction and the exhaustion of relationships.

Now, everybody doesn't feel this way. People who have Venus in Capricorn generally do not become exhausted by relationships, because they don't experience them so intensely. They are much more moderate about the whole thing. But not Jupiter and Venus. They do burn themselves out, they wear out, they say, "Oh, I've got to be alone because it's all too much!" Well, it's not all too much for everybody. So it must be rather hard on somebody! They can attract cool numbers like, say, Saturnian people, who think, "Well, what's all this about?" and it warms them up a bit, and then there is a contrast –

an intense person with deep emotions, always feeling everything and talking about it, and the other person who effects a balance or is a container for the excess of passion and, in return, is enhanced by it.

It could be very exhausting. Jupiter and its sign, Sagittarius, are associated with athletics, so you get this kind of Olympic experience with the Jupiter-Venus person. They can really wear one out with their intensity of expression or drive toward the ultimate goal. Again, of course, this does depend on signs. Like you said before, in the front, you have Venus and Mars in Taurus, with Libra rising, and clearly this isn't running rampant or on the rampage all the time because it's moderated by the desire to please. Taurus is a very gentle sign, if somewhat fixed, and it's very sensual and physical and sensitive, bringing the Venusian side to the fore. If the conjunction was, say, in Aries, it would then highlight the Mars function of domination and raw energy. Libra rising has the aesthetic quality of things to be concerned about, so there's a nice, passive lid on it all, but we still have Mars and Venus together, so there's a kind of volcanic passion lurking inside.

Jupiter and Venus together aren't always about marathon runs and Olympian feats, but I think, on the deepest, most fundamental level, the two planets conspire to do this, even if they are in Pisces, in which case it may be a marathon swim. Therefore, it may not be "personality", but it would be a deeply internal, emotional expression of passion and intensity – let's put it that way. It can be quiet, it can be loud. There are myriad other factors that you are going to feed into the combination of Venus and Jupiter.

Someone might be thinking, "Well, I have Venus in Sagittarius, in a square to Saturn in Virgo – so what's that all about?" Well, I would have to say, "That's like having an instinctive governor on the drive to experience boundary-breaking relationships." You could find the expansiveness of Venus in Sagittarius in conflict with an inner moral restraint – rather like having an Old Testament God sitting on your right shoulder, reminding you that you are mortal. That's a good lead into Saturn and Venus.

Saturn and Venus

Venus in Sagittarius might want to experience lofty ideals, eroticism and aesthetics in their relationships – all of it without the mortal side of life impinging. And Saturn will say, "Well, you know, you may want all of it, but you are going to have to control it. I will make sure that there will be people in your life who will do it for you, if you don't do it yourself. We'll find people who are really hard work, so that you get to exercise your high, lofty ideals and see if you can really do it. I'm going to give you a triple Capricorn opposite Saturn, to come in and say, 'OK, you think you've got philosophy and metaphysics and love all wound up together. Let's just see if you can really do that.'" There is usually a challenge involved within these ideal partnerships, because Jupiter and Venus are ideal partners, while Venus and Saturn are not.

There's no way around it. There's no point in pretending that they like each other. They don't love each other. I think they both regard each other with a very jaundiced eye, but remember the relationship between Saturn and Venus. The archetypal experience was that Kronos midwifed Aphrodite in an act of violence. He caused the separation of the archetypal parents, Earth and Heaven, and in that separation was born Aphrodite. And there's Saturn, standing around saying, "Oooh, what have I created, what have I unleashed?"

By nature Saturn is a very controlled, ambitious, mother-loving person, because, remember, he went against his father. That part is revealing. He acted against his father on behalf of his mother, and then, when it came his turn in time – when the Fates had to enact what they had written, that his youngest son would overthrow him from the throne – he began to swallow his own children. One after another, he popped them down.

This image brings to my mind that of a surrogate mother, because it is a pregnant man who holds his children inside of him, to give them secondary gestation. A secondary gestation – being twice-born – is a mythic signature of a godly or heroic origin. Saturn is very ambivalent in gender. Capricorn is a feminine sign, and in this way, so is Saturn. He's the midwife of Venus, he favoured his mother, he chose his mother over his father in the divorce. He then goes on to swallow his children, gestating them to maturity, ultimately giving birth to a new mythology.

Granted, it was a forced birth, or an induced birth because, of course, when it all came down, his wife, Rhea, fed up with all of this swallowing of her children, decided to hide one. This was Zeus, Jupiter, who was spirited away to the cave in Mount Dikte on the island of Crete, and was protected by the Kuretes, wild goddesses of Minoan origin, until he reached adolescence and the necessity of fulfilling what the Fates had proscribed. He then came to his father and disgorged the children, vindicating his siblings. This launched the epic War of the Titans, terminating Kronos' rule. And from that came the whole new mythology – the Greek pantheon as we know it today.

So, Saturn governed over a discrete period of time – the Golden Age – *Saturnia regna*. It was finite, it had a beginning a middle and an ending. Before that, eternity; after that, eternity. Saturn symbolises containment, confinement, gestation, nurturing – it's very positive on that level. It's very patient, it can wait, it's calculated and calibrated. None of these characteristics have anything to do with Venus. We've just spent hours exploring the domain and characteristics of Venus, and not once did we ever say patient, maternal, nurturing or safe – because that's not what Venus is about. She may be Venus Genetrix in the Roman role – that is, the goddess of agricultural fecundity – but we don't really think of Venus as a nurturer, because she is too independent, even in her guise as Pandemos. We can think of Saturn that way, however – protecting, supporting, enduring and safe.

Saturn-Venus might be a safe relationship – it could have a very protective relationship with Venus. Venus-Saturn people are not so much cold, isolated, removed, or manipulative, as they are protective of themselves and of others. I think Venus and Saturn together, in any combination of the chart, is a serious matter. Love is a very serious thing, creativity is very serious. You must be responsible, you cannot just be silly about this. It's got to be important. It's got a sort of "damn the war" attitude. They'll stick through anything. That's what I mean by faithful. It means they won't be deterred just because something is difficult. They will want to protect and nurture and take care of – even to a jealous level – anything that they love or are going to create. It has infinite patience, it can create beautiful things.

Saturn-Venus makes me think of the diamond cutter, someone who can actually take and make out of something rough and earthy and deep and buried, something truly precious and beautiful, and with great lasting value. There's something that's very, very positive, but there's also something about it that is a bit sad, because, I think, they take so very long to experience love in a way that is acceptable. Quite often the object of their love will have moved on by the time they have realised, unless they find somebody who really values that kind of patient, reserved nature.

I think it's probably more frustrating for the other people than it is for the Venus-Saturn person, themselves. There is also, too, the more uncomfortable side – the discomfort with the instinctive side, the more animal side, because I think there's a fear of being devoured. Venus is afraid of being devoured by Saturn, and so Venus will hold itself in very great reserve – we call it Saturn holding Venus in reserve, but actually it's Venus protecting herself from being swallowed by Saturn. Saturn doesn't really care much for the frivolous, exotic side of life at all. Even having fun is quite serious.

Audience: Would Saturn in Taurus inherently feel its emotional hunger, and if Saturn is exalted in Libra, does that give it special impact which is Venus-related?

Erin: First, about Saturn in Taurus – I think that is right. Taurus needs a lot of reassurance, physically. It may be that there wasn't very much tactile affection when the person was a baby, or they were uncomfortable with the way it was given. Remember, there is a preordination involved here, which mysteriously colludes with the infant's environment, so it is a both/and situation. Both the inherent feeling of the person, and his or her environment, "agree" to fulfill the individual's fate. As an infant, there may not have been as much of the type of sensual gratification that was needed – physical contact, assurance, lots of playing, touching and holding, unconditional fondling and love. Or the infant was reluctant to be born, what I call a reluctant incarnate.

Taurus is very instinctual, sensate and tactile, so the Taurus sign is going to be aware of being tenanted by grumpy old Saturn. Saturn square Venus does actually talk about an impoverished Venus, it does talk about being starved, hungry, didn't get quite enough at dinnertime, just not quite enough – it's never full. It's always withheld, and it does come from parents; it's very, very frequently not their fault, but that doesn't exemp them from having done it. Saturn in Taurus is super-conscious of rejection. As is Saturn in Libra, to get to your second question. Saturn in Libra can feel trapped in their feelings of love, or relationships can be so strong a focus that they smother themselves by relationship. Saturn in Libra's "heroic flaw" – *hamartia,* tragic flaw – is feeling alone with others. Saturn in Taurus' "heroic flaw" is feeling hungry when full.

It's too bad, because, obviously, what happens then is that they can act very aloof themselves. I'm thinking of someone who has Saturn in Taurus squaring his Sun-Mars in Leo – now, it doesn't sound terribly Venus-Saturn, but there's something about that quality there, too. I'm seeing that quite clearly. It may be that lack of self-worth is more to do with the diminished sense of one own love or beauty, thinking they are not very loveable or not very beautiful, or don't deserve to be loved.

Audience: Would there be a problem with money or materialism? I mean, could they feel that their spiritual path was in conflict with their physical, emotional and material needs?

Erin: That's interesting because its a very '60's dilemma. I remember it well. A lot of the front-runners of the consciousness movement in the mid-60's came out of the Saturn (and Uranus) in Taurus configuration. The 60's matured from the devastation of soul in the Second World War. That's something that a lot of us went through – working out how to weave the spiritual and the material. There was a strong bias against materialism, but weirdly, it flipped to produce its opposite. Jung called this phenomenon *enantiodromia* – when something becomes too polarised, it flips to become its opposite. It is about the natural laws of synthesis. In fact, spiritual and material are not split at all – we only perceive it as so. In other words, if we believe it, we see it. Now, we are in the middle of the social phenomenon of popularisation of ways of being beautiful, sparing no expense. Very interesting shift!

Audience: Venus-Saturn can be very guilty about pleasure and money and the sensual life, can it not?

Erin: Again, each of these is a whole workshop in itself, isn't it? Oh, boy, guilt and shame. Now, we need to address Aphrodite Urania – what have we got to be ashamed of except the fact that we are not perfect, we are not immortal? I have always said that *hubris* is next to godliness. Other than the fact that we are mortal, not gods, therefore not perfect, what have we to be embarrassed about? The sad part is that we can sit here all day, and be philosophical, analytical, psychological and astrological, and be right, but we might still go home and behave badly in spite of it. It really is a mystery, but that split is inherent in Aphrodite-Venus. We would not need shaming, nor would we need to internalise shame as guilt, if we did not have the two ways of experiencing ourselves in our own nature, either the Uranian ideal -perfection – or the Pandemic reality, the flaws of mortality. You know, suppress that monster, it's got two heads and a hundred arms, for god's sake, don't let it out!

The outer planets and Venus

Audience: Would Venus and Uranus play a role in that? The fear of the body, and its functions and issues? I have a friend who is a Cancer, and has Venus conjunct Uranus in Leo, who has a serious eating disorder – bulimia – and has had since she was thirteen. She has never had a period.

Erin: Oh, very much so. How sad for her. This is where Ouranos gets into the ideal and rejects the body functions – that is very descriptive of your friend. That it has suppressed her womanly functions of menstruation, reproduction, and so on is a graphic statement. Uranus in Leo would be the ultimate in perfection of image, ego and persona if it is distorted. Food, huh? And she's a Cancer, which has to do with nourishment and the womanly body – breasts, stomach, uterus, nourishment! Bulimia is a graphic reenactment of the suppression of the instinctual nature (the monsters) and the Saturnian disgorging ritual.

Somewhere along the line, she picked up that woman is inferior and man is elite. Uranus is the elitist in the solar system. Venus Urania is in charge here. Her mother may well have found her own body repulsive and projected that into the growing body of her daughter, your friend, who, in turn, being exceptionally receptive to mother's feelings as a Cancer child, felt herself terribly flawed, monstrous, especially as she began to undergo hormonal fluctuation in puberty. The body is never more "body" than in puberty! Or, in pregnancy, which your friend may have managed to avoid permanently with her condition.

In fact, Venus and Uranus have a very interesting relationship, when you get them together. Once we've crossed the border of Saturn, we move out into the outer planets -the trans-Saturnian planets. We start to move into an area which is quite mysterious, because they operate, by and large, as collective or social impulses that we go along with unconsciously until we reach a certain age. Although it's very possibly true, it would be insulting to tell someone of thirty that they weren't in touch with their Uranus, but it might be even more insulting to tell them they weren't at fifty. I think that as you reach your Uranus half-cycle and you begin to shift into that other side of life, the midlife, what Jung called the "unlived life" begins to assert itself. At this time, you become more consciously engaged with the process of individuating through the outer planets, that is, becoming more clear, more articulate, on what you want and don't want.

That's very Uranian – becoming closer to the spiritual aspect of the self, once you move into the late forties, fifties, and to the second Saturn return and beyond. Then, psychologically speaking, moving towards Pluto is a rather long, arduous journey, and very few people actually come into full Plutonian power until they get to be considerably older, if ever. This is why it's so perilous to be young and Plutonian, because if you live through it, great, it's just by sheer grace of the gods. Truly, to be young and Plutonian is a very dangerous thing, because you are walking with your mortality and threatening it every second, until you wake up and realise exactly who and what you are challenging! When you realise you've come face to face with the inexorable, then you begin to have respect, and as soon as you have respect for the outer planets, you start to have relationship with them. And that actually takes time. You don't expect somebody who's nineteen or twelve or even thirty-two to be standing around wanting to be respectful of the senex – the three old men of the solar system, Uranus, Neptune and Pluto. It's out of character. You're supposed to be carefree and not always analysing and individuating, actively, until you get into a certain time in life, when you're almost expected to.

Somebody said, "If you're not a Socialist at university and a Conservative when you get older, then you're completely out of synch with the whole of society." I suppose, to some degree, it's true, because, ideally, you burn bright when you're in the Mars age, according to Shakespeare; and then you begin to get a bit more avuncular and Jupiterian, "with belly capon-lined", and then you move into Saturn, "sans eyes, sans teeth, sans everything"! However, in these days, we go across that border into the outer planetary realm, which in Shakespeare's time had not yet been perceived. And that's when and where you get involved with the parts of yourself that have remained – probably fortunately – sleeping and waiting. Waiting for the slow processes of biology to take over, so that you can start to work with those powerful agencies, and become more clearly identified: through Uranus, more in tune with your own true philosophy and spirit; through Neptune into the realisation of spiritual fulfilment; and finally, to be aware of your mortality and your core centre of power – your existentialist stance, through Pluto.

When you have Venus with the outer planets, an element of the more celestial Aphrodite is introduced. In other words, you get a much more idealistic vision of things. People with Venus-Uranus, Venus-Neptune or Venus-Pluto contacts have a relationship with the collective in the sense that they will be forced by inner agencies or external events to examine their values more deeply for altruistic or humanitarian characteristics. Now, actually most of us have some contact of Venus with one of the outer planets, I'm sure. Just because of the way planets are arrayed, it would most be unusual not to have some contact, either through mutual reception aspect, dispositorship, sign, or whatever. Maybe you have Venus in Scorpio, or maybe you have Venus in Aquarius,. So there's always some touch, even if you have an unaspected Venus. I don't fully believe in an unaspected planet. I'll just preface the last part of today's seminar with that.

Uranus and Venus

Venus and Uranus is very, very special, because Aphrodite is the daughter of Ouranos, isn't she? She's a spontaneous, parthenogenic creation, the last offspring of her father. Essentially, there is a bond between the two of them that is unbreakable, and it embodies the male countenance of the female. Celestial Aphrodite is the most dominant, most masculine goddess in the entire scenario, in the whole pantheon, as we showed earlier. She demonstrates a masculine way of being feminine. She makes her own decisions, she takes her own lovers, she goes about doing what she's going to do, she has a vile temper, but also, she's kind; she's done lovely things for people and she's done terrible things to people in the myths.

It's an extremely powerful image. She's well articulated, Aphrodite is, and having Ouranos as her father says the two of them are celestial conspirators with very Uranian, mental, masculine, and objective ways of perceiving relationships. The individuation process through relationship with Venus-Uranus people has more to do with philosophy and ideals, not in the Jupiterian way, but in a way which means that they don't like to be confined. In plain old simple terms, Venus in Aquarius or Venus-Uranus says, "Don't fence me in, because I may have to go immediately if I am called."

So this aspect works better if there's a conscious devotion to a relationship with the collective or with the divine – any Venus-outer planet contact – or if a relationship has a purpose outside the love and nurture and romance side. It then becomes a much healthier and safer place. This means that it will take extra effort – which is where the process of individuation comes in, requiring the individual to step down the aetheric powers and bring them into real life.

It's one thing to sit on the mountain, meditating on love and divinity with your hand held up for forty years, but it's another thing to actually have a relationship with a person – anybody, a man or a woman. Intimacy is awkward and often difficult with strongly flavoured Venus-Uranus people. When you get to know somebody, you find out all sorts of things about them, and they start finding out things about you, and it's all very physical and not very idealistic. It's rather like those monsters that Ouranos didn't want to show their faces – all fifty of their faces.

It was the lack of perfection in the earthy Hekatonchires that Ouranos did not like; they were fearsome. Likewise, the Venus-Uranus person type often discovers that they really hate that feral part of themselves, and are hypercritical, or else totally removed from the animal-human. Thus they have said to me, "Why am I always so critical?" and, "Why do I always find flaws with the people that I love?" "Why is intimacy difficult?" Maybe because they are listening to some rules other than their own about intimacy, and they need to find their own way of being intimate, because there's nothing wrong with being a Uranian. There might be something wrong for them if they were in a Cancer-Pisces-Scorpio-ish type of marriage, though, where too much emotional feeling-tone smothers the airy feeling they need.

Maybe Venus-Uranus would be really uncomfortable in that type of emotionally demonstrative, womblike relationship.. There would be something unseen going on, if they appeared at peace with a very contained, restricting and conventional relationship. They need excitement, agitation – there can be a rejection of the body in favour of the soul, in fact. Like the functions of the body – in other words, sexual needs and various passions might be rather impulsive to the Venus-Uranian type.

This is fine as long as it doesn't upset or hurt them, or someone else. It will upset other people periodically, because they might not approve, or they think the person is weird. But maybe they're not.

They can be great contributors to the world of creativity. Their way of creating is so brilliant and spontaneous that it truly can indicate a kind of genius, Venus-Uranus, a creative genius. Granted, it may run along the lines of mechanics, but that doesn't mean that it's not creative. New systems, thoughts, for example, working in computers, for example, brilliant – creative, exciting, living in the ideal world in intra-dimensional forms. Plato would have loved what happens when you create something on a computer, or enter quantum dimensions or contemplate the existence of a black hole or space-time warps.

I do think that the "specialness" of Venus-Uranus finds everything a little bit gross. There is something kind of precious about Venus-Uranus types, because they really don't want to get dirty. There is a tremendous witness in the Venus-Uranus person – there's an inner witness that watches everything. That's what Uranus is about. Isn't it the split-off Heavens? It's observing everything in an objective and a positive sense, cool, very clear vision, sees everything, sees all. Says, "Hm. No judgements, but that's sort of interesting."

The inner witness of the Venus-Uranus person is very strong and they tend to watch themselves participating in their own lives. It can give them a sense of being schizoid, where they've got this part of themselves watching themselves – watching themselves doing what they are doing, which I would imagine is really kind of weird, at times. When you watch yourself giving way to irrational feelings, it must be rather odd. If they've got a good sense of humour, this would be good. I think this is very Monty Pythonish – you can say to yourself, "God, who are you? What are you doing?"

Audience: It sounds like Venus-Uranus people are actually seeking a heavenly father, one who lives outside their own mortal realm. It might be why women with Venus-Uranus seem to seek men who are unavailable, distant, much older, and so on, because then they don't have to have them around all the time.

Erin: The celestial father – that's a good point. This is where Venus and the outer planets find the celestial partner, and it can be either a mother or father. With Venus-Neptune, it is very likely to manifest as either. I think Venus-Uranus is more of the celestial father, if we are going to look at it like that. Venus-Pluto can be very connected to an otherworldly mother-archetype as well, but it would not necessarily be celestial – more chthonic.

Audience: What's that?

Erin: It means earthy. It can also mean there was either a harsh, powerful or erotic father in the picture, but it's a very motherly thing, Venus-Pluto. Venus-Neptune tends to see everything in a very multifaceted way. There is the soul of the visionary locked into the Venus-Neptune person, which can make it difficult to separate out exactly what's happening in the tangible world.

Neptune and Venus

There's very strong potential here for idealisation and projection of the Ideal – Venus-Neptune types of people can easily project their own inner beauty and divinity onto somebody else. One problem is love of a guru, or someone like that, who replaces the parent and who, in fact, carries the actual inner wisdom and beauty of that person, it being thrust out onto them. The thing about it is that the protean character of Neptune allows you to really love almost anything, because there's always something to love about everything. There is something beautiful about everything and this is where you get that spiritual quality and dimension of Venus-Neptune.

Obviously, it can be deluded and very dangerous, both to yourself and others, because you can become consumed by an awful person, having thought that they were beautiful, or allowed yourself to feel that they were beautiful, or maybe made yourself think it was beautiful so that you could rationalise the experience. It is such a creative aspect, such an imaginative aspect, that even the most painful, sacrificial relationship can be seen as exalted. I see the Christian symbol of Christ on the cross here, as if dying for others' sins is a path to redemption.

And then there's the other side of Venus-Neptune, where it is incapable of having an erotic experience without being in love. This has led to a lot of heartbreak for people, because sex isn't necessarily always going to be a divine experience, particularly in the emotionally younger, experimental period of life, where you can have Eros without the container of Love. There are periods of time in one's life where this happens, and you don't have to be in divine erotic seizure, but these people would find it very difficult to experience their priapic, lusty side, without having to say, "Oh, but I was in love!" So, there's always got to be love about – it's cosmic love. It's the memory of the ultimate, courtly love where the love actually remains contained in the womb, in Neptune, unborn and in the womb of potential, never tarnished with the reality of the body.

This kind of love never suffers the Fall, it never tastes of the apple; the individuals don't see the opposite, love is never tainted. If it could stay there, it would be lovely. It's just that in the real relationships of the world, the beautiful picture, the ideal sculpture, the book, or the person is clearly going to fall short of the mark, and then we get into comparisons and disillusionment. The perfect demise of Neptune would have to be disillusionment or deception. I don't know if Venus-Neptune could ever, ever experience its full capacity to love, I think it's boundless. That is why it's so suitable for cosmic love, for true dedication to the devotional path. That is what Neptune is partly about – the relationship between oneself and the divine is extremely powerful and compelling.

Clearly, it can be illusory. If you have a Venus opposite Neptune, we might be seeing divinity where it isn't. We may be projecting, we might be disillusioned, we might be very deceptive with ourselves and others, we might, in fact, be a liar, because we can't cope with reality. So, we make up stories. We can't tell the truth. Or we seem to attract other people who can't tell the truth, because reality is too harsh or boring. The problem with that type of creative urge would be that the ideal world is enough. The reality of creation is too difficult. But I have to say that I've seen far too many really productive artists of all types with Venus-Neptune very strong, and that leads me to believe that it is a conventionally creative signature. Especially music – it's classic – and film, photography, science, and all forms of transmitted media. It can bring the transcendent to the earth plane.

So it is romantic love in its most sublime. I think it might be made manifest through spiritual love, which doesn't mean that you don't have intimate, sexual relationships. But there has to be something spiritual about the whole experience. The interesting thing about the Venus-Neptune is that there is always something sacrificial going on. I get the feeling that there has to be someone crucified, somebody has to die, something has to be lost, something has to be given up, and there is actually something redeeming about it. Whenever you get the idea of sacrifice and sin, you always get the idea of redemption. They go hand-in-hand. It's just part of the Judeo-Christian heritage, which is becoming outdated. It's trying to break down but it's been awfully strong for about two thousand years, the whole issue around sin and redemption.

And there's something about the image of Pisces and Neptune, especially Venus-Neptune, which is about sin and erotica. That may well have to do with the whole Judeo-Christian ethos that permeates this epoch. I might not limit it to Judeo-Christian, but anything with a monotheistic ethos falls into this category and carries with it the sin and redemption motif, and the whole issue around sacrifice or murder of the wise person and the loss of self and ego. Perhaps that's what it is in the symbology that plays a significant role in love with Venus-Neptune people. If there is necessarily going to be a loss or sacrifice, then it could be something as psychological as the loss of ego, or the loss of the fantasy itself. You lose the fantasy and now you're stuck with reality. Even the loss of the beloved might have to be faced at some point.

Certainly, there's some kind of enjoyment around this, as well. Most people like themselves, really, deep down, so you might find that certain parts of your nature are troublesome and problematic, and you become obsessed periodically by complexes that do tighten up and start to constellate and aggravate and act on their own, autonomously. Therefore you might well say, "Oh boy, I don't like this part of myself right now." But, generally, people do like themselves, and if you have Venus-Neptune, then there is something good to be found in the sacrificial act; it feels good, there's something about being subjected to the loss of some ideal or goal that's really vital and is stimulating and exciting. It's as valid a form of love, as valid an aspect of love, as anything else. It actually helps to have a hard thing in your chart, a Sun-Saturn square, for example, or a Moon-Saturn sextile touching Venus in some way – something like that – a really good contact with Saturn, to make Neptune pull in and do some hard work.

Pluto and Venus

Now, who was it that said Pluto had something seductive and erotic about it? It was you, right? Yes, it does, and it's because...well, the story about Hades is actually sad. Ater the War of the Titans, it became time to divide up the spoils and allot manor and domain. Poseidon, Zeus and Hades drew lots – Zeus got the sky, and Poseidon got the seas and the rivers under the earth, and Hades drew the underworld. It wasn't because he was ugly or awful or nasty, it was because he drew the short straw, and so he was relegated to the nether regions.

Picture it: The other two are constantly having all sorts of relationships and carrying on, changing shapes and seducing this one and that. And poor old Hades – nobody wants to go and visit him. Guess why? So, there he is, all alone. Pluto is isolated and equally lonely. Thus he acquires an aura of mystery, he becomes charismatic through his unseen persona. He must therefore be quite seductive. There must be something about him, one imagines, something compelling, slightly threatening but powerful. The most compelling aspect of Hades is that he remains always unseen, and Pluto in the horoscope is the existential point in the chart which describes our own isolation and loneliness and "unseen-ness" – where no one knows us, and where we long for completion and union, but we will never get it. It represents everything that you have ever wanted and can never have.

Now, you might get it for a few minutes, you might get it for half a year, but you won't get it all the time and you can't take it with you. That's the essence of Hades, and that's what Pluto is about. He must have got very, very sad, very, very lonely, and, finally, just fed up, and he went roaring up in his chariot and grabbed the first virgin he could find, who happened to be Persephone, daughter of Demeter and Zeus. The stolen love theme is closely associated with Venus-Pluto, and this story of the abduction of the maiden – the descent into the underworld and the mystery marriage – is bound up with illicit or unorthodox sexuality, as well as the loss of virginity, a point of no return.

When we think in terms of Pluto as the last known planet at the limb of the solar system, beyond which we know not what lies, we get an inkling of the psychological terrain that Pluto represents. The ancient world-view of Hades was not like the biblical Hell, all fire and brimstone (only part of it was). Hades was a place, a locus, and in that locus were very specific other places, and in those places, like Styx, Tartarus, Lethe and the Blessed Isles, souls underwent transitional processes and endured tasks tailored to their fate-in-life, meeting it in death as well. Even though we are conscious, alive and present, there is a place in the soul that remains aloof. When we die, we don't know what occurs on the other side of that line, which is definite, it is a definite line. You can actually stand on the edge of it, and you can look over the edge, but you can't go across unless you have no intention of coming back.

Other people can be on that other side, they can call back to us as they depart toward the unknown, but they can't come back once set upon that inevitable path. There is a partition and a veil, and the coming and going between those two places, here and there, is not for the mere mortal. Indeed, there's only one god who does it on a regular basis – Hermes, the Psychopompos, the soul guide. There are a few heroes in the *Odyssey* and the *Iliad* who go, as it's usually required of a hero to go to the underworld and back. And in the *Aeneid,* when Aeneas goes down to visit his mother, Virgil says, "The descent into Avernus is easy, the door is always open, but to recall one's steps to the upper air, that is the labour, that is the task."[24]

And so there's a well-developed image of Hades and Pluto as the guardian of the riches in the bowels of the Earth – the container and

---

[24]Virgil, *The Aeneid,* trans. Allen Mandelbaum, Bantam Classic, 1961, Book VI, Lines 176-80.

the nurturer of the immortal soul. The story that Plato has at the end of Book Ten is beautiful, because it really talks about a great preparation in the underworld for incarnation. There's a lot of work that gets done in this place, this mysterious, strange place, of preparing to take on a new role as an incarnate person. Similarly, we do a lot of work in our own nether regions, in the deepest, inmost dwelling of the psyche – much of our nature lies in this place, in the in-between world of liminality – the place where we are without ego, somewhere between who we were and who we are about to become. A great deal of our so-called conscious work toward self-development actually occurs in this transitional place, in the Hades of our soul.

Now, there's nothing fun about any of this. It doesn't sound like a great place to go. Pluto doesn't sound like somebody you'd want to hang around with very much. But there is something mysterious and exciting about the whole thing. This is Eros, the vampire image. The most recent film based on the Bram Stoker variant of *Dracula* is fabulous. It demonstrates the lure of Hades absolutely beautifully. I think it's a film that could be watched many times, and out of it will come many images and symbols. It is *the* Saturn/Pluto movie. It was a Saturn-Pluto, Uranus-Neptune movie. That's what came out of the Saturn-Pluto square and the Uranus-Neptune conjunction in the last year [1993]. That was the epitome of the final passages of those dark aspects – the imagery was perfect – all black and red and intense. It's darkly ethereal, distant and veiled; the images around the transmission of body fluids and blood, and the confusion of souls and place – it's very current in its message. But it's that kind of attraction that holds one in the thrall of Pluto – there's something quite beautiful about it.

There's something in there about love, too. The story about the undead, and the image of the dead person who walks on earth without a soul and searches for love – it's very much Pluto, very much Hades. And in this particular version, in the Bram Stoker version, Dracula comes off as a really sensitive person, who realises his love is so great, that love itself is so magnificent, pantemporal and profound, that he cannot make his beloved undead. He says, "I will not make you undead." And so he sacrifices his own immortality and his own passion – and if you love Hades, you love the inevitable, you love death. When Venus and Pluto are together, there is a fascination with it. A Plutonian Venus loves death.

Now I don't mean that in the bodily sense, necessarily, although it can be translated in that way in extremes. I mean that this is a person who has to experience their existential aloneness and isolation, and has to undergo a descent into their most hidden self in the course of creativity or in relationship. And they find Eros in unusual, dark, and unpopulated areas. Now, depending upon the individual, that will be translated in as many ways as there are Plutonian Venuses. Because Hades had to steal his love, there is something about the need to experience love in a hidden way. It's very secretive, there's an element of the stolen lover or love. Nobody wanted to come and volunteer to be his partner, so he had to go and steal her. And then he had to negotiate and contract their time together, even though he had tricked her into a marriage. In the end she still leaves him for half the year.

Thus, it's about stolen love, it's about having it stolen, it's about stealing it, it's about feeling that it's going to be stolen. It's about the person dying, it's about you dying, it's about dying if you fall in love. It's about ego death, because, you see, the ultimate for the Venus-Pluto type of person is to experience the loss of ego and identity in love. When the French speak of orgasm, for example, it's called *le petit mort*. Ideally, if you have a good sexual experience, you ought to have lost your ego, died a little bit.

So it strikes me that this is where we find two very interesting and polarised conditions. On one hand, Venus-Pluto can be a person who is highly sexualised, where erotic experiences are always sexualised. On the other hand, we have the celibate, where Eros is never sexualised. Both are about control and power. Now, there are so many Venus-Pluto types falling in the mid-range of the Plutonian spectrum, that it would be difficult to delineate them all. However, an excellent example of both ends is Mahatma Gandhii. This Scorpio Venus, conjunct Mars and opposite Jupiter and Pluto, suffered from a relentless sexual drive. When his father died, he had been having sex with his wife, and something in him told him that this was a message to transmute the sexual energy and turn it into something profoundly different and powerful in an energetic way. Now, he stands as an icon for passive resistance! This is one function of Pluto-Venus power at one of its most transformative levels.

Celibacy doesn't mean the person doesn't have sexuality, it means that they have found somewhere else to put this energy, and in some cases I'm sure it's really very productive. We've seen some distortions of it when it's forced or imposed, in religious sects like Catholicism, for example, where the priests have a tacit tradition of exploiting young boys for their own sexual release. This is becoming more exposed these days, so to speak. Enforced celibacy can become distorted and sick, as it can be a result of a distorted emotional, feeling core. But when it's voluntary and it's experienced because of a spiritual call – something deep, deep, deep within the soul – then an individual may indeed have a very serious, truly religious experience in his or her celibacy.

This appears to be dualistic, doesn't it? An over-sexualised person celibate? The seemingly different behaviours have the same psychic origin – it's about intensity, power and control. The whole *raison d'être* is to capture and captivate – to have and to hold. It's Freud's Eros and Thanatos polarity – the life-force versus the death-wish, the seduction by death, the terminus that is always met in the erotic sphere. The fact is, sometimes we are stimulated by our death in a philosophical way; sometimes our creative abilities are facilitated by things like deadlines, endings, completion and so forth. Part of the thesis of existentialism is: "The only reason I do anything in the world of creativity is because I am going to die some day." You don't think about it, I hope. I mean, how often to you get up in the morning and cheerfully say, "Oh my God, one day I'm going to die and therefore I'd better get this done!" If you really thought like that, you probably wouldn't get anything done. You would likely fall into a depression, because it wouldn't matter, would it?

It can be deeply, unconsciously stimulating, humanity's knowledge of its ending, of its terminus, of its death, because it does mean that we have a relationship with death which is very erotic – it stimulates us to do something, to create order out of chaos and be productive and procreate. When that stimulus is hit, then you get the highest level of Plutonian contact to Venus. Being aware of entropy is also Pluto-Venus – eventually, everything will wind down and die in order to be reborn. So there is this constant touch of intensity to everything emotional and relational.

Now, the fascination with death in love and the death of the ego can actually render two beings in this sort of state rather senseless with intensity. The intensity of a Plutonian-Venusian type of relationship doesn't appeal to everyone, obviously. It can be exhausting and draining, and, in fact, when you have Venus-Pluto type relationships, you almost do feel that you have had your blood drained, because that kind of passion can occur. But then, of course, we've also seen that there is this other side where the celibate in fact turns that intensity into a powerful control of the senses. So there's no real model and it hasn't got anything to do with promiscuity – a lot of people think it does.

Audience: I have always been dismayed at the traditional treatment of my Venus in Scorpio square Pluto. It is always portrayed as a sex-mad creature, or someone of loose morals, or a rapist, or a victim of rape. This makes a lot of sense to me, and feels right because I have gone through various stages of what you are saying – I've been celibate by circumstances, I've been married and I've had many types of lovers, but I am very, very cautious and discriminating about my intimate relationships. I don't feel immoral.

Erin: Good. Because if you don't feel you have a problem...

Audience: Oh, but I had problems – at forty-six, they are not what they were, but because of the puritan moral upbringing, I did think I was nasty at times.

Erin: OK, that's what I was about to say. That's so true, what you say about your experience of how your received values have contrasted with your own personal experience. There is an archetype for this way of being, you know. The vestal virgins were not sexually innocent. They had sexual relations with the men of their choice in ritual circumstances, but they never married and they never gave their souls to their lovers. They remained chaste and pure in their hearts for the goddess. Their bodies were not their souls. This is another aspect of Plutonian-Venusian sexual love. This is why it is not promiscuous in the spiritual or archetypal sense.

Sex has to be religious – you've got to see God, or not bother, basically. That would be a great way to meet somebody. Introduce yourself... "I've got to see God, what about you, oh, OK... Next..." So I think that is about fascination with sexual control, isn't it? It's found in common with celibacy and sexuality. They're very similar in that way – power, submission, submitting, and so on.

Audience: You said you'd talk about Venus retrograde and unaspected Venus.

Erin: Yes, but I lied. Look, it's not a ploy to sell books, but I really did cover it pretty thoroughly in *Retrograde Planets*[25] and we are running out of time, and I would like to fulfill at least half of my promise and talk about unaspected Venus. Retrograde Venus is covered in the book much better than I feel like doing it today.

Unaspected Venus

Now, unaspected Venus... First of all, let me say that there's no such thing as an unaspected planet. Having said that, what that term generally means is that there is no ptolemaic aspect between the planet Venus and any other planet, that's all. But if you look more closely, in some way Venus is going to be interactive with other planets. The thing to do when you see an unaspected planet is to say to yourself (or anyone who will listen), "OK, first of all, what is the last aspect that it made? What is the next aspect that it will make? What is the last planet it passed over? Is it at a midpoint of two other planets? Is there an harmonic linkup?" Then, other things to remember are: It does rule two houses in the horoscope, possibly more if Libra or Taurus is on the cusp of two houses. Venus is in a sign, and it is in a house, and you may even have a planet in Libra or

---

[25]Erin Sullivan, *Retrograde Planets: Traversing the Inner Landscape,* Arkana Contemporary Astrology Series, Penguin, London, 1992, Venus Retrograde Chapter.

Taurus. You then have all that information. Working with that should keep you fairly busy finding the subtleties and nuances of a quiet, unaspected Venus. In fact, you might do all of the above anyway, to thoroughly examine all possible aspects of love and creation.

Now , having said all that, I do think that Venus without a ptolemaic aspect is special. In some ways, it is like a singleton planet, all alone, with no obvious relationship to the gestalt of the rest of the horoscope. In some way it has deferred participation with the collective collaboration of the rest of the planets. And, if this is truly the case, and it is not making one of the more obvious ptolemaic aspects, there is a lack of compulsion. There's no real sense of challenge or specific task assigned to Venus. When you have planets aspecting other planets, the one that's closest to the Sun is making the aspect to the more distant planet. But it is the "heavier" or more distant planet which is challenging or charging Venus (or any planet) with a special job. And when Venus is not making an aspect to any planet beyond it, it's not being channelled to do something specific in relation to another member of the family of planets.

It means that Venus is more malleable and without definition. It also means it lacks a bias or a focus, and thus can be easily manipulated. There is a kind of flaccidity about an unaspected planet – it is somewhat like a retrograde planet in that it develops and matures in its own unique time. Therefore, it is rather like a retrograde Venus in that it doesn't have the same kind of impetus to relate as a really busy Venus would have. It will form its values in its own time. It can be hanging around, waiting to be activated by another person to help shape and form the values, ideals and desires. I saw the horoscope of a little boy with an unaspected Venus, and his mother was not particularly maternal nor interested in him. He lived with his granny, and with his unaspected Venus in Capricorn, to have an "old mother" as a replacement might just suit the little fellow fine!

It takes full conscious effort to apprehend your own personal values, your own needs for love, the capacity to love, the feminine images that are around. It takes a lot of quiet exploration of your own inner world to mature and give birth to your creative needs. It's like being so flexible and so multifaceted that it's very easy to see everybody else's viewpoint. It may be a real late bloomer. It likes to spend time by itself. It doesn't always have to be chatting to other people. Remember, too much activity in the horoscope can actually create confusion – busyness versus business. If it's simple and clean, you've got one aspect, so you have one job to do, you go and do it and don't worry about anything else. But if you have no specific jobs handed to you, it means you have to find your own. Sometimes it's a bit more difficult, and it may, in fact, take longer...what am I saying? "Longer?" One's personal development is relative, isn't it?

Rather, we could say that, according to their own self-perception they are late bloomers when it comes to relationships, experiencing their own creativity, and when it comes to expressing values. There maybe a quiet watchfulness, interest, curiosity and philosophical observing of other people's values, but not very much content in their own set of values until they grow up and have had experience in the world. If you have a lot of aspects to Venus, then you've already got a strongly inclined Venus "attitude". But if you don't have any aspects, you don't really have a *pro forma* Venus "attitude". This means that you are more likely to pick up, observe and take part in other things, and find out willy-nilly what your value system and your creativity are about.

Audience: An unaspected Venus sounds a bit like Eros! Something, all full of potential, waiting to happen! More primal, less civilised or socialized.

Erin: That's a really good point, because, isn't chaos, as Jung called it, the pleroma? All things in an hiatus, waiting to happen? It isn't the void, but the full void! It's when all the parts begin to constellate and articulate themselves, differentiating the basic elements, forming a solid entity – or, in this case, identity. And wasn't Eros the "quickener", the cosmic attractor who pulled all things together and made matter?

So, it's the first thing – well it's not really the first thing according to the myths, but you'd think they would have started to organize air and earth and fire and water, and separate those things and make them into shapes like continents, seas, and wind, and such. Venus is the primary conduit for the erotic impulse to live, to be to be something of value and worth. I would think, for instance, that an unaspected Venus would imply that there isn't any direct challenge to turn anything erotic into anything in particular, but that it's actually a free agent – this can be a problem if there are a lot of slack aspects, but it can also be a real talent if there are strong aspects from the Sun to one of the outer planets and Saturn. Does any of this ring true for you because you have an unaspected Venus?

Audience: Yes, I never found my sense of creativity until I was about forty – I lived in my head and thought I could never produce anything as perfectly as I saw it in my head. Oh, that's the Urania side of Venus, isn't it? I think I read somewhere that it could it mean that there was too much Venusian experience in a past life and that it's a karmic aspect.

Erin: I wouldn't actually know that for sure, but I also wouldn't worry about it, either. I wouldn't know about the previous lives, however, I would think that in this one, there are plenty of dilemmas to solve and things to do that are directly related to your own personal history. As for karma, that is what aspects are – karma! Its everywhere, in every planet, and locked into every breath you take. I wouldn't be comfortable hanging such a profound concept as karma onto a single planetary signature alone – it's all karma, isn't it? I don't think that it's a problem. I think you should forget about it, don't worry about it. In fact, we might even look at an unaspected Venus as a life off. As for the "living in your head", and not feeling you could externalize your creative impulse until after forty, that's about the time of the Uranus half-cycle, isn't it, when the unlived life starts asserting itself. If you were Urania for half the life, then you must propitiate Pandemos for the next part!

Seriously, let's look at it this way: There are no encumbrances, there is no task, there is little bias hung on to Venus. It's like free space, choice, opportunity, chance. You have problems elsewhere which you cannot avoid, whereas you could avoid this one, but I wouldn't recommend it. Your problem is somewhere else. Your connection with Venus may actually be unencumbered by particular karma – that's how I would put it. This may where you're more subject to collective things – like the wind blowing love, potential and opportunity your way – but you have to act to take the responsibility for it. It's rather like the wind coming up, bringing a selection of Venus attributes to you, and you stand there saying, "Oh, goodie, here's some Venus." And then the wind blows on, and you're not there with it. It needs a container, it needs to be embodied and manifest in a more conscious way, but there may be more choices open to the completely unaspected Venus.

That brings us to the end of the day – see you next seminar, and thanks.

Bibliography

Dreyer, Ronnie Gale, *Venus: The Evolution of the Goddess and Her Planet,* Aquarian Press, HarperCollins, San Francisco, 1994.

Foucault, Michel, *Madness and Civilization,* Vintage Books, Random House, 1965.

Greene, Liz and Howard Sasportas, *The Inner Planets: Building Blocks of Personal Reality,* Seminars in Psychological Astrology, Vol. 4, Samuel Weiser, Inc., York Beach, Maine, 1993.

Hesiod, *Theogony,* trans. Dorothea Wender, Penguin, London, 1973.

Jung, C. G., *Collected Works,* Vol. 11, Bollingen Series XX, Princeton University Press, 1969.

Lucretius, *De rerum natura,* trans. Rolfe Humphries, Indiana University Press, 1969.

Person, Ethel Spector, *Love and Fateful Encounters,* Bloomsbury, London, 1989.

Plato, *Phaedrus,* trans. Walter Hamilton, Penguin Classics, 1973.

Plato, *The Symposium,* trans. Robin Waterfield, Oxford University Press, 1994.

Sappho, *Poems and Fragments,* trans. Josephine Balmer, Bloodaxe Books, Newcastle upon Tyne, 1992.

Sophocles, *The Antigone,* trans. Elizabeth Wyckoff, The Greek Tragedies, Vol. 1, University of Chicago Press, 1960.

Sullivan, Erin, *Dynasty: The Astrology of Family Dynamics,* Arkana Contemporary Astrology Series, Penguin, London, 1996.

Sullivan, Erin, *Saturn in Transit: Boundaries of Mind, Body and Soul,* Arkana Contemporary Astrology Series, Penguin, London, 1991.

Sullivan, Erin: *Retrograde Planets: Traversing the Inner Landscape,* Arkana Contemporary Astrology Series, Penguin, London, 1992.

Virgil, *The Aeneid,* trans. Allen Mandelbaum, Bantam Classics, 1961.

Von Franz, Marie-Louise, *Creation Myths,* Spring Publications, Dallas, Texas, 1972.

Yeats, W. B., *The Second Coming,* MacMillan, Papermac, 1973.

Part Two:
The Justice of Zeus and the Astrological Jupiter

This seminar was given on 13 June, 1993 at Regents College, London, as part of the Spring Term of the seminar programme of the Centre for Psychological Astrology.

Introduction

Today is Jupiter day. We'll explore as much of Jupiter/Zeus' domain and character as we can, and find out how the astrological Jupiter embodies much of the Greek god's character, and, in turn, how we use the agency of the astrological Jupiter in our lives to learn, understand, rationalize, absorb and differentiate between truth and dogma, inherent beliefs and received beliefs. Part of studying Jupiter should involve us looking at the mythology, philosophy and methods of rationalizing myth and the gods of the ancient western civilization.

If we are going to enter the realms of Jupiter, Sagittarius and the 9th house, then it means looking at some of the areas it rules, like history, education, classical studies, myths, psychology and philosophy. To really embody Jupiter, I wanted to bring a lot of information to you for processing and assimilation into your own Jupiter, 9th house, and the Sagittarius part of your horoscope. Jupiter and its domains rule the Big Picture – the overview, the future, and the potentials that lie in the present leading to the future. In this way, Jupiter has rulership over astrology. We are in the habit of thinking astrology is "ruled" by Uranus – groups, systems, and so forth – or by Neptune – mystical, spiritual, and the collective unconscious; or even by Saturn as the old ruler of Aquarius. Actually, this is a bit closer to the truth, as Saturn seems rife in the astrological world as a tribe, but so is

Jupiter. There are the Jupiterians and the Saturnians in astrology, for better or worse, it seems!

It does seem fitting that a seminar on Jupiter should be done today. We are sandwiched between the station-direct of Jupiter five days ago, and the station-retrograde of Saturn in four days' time. The heavens are engaged in the mythological battle of Kronos and Zeus, for the birth of a new mythology out of old, archaic paradigms. When you think in terms of the kind of work that we're engaged in as astrologers, symbol readers, it is interesting that we both attract and create that which is about and within. Generally, a station-direction of Jupiter brings all chaos to the fore and unleashes religious, ethical, moral and ideological forces – creating pandemonium in various aspects of both social and personal life. However, such are retrograde cycles that this particular station-direct seems to be somehow blocked or stifled. There's a sense of built-up tension, of waiting for something, and nothing is happening. That is because, within days now, the transit of Saturn will station and go retrograde. So what we're looking at is a blockage between Jupiter's station-direct and Saturn's station-retrograde.

The feeling is one of suspended animation, wherein we suspect – know in our bones – that something big is going to happen. It feels like we're going to make some kind of breakthrough, and yet it is arrested, perhaps needing more incubation, more interior development. The cycles of Jupiter are fascinating in that Jupiter is the perfect solar system paradigm of all planetary apparent motions – that is, their direct and retrograde periods. Each successive year, Jupiter stations retrograde exactly one month and two days later, and then, four months later, stations direct about a month and two days later than the previous year, slowly, gradually increasing in degree-number each time. It is absolutely perfect. There is much in the physics of a planet which reveals its true nature. The Greek word *physis* literally means "nature", hence the term astrophysics, which is the study of the nature of the planets. Thus, I will weave some astronomical and astrological patterns together in working with Jupiter.

Digression aside, let's move right along to the subject at hand, and the seminar as I have designed it! I think that it's quite important, considering that we are doing a seminar on Jupiter, which has to do with all things 9th house and all things Sagittarian, that a larger picture is brought into being which will then lead us into specific ways of approaching Jupiter in the horoscope and the astrology of Jupiter – how our own Jupiter works in our lives. To do this, I've gone back a bit in my own studies and Jupiterian-9th house interests, to review some areas that, for me, were particularly inspiring at a time in my life when I encountered a test in my work and faith that happened to coincide with transiting Uranus in Sagittarius opposition to my natal Uranus in Gemini – the advent of mid-life. Since Jupiter has to do with beliefs, ideologies, faith, philosophy, and one's deepest sense of moral and ethical commitment, I think it is fitting to be a bit self-revealing for a few minutes. This is more than self-revelation, it is the epitome of a Jupiterian experience.

In 1987 I embarked upon the mid-life transition, which, in itself, is fraught with myriad implications. But the mid-life herald of the Uranus half-cycle coincided with a specifically tight coincidence of natal Uranus being 25° Gemini and my progressed Sun at 25° Sagittarius – exact opposition – and, that year, transiting Saturn and Uranus were conjoined at 25° Sagittarius! This was not just a mid-life crisis, it was an entire deconstruction of my working mind and deep psyche, and resulted in reframing my way of viewing what I had been doing. It happened to coincide with a threatening loss of inspiration and a strong need to broaden a philosophical basis for astrology. I had been reading astrology since 1963, practicing, teaching, and writing since 1970, and had come to a crossroads within the vocation.

As with all mid-life experiences, suddenly, whatever I had been doing just wasn't enough, and I felt hypocritical – I felt that I'd run up against something, that I was doing something that I didn't understand fully. I felt I needed to know something more, and I didn't know where to find it. I needed an answer and didn't even know how to phrase the question! Very Jupiterian. So I started to cruise the university (ruled by Jupiter, Sagittarius and the 9th house) and I thought, well, psychology isn't exactly interesting in this format, because when you take it at university, it's all rats and stats.

There was no challenge, nothing to be explored which I hadn't explored thoroughly on my own.

Then, I looked at astronomy, because I thought that could be stimulating, and it was. My survey of solar system astronomy and studies of astrophysics were profoundly stimulating for astrology – I continually saw meaning which was apparently not there. I taught my professor to cast a horoscope (it took him about 15 minutes to grasp that, but when it came to transits, his mind could not comprehend it).

However, I fell into the Classics department. This was by "accident", having always been interested in words and what they really mean, and how we might further our communication and understand more about what we're really saying. This led me to a class on Greek and Latin origins in modern usage. From there, I was off. And this humble origin led me into the marvellous world of the Homeric period through 5th and 4th century Athenian culture. I felt I had found a home there, and my reading of Classics brought me into a familiar place – loss of gods, loss of culture, loss of ethics – in short, the disenchantment of the collective, of which I was acutely aware in coincidence with my own personal disenchantment. I had found a parallel culture and literature to go with it!

This led into three years of the exploration of the root-origins of Western consciousness – where we come from, how we think, why we think the way we do – and in that foray into the world of classical myth and reading translations of original material, studying Latin and a rudimentary Greek, within months I was completely revivified. It meant I'd embarked on a new path, which not only enhanced my astrology, but had blown open something else. I needed to know why it is that astrology can incorporate, not just the modern experience or our current frames of reference, as well as timeless images, but also eloquently describes the individual's inner world and reflected outer world. (As to why it works this way, I still do not know.) It is a question I still can't answer, but I understood more about the richness of the mythic mind through the exploration of the philosophy which is the underpinning of our Western world-view. I became immersed in the experience of the ancient mind, forming an intimate relationship with it. It wasn't something I could impose my world-view onto – refreshingly, I didn't know enough to do so.

Discovering another culture, another time long ago, that was directly relevant to me and my own cultural ethos – albeit a global culture, rather than the small, Athenian world – brought something that I needed to give me a greater sense of my own participation in my world, and made me realize why our own culture is so biased toward a masculine, intellectual, rational way of life. In fact, I began to think our culture was still in the domain of Zeus Tyrannos. It made me acutely aware of a sky-god, a masculine partiality which has gripped the western world since the last shred of the goddess-based Minoan culture was submerged around 1200 BCE . The invasion of the celestial sky gods from the north quelled the peaceful domain of earth-grounded worship and coincides with the time of what we might call the origin of solar consciousness.

So, rather than it deviating me from my work – the vocation of astrology – it refired it and, in doing so, kindled something larger – a more comprehensive understanding of how we've developed as a Western collective, and how it has affected our astrology. My mind grew, my vision expanded, and my astrological framework became deeply enriched. Therefore, I thought I would like to give you a small part, an introduction to this bigger picture, too, because as I said, anything that is Jupiterian, 9th house or Sagittarian has to incorporate the past and the present, and have intrinsic value for the future. It should be incorporated into a multiverse context – the present moment, the NOW, is consciously more fully appreciated if it is contained within a past and future. There must be a context, rather like parentheses around a word. To be able to be in the present, and to live existentially, is a very rare and very unique experience, and it doesn't usually last very long. As an aside, the existentialists – the philosophical purists, that is – were largely clinically depressed, cynical and suicidal. I think if we can see where we are now with respect to where we came from, we may actually be able to feel more comfortable or, at least, more in tune with our future, both collectively and individually.

The background of mythology

Anything that falls into our subject material which encompasses Jupiter, must incorporate both a global and a local perspective. This introduction to mythology can bring us closer to understanding how our own capacity to think rationally and also magically is "ruled" by Jupiter. I want to incorporate as much of Jupiter's domain into the day as I can, before actually interpreting the astrological Jupiter. Today we want to come away with a full Jupiter experience. Jupiter needs to be seen in the context of its own domain – within a historical, mythical, ideological and astrological context. Jupiter rules all of that *nous,* mind, and so forth. We need to explore how we rationalise our work, and where we can perhaps enhance our awareness of the astrological perspective by understanding more about the various realms of Jupiter's domain.

Now, in order to do this, I want to talk a bit about the rationalisation of mythology. Because we're dealing with Jupiter, we're talking about the higher mind, the capacity to see the divine or the religious in everything. And I think it's also very important to recognize how the power of myth underlies astrology, and how it has permeated the cultural world-view we live today. Myth is not astrology – you don't want to mistake our use of astrology and astrological symbolism with psychology or mythology, but it's interesting to see how they feed into each other.

Since the birth and maturation of rational thought, people have tried to understand myth and legend in the context of their own world view.[26] As a result, there are several ways mythographers have outlined the "meaning" of myth. The function of myth has been contemplated by some very innovative thinkers, whether they were archaeological, sociological, psychological, or classical scholars. It seems to me that it's very important, especially now, in these de-sacrilised times, to understand the need for humanity to maintain a relationship with the divine. In other words, we need to be in touch

---

[26]See G. S. Kirk, *The Nature of Greek Myths,* Pelican, 1974.

with *cosmos,* which in Greek literally means order – order is birthed out of chaos.

Generally, what you will find in an in-depth survey of the study of mythology – that is, the rationalisation of mythology – is that myths scare people. They have been distorted in every era by every intellectual who fell upon them. Historians have been so horrified and revolted by the tales, the *fabulae,* of the archaic Greek world that they have spent a great deal of time analysing and trying to find a way of "knowing" what they were.

The word myth derives from the Greek *muthos* – which simply meant "word", "speech", "narration", "news", "tale", "report", and so on, in its original usage. It had no connotation in the archaic Greek mind separate from *logos* – word. However, 2,600 years have deconstructed not only the meaning of *muthos,* but also the tales we now know of as mythological. It is a tiresome, pedantic world of deconstruction of something very simple in its origin, but, in its development, highly complex to our current received wisdom.[27]

Unfortunately the use of the word "myth" has degenerated, and thus degenerated the power of the tale. Myth is commonly used incorrectly, to describe a lie, an untruth, or a ridiculous belief. Clearly, there is more to it than that. We assume myth originated in preliterate times and was transmitted orally. It was born out of a culture where the transmission of ideas and information was passed on from generation to generation, usually by gifted speakers, people who were able to orate and to narrate. They used formulaic methods such as mnemonics and breath, as the vehicles for long, epic poems of cultural and heavenly activities.

The myths that have descended to us from the Greeks, in fact, are no different from any other myths from any other culture. There is a cross-cultural connection between the monolithic myths of each culture that's pretty fascinating. In his book, *The Hero With a*

---

[27]Marcel Detienne, *The Creation of Mythology,* trans. Margaret Cook, University of Chicago Press, 1986. See especially Chapter Three, "The Mythic Illusion". This book discusses the origins of myth and how it has been treated, and proposes a new way of receiving myth today.

Thousand Faces (written in 1949), Joseph Campbell outlines brilliantly the paradigm of the heroic journey as the "monomyth", a term coined by James Joyce in *Ulysses*. It describes the similarity between heroic myths from all cultures and ages. The relationship that individuals have to origins, archaic and historical, retained unconsciously in the psyche, is part of why astrology works in the way we use it. Through this magical connection, we are in a timeless place.

The monolithic myths have paradigms which are rooted in all cultures. Some of you may have knowledge of Indian myths, South American myths, native American myths – they all have stories that are fundamentally the same. There's always an origin myth, a trickster myth, the birth of the world, the slaying of a monster, a mystical marriage, overthrowing of old gods, explanations of natural events (thunder, where does it come from? – fire, where did it originate?), explanations of celestial events (lunar phases, eclipses), the deification of the god, immanence in animals and nature, and totem myths. All remain relevant to today's consciousness. How we come to terms with that, and use that information and high-level rationalisation, is interesting. Astrology is one way of employing the past for present creation.

Audience: I have found, in my own experience, that I am both excited and frightened by the apparent inevitability or predictability of my and others' behaviour – I mean in the sense that myth is enacted today! It is both depressing and encouraging that nothing has really changed on the level of the archetypes.

Erin: As I mentioned earlier, some of the best minds have been alarmed by the very fact that myth exists! To allow oneself the luxury of being part of a collective unconscious *muthos* can be very worrying. We are so individuated today, that to think we are eternally repeating a variation on a single theme is insulting to some people. People like to think they have "progressed", or become civilised. Indeed, when I talk about Jupiterian complexes and aspects of Jupiter, we can see that we do vary these motifs somewhat, and through our own individuality, we "individuate" the archetypes. The archetypes come through us, so to speak, to become further refined and more useful, appropriate for our times. However, they do not change in and of themselves. And there's something about the power of these images, these transcendant images, that lends astrology something that's vital. Again, we may not necessarily use myth as a way of interpreting behaviour, although we can use it allegorically or as storytelling, which enhances and validates the human experience. In magnificent mythic acts of the immortals, we see ourselves reflected.

However, you must keep in mind that the myths we relate to are not from the beginning of time, so to speak; they are relatively current in the Big Picture. That is, they are not myths from the cave days, nor are the Greek myths even as old as the Egyptian myths of the Age of Taurus. Greek myth stems from the Age of Aries, and the "tail end" of the Age of Aries, at that! And they have been food for the Piscean Age poets, artists, writers, painters, classicists, philosophers and, more recently, psychologists, and so on. Whether or not these myths will survive through the Age of Aquarius remains to be seen. However, we have around 2100 years to find out, so there is no hurry. Basically, the myths of Zeus and Jupiter still have strong resonance for us today, and likely for a while longer.

We will also see that something has been lost, an age of earth-based reverence in the transmission and study of Greek myth, the current usage of it, and its relevance within our modern psyche. Myth needs to be defined within a certain context, separated out from fable or saga. Myth is anonymous, we don't know the origin, it is ancient, and has emerged out of the kind of mind which appeared to participate so wholly within its environment that there was no conscious separation between human beings and their environment. At some point way back, our consciousness was so fully enmeshed and fused with the environment, with nature, there was no sense of separation with self, and there was an ego-less state. The term that is used – *participation mystique* – is something that is reemerging in a different way, and that's part of that Uranus-Neptune aspect that's taking place now (1993-95).

The mythopoeic mind – the "mythmaking" mind – is a state in which we find relevance in consciousness of things magical and nonrational. In the *Iliad,* when Peleus entrusts the magical horse Phoenix with the education of Achilles, he asks him to make of his son a good "giver of advice" – a *muthon rheter*.[28] So, the "giver of advice" is the orator of myths. Apparently, when addressing deities, men were to sing with auspicious texts *(muthoi)* and pure words *(logoi)*.[29] This implies that the *muthos* is the content and the *logos* the manner of expressing the content! We could go on forever with this, but I hope you see the point.

Audience: I think the difference you are making is that one of the terms, myth, is about an experience, and expressing the experience needs a container or a word. So myth is an experience, not a story.

Erin: Exactly. Like myth, astrology is an experience as well, and we use our logos to tell that story. This, by the way, is all Jupiter's realm. You are engaging your Jupiter to understand what large frameworks are about.

Differentiating between myths, which are stories with a high moral content, and fables or legends, which are actually rooted in social organisation, is important. Furthermore, fable and legend have to do more with moral issues and social patterns, with laws which are concerned with the culture – fables and legends are really in some way rooted in historical fact. They are quite different to myths in that way. One way of defining myth would be that, primarily, myths are tales or stories concerned with the gods and humanity's relationship with those gods.

One of the most marvellous Western tales of gods, heroes and mortals is the *Iliad,* Homer's epic poem. The *Iliad* was written down somewhere around 800 BCE, and is a story about the last few days of the war between the Greeks and the Trojans. But more significantly for us, it is a story about the relationship between the gods and the mortal heroes. If we look at it in a certain way, it appears that the gods needed human beings to act as their mortal representatives. The

---

[28]Homer, *The Iliad,* trans. Richard Lattimore, University of Chicago Press, 1951, Book IX.443.
[29]Xenophanes, "Xenophanes on Drinking-Parties and Olympic Games", Frag. 1.13-14, Illinois Classical Studies 3 (1978). This is a journal article.

Iliad is a story of "upstairs, downstairs", that is, about the gods above and the mortals below. You perceive a picture of some gods above the earth acting in ways which are remarkably human, but writ large. I mean, they are filled with petty jealousies, always power-tripping and manipulating. Achilles sulks his way through the entire first half of the poem, because his girlfriend was taken away; he's in a terrible mood the whole time. Meanwhile, there's all this petty action going on in the god-zone as well, all reflected on earth! Achilles blames Zeus for this madness and claims that he has taken his wits away, and Zeus complains that men always blame the gods for their own misdemeanours!

In the *Iliad,* the actions of human beings are in some way related in or parallel to the actions of gods. It is as if the gods are puppet-masters, who have created mortals in their own image to do the "human work" for them. For example, the goddess Aphrodite, who couldn't do certain things because she was immortal, had Helen act it out for her. Helen of Troy was Aphrodite's human simulacrum. So you have these personifications. All the mortals act in accord with the nature of the gods. There are many ways of looking at this – how do we relate this, what is this story really about?

The origins of myth today are lost to us, really. The only real way to be in touch with the mythological world today is through the individual's relationship with himself or herself, by being closely connected to one's own interior world. Astrology makes that bridge from the archaic world of gods and symbols to the conscious world "out there", with which we all are intricately involved. And in some way, everything that we do today is not dissimilar to the behaviour patterns found in myth and in the stories of the gods. We can look at them in that way. But the thing about myth is that it exists outside our concept of linear time, outside the rational mind. It is nonrational, magical – it has nothing to do with how we think and how we actually can control or create our future. It has something to do with our instinctual side, perhaps even with our religious side.

The cultural need to rationalise myth arose around 500 BCE – it became increasingly important because of the developmental pressure of the emerging democracy on civilisation. The organisation of the state and church, and the separation of nature and culture around the time of 5th century Athens, were the direct result of a time not unlike our own today. The Greeks were situated between two worlds – a world in which there was a general acceptance of divine ordination and natural law, and a world in which they were also compelled by increasingly organized human-made laws.

Moral issues arose between "civilised" behaviour, as dictated by social order, and the mythic activities of the gods. One could cite one's bad behaviour by saying, "Oh well, Zeus made me do it." In the Iliad, Zeus may well have taken Achilles' wits away by instilling *Até* – witlessness. However, this would not hold up in the newly forming courts of justice in Athens! Something had to be done. For example, in 5th century Athens, society was getting organised – you could not send your slave girl out to the market to buy things, have her raped, and then let the rapist get off in court by saying, "Well, Zeus did it, why can't I?" Quite. Zeus could transform himself into a Swan or a Bull or a Golden Shower to have his way with a mortal woman, but could we allow that for your average citizen? Not likely. So they had to have some sense of order around things.

As a result, there erupted a great schism in the participation of humans and gods in collusion, because people began to see that the behaviour of the gods could no longer effectively mirror, in any sense of the word, our behaviour as human beings. Essentially, what happened was that there was a shift to a kind of culture in which motive had to be understood in relation to action – *mens rea*. Volition, conscience, and intent began to take shape. The earlier cultural ethos was what is now called the "shame culture", wherein what you did was more important than your motive, that is, why you did it. Other people would observe you, and what you did was important because it had to do with the gods. In other words, why you did something was never really in question, but it started to become very questionable later on, as Western civilisation began to develop. And that's where the concept of guilt began to emerge. The transition from a "shame culture" to a "guilt culture" is deeply connected to the rise of Jupiter/Zeus consciousness, where Zeus becomes not just the external god, but an internal moral code.

In the course of that shame-to-guilt evolution, the rationalisations for myth became very psychological. The plays that began to be written and dramatised in the Theatre Dionysos on an annual basis had to do with the portrayal of the actions of gods, heroes and mortals, and their behaviour patterns, and what happened in those relationships. A great deal of struggling to understand the human condition began to appear as themes and motifs in the celebrated tragedy plays. I think a lot of what we were doing in that time was trying to come to terms with the very uneasy emergence of individualism and self-consciousness from the collectivity of mass consciousness. In other words, to become individual takes a great deal of energy, it takes a great deal of effort and a lot of courage. That includes not only our becoming more of ourselves as individuals, that is, individuating, but also cultures as they separate and individuate from their own collective past.

The uneasy birth of rationalism in consciousness has resulted in our state of mind today, where we are in some way deeply aware that we have lost something valuable, something luminous, something magnificent, something bigger than us. But perhaps it also has a purpose to it. Maybe all of this separation and differentiation and the birth of individualism actually does serve a purpose, because we are approaching, and indeed, are continuing to approach, what I must assume is a much more efficient and higher level of being, where we can consciously participate in the collective, rather than unconsciously.

But what I am leading up to is the ways in which traditional classicists have developed for the interpretation of myths, and it leads me into where we might be able to use the interpretation of the myth in our own work. Or, perhaps, just by knowing of it, we can enhance our philosophical view and the work that we are doing with other people – knowing how we behave in ways that are archetypal, as opposed to stereotypical, and, in these times of chaos, of radically shifting values, ethics, beliefs, relationships and world politics, finding a bigger picture within which to frame our personal lives.

Audience: Do you think that this cultural split between nature and culture, or the evolution toward greater self-awareness you are describing, has to do with the way we perceive our own selves as "good" or "bad"? Does Jupiter in the chart have to do with the way we judge ourselves and weigh our "good" side and our "bad" side, based on what we know from the deep archetypal level, and measured against what our parents or society has taught us? How does personal shame differ from guilt?

Erin: To answer your first question: Absolutely. Yes. Jupiter is the moral arbiter, its placement holds the key to our capacity to rationalise myth – our own mythic image – and to differentiate between being "shamed" (that is, being observed as "bad" by others) and "guilty" (that is, feeling an internal, instinctual, self-aware unease with a moral or social act, or a feeling that we might have about something we did or felt). Jupiter is also "borrowed wisdom", as we shall see in his myths – a wisdom that comes from the time of great mother-religions, but could not survive in the sky-god, male-dominated society which followed it. Zeus had to swallow one of his consorts, Metis, whose name means "wise counsel". In the eating of "wise counsel", Zeus incorporated wisdom, but he was not created wise.

Now, about shame and guilt: Shame is something we feel when an outside force, often a parent, has pointed out a shortcoming. Guilt is what we feel when we know we have done something that goes against the grain of our own "rightness" or goodness. Obviously, some people are more prone to shame or guilt, or both. Jupiter in the chart will help us understand about this complicated duality. Jupiter is also where we can inflict shame or guilt on others – when one imposes one's moral code upon another, and they feel judged.

When we get into Freud's and Jung's use of myth, we'll see that there is in some way a separation of stereotypical behaviour and an awareness of more archetypal behaviour – in other words, something that is the underpinning of all humanity, that ties us together, a type of collective pool, if you will, of consciousness. It means that we are related cross-culturally, and that we are in fact interdependent. Stereotypes arise within specific cultures, they come out of our families, they come out of local frames of reference, rather than global frames of reference, but at the root of stereotype lies the archetype itself. And, essentially, whenever we view anything as magnificent and as big as myth, we sometimes can't help but impose our own world view.

It's very difficult to participate in an ancient world. A big danger lies in projecting upon a culture or people our own, current world-view – that's part of what the difficulty is in comprehending what myth has to offer us. We don't really know how the ancient human actually experienced his or her world. Our tendency is to see archaic humanity as rude savages, primitives, scraping along in ways that we wouldn't think or dream of living, and yet there's a great deal of evidence that they were highly civilised, that they had a tremendous amount of awareness, and that there was certainly art and beauty and harmony. Twelve thousand years ago was a time when humans and animals existed together in mutual participation. The cave paintings, for example, at Lascaux, show that there was some sense of everybody doing what they had to do because that was the way it was done. There likely was no arguing about whether men should be doing this job and whether women should be doing another. These are stereotypes – that men and women do this, certain types of people do that, this kind of culture does this, and so on. The archetype allows the freedom of difference, but knowing that difference in fact joins and creates a sense of wholeness.

The rationalisations of myth

Moving on to several accepted rationalisations of myth: There are a few key individuals who have contributed to the categorisation of the study of mythology, and have codified certain ways of approaching it. In order to get to where we are, to our own bias, it might not hurt us to outline a few of these historical megalithic theories.

Nature myths. Max Müller, an Oxford professor, identified myths as "nature myths". In other words, all myths refer to natural or cosmological laws – they explain nature. This is very close to the aetiological interpretation which we deal with next. What this effectively does is explain all natural phenomenon – largely meteorological and cosmological – through the actions of gods. In other words, in the mythopoeic mind, thunder and lightening *are* Zeus – they have nothing to do with the convection principle. Myth is an explanation of that which cannot be rationally comprehended, so early humanity created stories to help them come to terms with floods, fires, plagues, and so forth. Just as Zeus is lightning, earthquakes are Poseidon, and the winds are Boreas or Aeolus.

This view explains rituals of archaic peoples around sunrise (banging of drums), sunset, eclipses, lunar phases, and so on. Rituals to aid the sun to rise were employed to help the sun in its path through the heavens, and again, as it set, other rites would be enacted, to assure the sun that it was wanted and would be welcomed back after its descent into the underworld. This view was disregarded as false and derided by Andrew Lang who introduced his idea that all myth is an attempt to cite the origins of things.

Aetiological view. Andrew Lang based his views on the concept of *aition* – beginnings, causation and origins. This view of myth has the myth-maker as a kind of primitive scientist, using myth to explain facts that otherwise cannot be explained within the limits of society's comprehension at that very time. And that doesn't seem to be particularly satisfactory, either. Origin myths explain why things are the way they are because the rational mind cannot stand chaos, a vacuum. We are still in this stage of trying to explain the origins of things! We are still trying to do this. Our Jupiter needs to "know" why things are the way they are.

Charter myths. Another way of looking at myth was developed by Malinowski. He decided that there was an intimate connection between social custom and myth – as if myth was created by a people who were aware of their social customs and needed to use myths as a way of creating law and order. And so the "charter myth" rationalisation, which is again another valid way of looking at it, establishes a kind of quasi-legal situation, where there are precedent cases for moral codes. For example, the gods would have meted out particular kinds of punishments for certain moral affronts, like incest or murder, theft, and therefore there would be set structures. So you would refer to myth to say, "All right, I'll recite the case of so-and-so in order to determine what the punishment for the mortal sin would be." The charter idea is that we use myth as a way of organising ourselves in social ways. It also implies that myths were created, rather than emerging from the great collective unconscious, as certain other mythographers believe.

Audience: What are some of Malinowski's books?

Erin: He's written several, but there's one in particular called *Myth in Primitive Psychology,* which outlines the "charter" idea very well. It was written in 1926, so it is around the time of the emergence of what we now know as modern psychology. He makes every attempt to relegate myth as a construct of the conscious mind, rather than something that spontaneously emerged out of a collective psyche. I don't know where you can find this book.

Audience: It makes sense that laws should emerge from myths, that we should pattern ourselves after the gods and what the gods do and say. This way of interpreting myths seems closer to what we do in astrology.

Erin: It's getting a bit closer, because it acknowledges the power of immortal beings and their participation in our own society, in our own culture. This way of looking at myths is rather legalistic, in that the acts of the gods are precedent cases for social and moral codes.

Ritual interpretation is the next major grouping. W. Robertson Smith tried to reduce all myth to explanations for rituals performed by archaic and ancient peoples. J.G. Frazer wrote the definitive "ritual" interpretation of myth, *The Golden Bough.* Has anybody read it? It's a classic. What Frazer was doing in his work was attempting to rationalise myth in a particular way. And what he saw – and this is quite important – was an analogy between tribal rites of primitive man, and high classical myth. Therefore, he felt that all ritual behaviour was an attempt of the "savage" to ascend to the level of a god. Frazer's explanation of mythology is called the "ritualistic" interpretation. Frazer was saying that myth was created to codify tribal ritual and explain those rituals. Clearly, there's a tone of elitism in Fraser's work, as amazing as it is.

Audience: How do we come to understand the character of the horoscope through mythological connections? It seems that there has been a lot of going on about myth and what it is. Is this because Jupiter rules myth?

Erin: Yes, that is why, because the 9th house is about rationalising divinity, trying to identify the godhead. For us to take a look at the big picture, we will incorporate some Jupiter. Sorry, so far it does seem to be a dissertation on the history of myth-rationalising! But, as I mentioned in the beginning, Jupiter's realm is the realm of high rationalisation, and the domain of the 9th house, wherein we seek to find a reason for being. I am trying to activate your Jupiter in as broad a way as possible, to send you away with a huge question in your head that allows you to get to the root of your own cultural biases, your own essential truth and your greater understanding of the Big Picture.

The Jupiterian realm is one in which we look further and further to the horizon for new life, new ideas, new understanding. And it is the place where we create belief systems, dogma and highly structured containers for the ineffable. It think it is generally agreed that there is a sense of the divine within all cultures, but how those cultures contain that vague spiritual experience is the 9th house, Sagittarian, Jupiterian manor. I hope to impart a full experience of Jupiter's offering – a survey leading to the origins of our own use of myth in the horoscope, and just how it is that Jupiter acts as lord of the mind.

So far, none of these particular ways of approaching myth actually explains or helps us in understanding myth – where it "came from", what it is, and why it is that all cultures have archetypal tales of divine beings who have a deep impact on their mundane lives. The fact that so many great minds have grappled with it means something – there's something deep here, perhaps, to be accessed. But none of the above explanations allow for some of the more imaginal or metaphysical aspects which I feel are the more true experience of myth – that there is, in fact, a numinous life, that there's something bigger beyond us, within us, around us.

There is another view which I particularly like and find very reasonable and useful:

Re-enchantment, or rites of passage. Mircea Eliade believed that, in reconstituting an era, one could also revive its power. By reenacting myth and ritual, and invoking symbol, we can reunite with the magical past. I call it re-enchantment, but the accepted term is "creative era". Now, Greek myths are not actually terribly magical, nor are they numinously religious (not taking into account the mystery cults, which, true to their name, remain shrouded in darkness – such as the Orphic mysteries, Mithraism, the Eleusinian mysteries, Bacchic revels, and so on). Our Western culture stems from a logical positivist type of mythological culture. So, rites of passage do work – the re-collection of the origins and magic of participation in a culture long gone could bring back the gods to the disenchanted world we are now living in.

I particularly like Mircea Eliade, and recommend his work to read as an important part of your studies. The re-connection to ritual and rite of passage is akin to what our most modern mythographer, Joseph Campbell, does (or did) in his work and writings. This "creative era" solution to the mystery of myth does not attempt to rationalise it in as deconstructive a way as the other four types do. It doesn't impose as much of our own world-view onto an archaic culture, nor does it try to explain anything. It allows myth simply to be, and further, it helps us understand why we need markers along the path of life. Passages of life need recognition! Astrology does that brilliantly – it clearly demarcates phases, time periods, and events in the life in a context which gives us a personal mythology. My bias is toward this kind of use of myth in astrology – that of reawakening individuals to their own power, sense of timing, and place in the world.

So a bit of background on the history of the attempt to rationalise myth now leads us toward a new way of approaching myths. Until the 20th century and the advent of modern psychology, myth remained in its old place,. However, it was re-enlivened with Freud. In some way, Freud takes us back to Plato and Aristotle, because fundamentally, all the developmental psychology that we use now harks back to those times, back to the times of the pre-Socratic and subsequent Greek philosophers asking to understand why we behave the way we behave. Freud began to see myths as prototypes of the human experience – which is pretty enlightened. For an early 20th century scientist (which was what Freud was) to have a religious experience, and to use mythic analogies in working with the psyche, was a major breakthrough.

These mythological prototypes of human psychic and behavioral experiences were a great revelation for Freud. They recall the time when, in the 4th century BCE, Aristotle was trying to figure out what made people tick, how we do things and why. He developed the idea of *katharsis,* based on the tragedies, the plays in which great heroic acts were dramatised in the Theatre Dionysos in Athens each year. Aristotle came up with the theory that the observation of, and vicarious participation in, the drama produced a catharsis – a purge – and that, in the experience and telling of the tale, one could heal oneself. The cathartic experience is something we introduce in psychotherapy and astrology today. In the telling of the tale, the healing can occur, and if we realise that we are participating in something much greater than our own singular life, then clearly we are relieved of a certain burden – the burden of alienation and isolation. This is why Jupiter seeks out "tribal" familiars, and will travel far and wide to find like minds – or, on the other hand, will seize up and become rigidly, protectively, xenophobically dogmatic, ruling a small group or tribe with an iron hand.

Freud and the myth of Oedipos

Earlier, I mentioned a transitional state in the ancient world, in which the prevailing culture-consciousness seemed to shift from shame to guilt. This transition lasted centuries, and even long after 5th century Athens, and in the "new enlightenment" and the birth of psychology, there were still very strong shame attributes. It is very difficult to separate out the two, but basically, shame has to do with a standard of behaviour in relation to society (Freud's superego), while guilt involves a personal feeling of having transgressed a divine law or acted against our own sense of divine correctness. One of the things Freud was obsessed with was guilt and sin. Fundamentally, he was an Aristotelian, because his ideas were formulaic, and he was always searching for the primal cause of psychosomatic illness.

This is an oft-told apocryphal tale, but it rings true – perhaps the details are a little bit off. One night, Freud was going to the theatre in Vienna, where an ancient Athenian theatre production was being done of *Oedipos Tyrannos*. In those days, many scholars read ancient Greek, and Freud, like a good scholar, went off with his copy of the play and sat in the audience watching and observing.

Briefly, the story of Oedipos: At his birth he was exposed on a mountain top, left to die, but was then discovered by a humble couple, who took him home and raised him. The oracle had stated that he would eventually marry his mother and kill his father and, in the course of his life, these acts came to pass. However, there was a point in Oedipos' life where he was still completely unaware that he had done this foreordained act – that the man he'd killed at the crossroads was his father, and the woman with whom he had been living, and with whom he'd borne a child, was his mother. He didn't know this, but his mother had come to realise the awful truth.

It is at this critical turning point in the play where it gets very, very intense, because Jocasta, his mother, is aware she must tell Oedipos of this, and she is terrified of what it will do to her son. And so she is trying to find ways of soothing him, and he's worrying about it (and the chorus is wild with fear and dire warnings). He's saying, "What's wrong? Why are all these terrible things happening? What is this curse that has befallen us?" And she's saying, "Look, everything's fine. It's OK. Don't worry. It will all work out." And the revelatory quote is: "Many men in dreams have lain with their mothers."

Well, apparently, at this stage Freud leapt up, rushed out of the theatre, streaked home and spent the next forty-eight hours in a frenzy of writing, developing his thesis. And he spent the rest of his life defending it.

And so, of course, now we're stuck with that wretched Oedipos complex for as long as we can possibly stand it. But then, you see, what happened at this moment of epiphany was that Freud opened the door to something that has led to our awareness of our participation within a greater whole. He implied that if, back in 5th century Athens, Sophocles, who was clearly a psychologist by nature, was portraying this story, then it must still be a useful allegory for the erotic component in contrasexual family relationships. Well, anyway, Oedipal relationships do exist, and they are still at the root of some severe relational problems. Obviously, Freud connected personally to the story, and then recognised that it was likely that his own experience and the experiences of his patients might well be explained by archetypal situations. As astrologers, we often work in this way. We tell clients relevant stories, we relate these stories to something within their own personal experiences, and thus relate their lives to something greater and bigger.

The problem with Freud is that his use of myths and legend, though legitimate and valid, actually served to stereotype things. He himself crystallized and stopped growing at the critical midlife juncture. But his foray into that area opened the door to a future mythographer, which is where Jung stepped in. One doesn't have to believe in a myth for it to be reenacted, I assure you! It is rather like saying you don't have to believe in a screwdriver to get it to turn a screw. Generally, though, it is abstract thinkers who take myth seriously.

One Jupiterian story is the moving tale of the Minotaur and Theseus' journey into the Cretan Labyrinth, to kill it, retrace his steps, take a wife, go home to his country, vindicate his father, and set up a new order. This theme cleaves perfectly to any act which requires going to the core of an issue and facing it, killing off the "bad" part, and finding the way out and home. It's something that we have to do quite often. For instance, we have to go back into the matrix of our families on a regular basis, either psychologically or literally, to claim parts of ourself left behind; or trace our steps through the labyrinth of the psyche, into the core of the centre, to wrest out some lost treasure of Self, or slay a shadow-dragon, or rescue a maiden-self, or in some way go back into the centre of our origins, where something may be eating, destroying or devouring our creative essence. This is a repeated theme – at certain points in our life we must do this.

For instance, Picasso's midlife involved an interior journey into the centre of his creativity, and the Minotaur became an emblem of his excursion into his own soul. He was gripped by the image of the Minotaur, and he made many beautiful paintings and drawings of the Minotaur and the experiences around the Minotaur motif. Interestingly, as Picasso was a Scorpio, his "shadowed sign" was Taurus, so his own opposite was his redemption. He literally had to meet his opposite – his Minotaur period was prolific. He became obsessed with this sad monster, and, metaphorically, it was eating him alive, devouring his most precious creative source.

So for Freud to introduce the idea that we might be able to reflect these big pictures, and use them, was a breakthrough. And we do, because everybody here has related to times when they have wandered in the maze of their own psyche in order to get to something that seems to be devouring them at the core. The pioneering of myth and the use of the Big Picture, which were introduced by Freud, were further developed by Carl Jung, and taken much deeper. They had a tremendous rift over this. Jung had a dream, and because he and Freud were doing analysis together, Jung told him of the dream. He dreamed that he had gone into a house, down the stairs and into the cellar, where he had been before. But then he found a trap door and opened it, and went further and deeper, into a remote area of the basement in which were all these skulls and bones lying about. Jung interpreted this as having broken through to another level, a much more fundamental level – an archetypal level, if you will – wherein the procession of the ancestors made themselves available, that we might access them and use them in our daily lives.

When he presented this idea to Freud, he freaked, and he couldn't cope with that concept. He said that this was blasphemy (against his own, Freud's, dogma) – it wasn't possible, it was ridiculous, and it couldn't happen. The collective unconscious, as Jung was describing it, was simply impossible.

So, Jung offered a new treatment of myth, and in doing so, a tremendous amount of freedom was unleashed. His work, especially the archetypal work, stands as a great breakthrough in thinking.

Obviously, Jung was a man of his time, and constrained by it – he too was born in a time of obvious conventions and cultural restraints, which he had to work within and fight against. Jung felt that the split between the soul – *psyche* – from the body – *soma* – was too polarised, and Freud's treatment of the body as separate from the mind, and his inability to blend and bring them together, partly fuelled Jung's work. Freud stressed the more logical *(logos)* side, as opposed to the side which is more nonrational and more archetypal *(muthos)*. So I would say that, for Freud, the logos was more important in psychology, whereas Jung's ideas of archetypes allowed for a universal psyche to exist, which Freud didn't recognise. He felt it was a feat of imagination that this should happen.

And so Jung's philosophy, especially his archetypal work, opened the door to something new in the interpretation of myth. I guess this would be number seven to Freud's number six, in he list of monolithic theories about mythology. All of this is terribly Jupiterian – the discovery of a new perception and the resultant dogmatisation of it. So, more dogma on myth!

Planets, themselves, are archetypes. And using the realm of myth is bringing the allegorical and creative era back to life, which Mircea Eliade believed to be the point of modern use of myth. The concept of an archetypal experience, which is common to all humanity, opens the door to a common human experience which underlies all psychic action, and relates back to a prototype experience. In fact, the inclusion of the mythic experience into modern life is a conscious attempt at reconnection to nature. This might be where Jung probably did his most creative work. His concept that we could reconnect with nature and participate with it, and that we were, in fact, at one with it, was a breakthrough. And holiness or divinity, in his view, was immanent – it wasn't external – and in fact he had a terrible struggle with the idea of the Old Testament God, and had real problems with it. He never could get to Rome, for example – he finally got up enough courage to arrange a trip, but he fainted in the ticket queue. He simply could not get on the train.

So I think that the greatest value of Jung's uses of myth is twofold. Firstly, he emphasises the psychological dependence of all societies –

both primitive and sophisticated – upon their traditional myths, which are often expressed through their religion, art and ritual: rites of passage. And the second one is the obvious one – it includes the individual within a collective. We are not isolated, alien, separate, alone. We are existential, but we are not without connection to each other.

To close this introduction to Jung, Eliade, and Campbell, and their contribution to the understanding of mythology and psychology: We often relate psychological and mythological motifs to astrology, but myth is not another explanation for astrology. Astrology in itself is elegant and beautiful, and stands alone – it doesn't need other models, you don't have to marry it to another system or model to validate it. It is a perfect model of one's own individuality, and is useful in itself for furthering our understanding of the interaction and relating that occurs within our own selves, as well as between us and others.

Myth and astrology

You can look at the horoscope as is if it were an inner pantheon, with each planet a god-image jockeying for position. And in the normal course of events, it means that at any one time, one planet is going to take dominance, and another planet is going to be submissive. There's always going to be some kind of tension that goes on between individual agencies within ourselves. And if you look at the horoscope as a kind of living and mythic representation of the psychic state, and you look at each of the planets as an individual member of this interior pantheon, then you find various components of your own self, with all their individual variants as well!

Each planetary agency has its own power; no single planet has more power or more substance or more dominance than another, as far as its fundamental influence and its inherent characteristics. But at certain times there is going to be more emphasis placed on a certain configuration or a specific planet – sometimes a particular planet at one time, then another planet or a configuration at other times. All planets are of equal power in and of themselves, but they have different dimensions and domains, and certain times when they transgress the boundaries between themselves and others in the horoscope.

The first astrology book I ever read was *The Lunation Cycle* by Dane Rudhyar. And although from 1963 on, I knew that astrology held something familiar to me, a language which I recollected, I couldn't quite believe that planets "did" something to you. How could I relate to astrology as something that was cohesive, that actually made sense? If you read a cookbook, you will see that Mars in Leo means this and the Moon in Scorpio means that, but why? I mean, is it possible that astrology actually can define things so finitely? Isolating a planet and drawing a conclusion about the nature of a person doesn't really work – it would be rather like analysing a cell from my fingernail and drawing a personality profile, or determining the condition of my soul.

The only way we can further the understanding of astrological positions relative to human behaviour is when planets are in a relationship with other planets, as seen from a central viewpoint – in other words, from ourselves. And so the relationship between planets is akin to the relationship, for example, of god images with each other, or better yet, between aspects of ourselves in relationship to other aspects within ourselves.

I don't think there's anybody in this room that could actually say that they go through the course of an entire day without something accomplished, something realised or some inner tension which developed a new perspective. We need to identify what components of our inner psychic selves, our nature, are in conflict with which other components. If you relate it, for instance, to a planet – a planetary energy or characteristic – you are well on your way to understanding more about astrology. Sometimes I might explain the horoscope as a board of directors, in which we have the Sun, Moon, Venus, Mercury, and Mars, Jupiter, Saturn and Uranus, Neptune and Pluto, all around the table; and one of them is going to try to run the show or be credited. Then, there's always going to be the planet who's been usurped. And there's always going to be a need for resolution of inner conflict. I think the planet Jupiter holds the key to our ability to render things sensible which are intangible, to rationalise and understand our mysterious selves. It is also the planet that acts as the disseminator of our newfound wisdom! We all like to teach things we know, don't we?

The myths, and the knowledge of the planets as characters, as mythic characters who in some way play out or enact a drama in the horoscope, is one way of looking into yourself and recognising yourself as more than just a mere mortal scrabbling along, trying to pay a mortgage, foraging for food, and that kind of thing. There is that side of the kind of work that we do – to bring us up and out of ourselves, to the degree that we actually participate in something bigger than our own selves. The spiritual focus in life has been largely secularised in our culture, and astrology can put one back in touch with the spiritual realm – one's own personal spiritual guide is found in the gestalt of the natal chart . So the concept of using myth in astrology does help. If astrology has anything to offer at this stage in history, it helps us return to the place in which we participate consciously in our environment, and with the heavens. So, it really is *participation mystique,* only with consciousness.

Archetypal astrology is about relating to bigger pictures, mythic images – psychological dramas which are enacted by each individual in some very personal way. I would think that we would want to use images from our various mythologies to enhance the timeless soulfulness of life, rather than as an explanation of astrology. It's not an explanation, but more an illumination of how we might understand more about the timeless nature of the heavens, its planetary patterns, and the human experience. And with respect to Jupiter, it's specifically the planet of understanding, expanding the mind, exploring new dimensions of thought, establishing power in the masculine realm of philosophy. Jupiter, as we shall see, is not only the planet which acts to reclaim our mythic history, but it is also the agency which can vanquish acknowledgement of our instinctual nature.

Jupiter is a tyrant, a god of ruthless arbitrary judgement. Jupiter's realm is just one level "lower" than Ouranos' – it is the visible skies, whereas Ouranos ruled the upper aether, the archetypal realm of the perfect forms, the Ideals. As Ouranos' grandson, and a descendent of the original severance of the heavens from the earth, Jupiter is dedicated to culture and the cultivation of the mind, *nous,* over matter, nature. Look at the order of the planets from Uranus: Uranus is the father of Saturn, who stands between him and his own son, Jupiter. Jupiter is on the other side of the Saturnian border. His job, therefore, is to bring the Uranian ideals into the world we live and socialise in. Jupiter rules mankind's translation of those ideals, those perfect forms, and thus is almost wholly confined to the *Zeitgeist* – the spirit of the times. In this way, Jupiter is biased, bigoted and chauvinistic – he is only able to come from the collective as it is in current time.

Jupiter also rules psychology, which is a "step down" from the spiritual development of humanity. The psychological realm is very important in human development, but we've already seen, just briefly, how philosophy, psychology, and all ideology change shape with the times. This is why we have to watch our own Jupiters very carefully for judgemental attitudes, bigotry, xenophobia, excessive egoism, pedantry, fear of nature, and ideological crystallization. Pure, raw Jupiter, without the mediation from other perspectives – that is, other planets in aspect with it – is dangerous and limiting. It is its interaction which gives it the depth and breadth of understanding, knowledge, and, possibly, even wisdom. Jupiter is a usurper, a stealer of cultures, of ideas, and of soul, if we are not careful. It is easy to substitute psychological models for spiritual development.

The birth of Zeus-Jupiter

This afternoon we'll talk about Jupiter within the context of aspects to other planets, because it's how Jupiter is viewed by, or views, other planets, that gives you the context of Jupiter's *largesse* in your own lives. There are times, under particular transits, when we may not even know that we have a Jupiter. I'm certain some of you will have experienced times in your lives when aspects or planets in your chart are virtually unreachable – you just simply cannot get in touch with that side of yourselves. Or you think it's gone, or over, or lost. That it might be subordinate to a current planetary picture is worth considering. For example, if Saturn is transiting Venus, you might not even realise you have a Venus. There are times when certain parts of our nature take a back seat and go into hiding. They go into a kind of gestation period, to evolve and mature in private.

In the beginning was *chaos,* and chaos was the genesis of all things. I think that's something we might do well to remember these days! Out of chaos emerged Gaia, the underworld, and Eros. Eros connects things to other things – people, ideas, and so forth. Eros is needed to inseminate and infuse primal life with raw creative power, to create a spark of love, really, between one thing and another, so it creates a new image, a new picture, a new feature, a new face. Gaia then created Ouranos, because she found that she was alone. In order to fulfill the mysterious feminine principle of seeding, gestating and giving birth, she needed a consort, and what more handy one than the one that surrounds you? And so, being surrounded by Ouranos, she then mated with him, and gave birth to several offspring.

The ones that I'm concerned with right now are the Titans – the youngest of whom was Kronos. When he achieved a certain age, he became the confidante of his mother. She had conceived some monsters which were repressed by Ouranos. In the seminar I gave on Venus,[30] I spoke a lot about the father's ideal image of perfection, and being unable to reconcile the image of perfection with the actual earthy primal seed of his own creation. As you know, the suppression of these monsters, the offspring of Ouranos, was so painful that Gaia asked Kronos to help her in the delivery of the monsters – to bring forth the primal instinctual nature. The old saying, "a face that only a mother could love", applies – there's something about the instinctual nature that is fearful to the archetypal masculine, and the instinctive nature is what Kronos midwived.

As an astrological figure, Kronos-Saturn is well defined, because the act of separating heaven and earth created Time. The concept we have of linear time was born out of Kronos' sickle. In the beginning there was infinity, which ended with the Golden Age, ruled by Kronos. The story of Kronos and the Golden Age is well known, but

---

[30]See Part One, pp. 26-30.

it's terribly important in this context because it's the termination of the Golden Age that brings about the rule of Zeus.

The reason it ended was because Kronos realised he was fated to be usurped by one of his sons – another one of these cyclic, ageless and contemporary stories of one generation having take over the next. Kronos didn't like this at all. He was terrified, and so, as a result, every child that his wife Rhea bore, he promptly swallowed. And there were five of them – Hestia, Demeter, Hera, Hades, Poseidon, and the final one, Zeus. Because Rhea didn't want to have all of her children swallowed up, she tricked him by feeding him a stone, and had the last-born, Zeus, smuggled off to live in a cave in Mount Dicte, where he was cared for and fed by the goat-goddess, Amalthea, and protected by the Kuretes. The Kuretes were wild women of nature, attendants of Rhea, who drowned out his infant cries with the clashing of their weapons. So, Zeus was fostered by earth-goddesses until his adolescence.

His story is the monomyth of the heroic cycle. The birth is endangered – threatened at the beginning; he is then sent off to grow up in a cave, close to nature and wild animals – that's very important, he had special care and tutelage; he returns to overthrow the father (asserts himself on behalf of the next generation); he faces specific challenges (the need to establish a new rule of order, a new dogma); and then he takes that knowledge into the formation of a new culture – in this case, an entire new pantheon, a new religion, a new mythology and a new collective epoch. The olden days are over, the Golden Age is done. Jupiter's overthrow of Saturn now symbolizes the necessary shift from one generation to another, bringing new ideas, new wisdom and new order to society.

Jupiter's reign

Jupiter cycles are twelve years long. At age twelve, we begin, emotionally and psychologically, to separate from our nurturing family, and begin preparation for adventure in the world. Our philosophies are well on their way to development. There is a strong sense of spiritual questing in the twelve- to fourteen-year-old person (between the Jupiter return, and the Saturn half-cycle), and with each successive Jupiter return, we reorganize our beliefs in accord with cultural and social demands. It is our Jupiter and its timing that tells us when it is time to explore horizons beyond the given ones. Jupiter is our instinct to create new philosophies, develop expanded knowledge, and cross over into unknown territories, familiarising ourselves with strangers and foreign things. Jupiter is our "rebellion clock" – it tells us when to look at our involvement with society, and whether or not we or it need revision. Our relationship with the swift-moving flow of cultural moods and fads is in constant flux, and our Jupiter shows us how we are inclined toward cultural and social norms and standards.

Jupiterian rites of passage include: moral development; spiritual ceremonies; educational shifts; social responsibilities; political awakening; changes in ambition levels; shifts in social status; and the advancement of natural ageing cycles (unlike the harsh seven-year ageing cycles of Saturn, his father, the Jupiter cycles are more synchronised with mental development, hence less shocking). Essentially, the Jupiter function is to keep the blood flowing and the interest level up! Drawing the allegory from Jupiter-Zeus' origins, our natal Jupiter is our heroic point. The place where we most need to have authority over both nature and society, and where we are challenged to arrive at a sense of well-being and spiritual security, are often found in the Jupiter regions in the chart – Jupiter itself, in the 9th house, and where we find Sagittarius in the natal wheel.

Jupiter's release of his siblings, and the vindication of his own generation, are typical of a kind of Jupiterian experience that we have in our lives – when we reach a heavily restrictive, authoritative boundary, cross it, grab something, deliver it, or force its birth, and then civilise it and turn it into something that's going to be useful in our daily lives. Too, Jupiter's allegiance to his siblings is symbolic of our own allegiance to our "tribe" or familiars. We are as protective of our friends and significant tribal members as Jupiter was of his siblings. This is one of the archetypes of sibling relationships and familial/familiar tribalism. The first act of this avenging, Jupiterian type is generally in the adolescent stage of coming into self-realisation. We tend to follow that paradigm at each successive Jupiter return, at twenty-four, thirty-six, forty-eight, sixty, and so on.

What's really interesting, with respect to the translation of myth, or the interpretation of myth, is that the Zeus-Jupiter myth actually does relate to an historical experience. It was around 2,200 BCE that the invasion of the sky gods occurred in the Peloponnese and in the Aegean Greek Islands. Prior to that was the Greek Bronze Age and a culture known as the Minoan period – which was primarily based upon the worship of the earth goddesses.

It's an entirely different mood – the cultural ethos shifted from an earth base to a sky focus. It has to do with a natural evolution or a natural assimilation of one culture into another. The absorption of one culture by another is usually initiated in stages: firstly, the overthrow, then the usurping and assimilation of gods and goddesses and the merging of them into the dominant culture. There often appears a kind of seamlessness between the previous culture and the current culture, but that is because Kronos gave us linear time, and we cannot understand the vast, slow-moving epochal changes while they are in process.

About four thousand years ago, the Greek Zeus came into being, as part of an apparent surge from the north of a realm of sky-god worshippers. By about 1200 BCE, the death of the Minoan goddess culture was fully complete. That would have been around the time of the fall of Crete, which is the last known place where the earth goddesses and the fertility cults existed. Crete: King Minos, Minoan, Minotaur, Maze, Matrix, Mother – do you see the connections? Minos was the father of the Minotaur, and Theseus its slayer and the bringer of democracy to Athens, which provided the foundations of our own Western civilisation.

Thus, we are looking at the emergence and supremacy of a masculine-dominated hemisphere in the process of the "civilisation" of the Western psyche – the emergence of solar masculinity in consciousness, outshining the lunar-feminine. Jupiter/9th house/Sagittarius traditionally rules education, and it would be after the fall of the goddess cultures, and during the ascension of the sky gods, that literacy emerged, and the transmission of the old oral stories changed into literary transmission. There followed a rather rapid transitional period from orality to the crafting and use of alphabetic characters and symbols to tell the ancient stories of myth. And again, this begins to define and shape and change the dimension of human beings. So over a few hundred years only, an evolutionary leap, long in the incubation, took place.

But the arrival of Zeus, and the implications of an invading sky god, are easily translated into a few germane issues. From the time of the fall of Troy (which was around 1184 BCE), right through to the time it was written down in the *Iliad* (about 800 BCE), something happened. And there is a natural evolution in the great cycle of time in astrology – the great sidereal year, the Platonic year, the precession of the equinoxes which produces the (approximate) 2,100-year epochal zodiacal ages. Whereas about fourteen thousand years ago we were likely in a period of pure fused consciousness (Age of Virgo), we are now at the most radical polarisation of masculine and feminine consciousness as we approach the end of the Piscean Age. However, the Iron Age of the Greeks is pinned at about 1050 BCE, which would have been smack in the middle of the Age of Aries.[31] This is the essence of Zeus-Jupiter consciousness.

Audience: You might see Jupiter as the ultimate patriarch? I have noticed that Jupiter is not as "benefic" as it is often portrayed in books and in most astrology writing. Jupiter sounds more like a warrior god than a great benefic, and rather cruel – or at least unfeeling.

Erin: I can't associate "feeling" with Jupiter. I associate opinion and attitude and cultural mores with Jupiter. The tradition of the "great benefic" comes from the same world-view from which he emerged! Jupiter in the heavens, auspiciously placed, meant that the king would win the war. What about the millions of those who lost the war or the invasion? You see, we are still looking at Jupiter in context of his origins as a planetary deity. Times have changed, and a new

---

[31] *The Oxford Companion to Classical Literature,* Oxford University Press, 2nd edited edition, 1990. Dates are approximate - a guideline in the index of this text gives a list.

world-view is emerging, and that is one in which we see the great split between the mythological realm of the great goddess and the modern realm of solarisation of consciousness – the masculine-dominated collective psyche.

Indeed, where we have Jupiter is where we can morally judge ourselves very heavily. Jupiter is not always kind in the chart, it can encourage us to extend ourselves beyond our capacity, and thus, fail! It can urge us to indulge in fantasies which cannot be realised. It can find itself out of balance with the rest of the planets in the chart, and be underdeveloped, lazy, and slothful, so that we lay about and get fat. Or, it can metabolise too slowly or too quickly, causing a physical disorder. Jupiter and Venus, for example, show up strongly in the charts of families who have diabetes running through them – an over emphasis on the sugar (Venus).

Let's explore some more of the myths in which Jupiter-Zeus is dominant, and see the correlation to the astrological Jupiter as an agency in our own lives. One of the stories involves the founding of Delphi as the Greek oracle. Now, for millennia, the site at Delphi was occupied by a *drakon* – a snake, the Python. The Python, or Pythia, was the essence of earth-power and earth-wisdom. Today, we tend to align Delphi with Apollo, keeping them in the same context. However, there is no evidence of Apollo being worshipped at Delphi before the 8th century BCE! He is a latecomer to the area, and the shrine, located on the southern slopes of Mount Parnassus, is also home of the Muses, daughters of Zeus by Mnemosyne (Memory).

Apollo of the Sun and Artemis of the Moon are twins, being born from the same egg, and Apollo's first heroic feat was to seize Delphi for his own home. In doing so, he destroyed the dragon, Python, the guardian deity who personified the dark forces of the Underworld, the earthy goddesses. His pre-Greek origins are relatively obscure, but one of his epithets, Lykeios, and a mention in the *Iliad*, indicate he may be connected to Lycia. An accumulation of terra cotta figurines found there confirm the belief that this was a site of earth-goddess worship, right through to Mycenean times, terminating around the time of Homer. However, the point is that Apollo stands as a personification of the Greek standards of perfection in the male form – *arete* – perfection of mind, body and spirit. The male mind body and spirit, mind you.

The snake and the serpent represent earth energy. The Delphic snake was slain by Apollo, which is a metaphor for mind over matter. Oddly, even though it became a shrine to Apollo, an actual woman was employed to sit in the cave, on a tripod, and act as the oracle! So, the female form still had to channel the wisdom, riddling as it always seemed to be. Apollo then became the keeper of the Delphic oracle, upon which was then inscribed, "Know thyself" and "Nothing too much". This is more evidence of the schism that exists between man and nature. There is somehow now a dividing line that dictates that I exist outside of, and independent from, my environment. If I'm to know myself (which doesn't mean going into therapy and being analysed), then I must know that I am mortal, and I understand my relationship as subordinate to the gods. "Nothing too much" is really a statement about keeping within one's mortal limits.

"Nothing too much" doesn't mean don't eat too much chocolate cake or you'll get fat, or anything like that. It means: Do not attempt to ascend above your mortal limits, or attempt to become immortal. If you do, there will be retribution – and the term for this, which is very Zeus-orientated and very much a Jupiterian experience, is *hubris*. This happens to mean the desire to go beyond mortal limits and achieve the status of a god, at which time you will then be smote or struck down, or in some way face some dreadful punishment. It is rather biblical, in that Eve's sin – informed by the snake (feminine wisdom) – was to eat the apple of knowledge, and thus to know only what God (male) is to know!

In Robert Graves' *The White Goddess,* he says, "The memory of the man who first tilted European civilisation off balance, by enthroning the restless and arbitrary male will under the name of Zeus and dethroning the female sense of orderliness, Themis. The Greeks know him as Perseus the Destroyer, the Gorgon-slaying warrior-prince from Asia."[32] Now, I have to admit, Robert Graves is a bit over the top, and not terribly scholastic in this book, but more

---

[32] Robert Graves, *The White Goddess,* Faber and Faber, 1961, p. 486.

mythopoeic. His dedication to the goddess guides every poem of grace and beauty written, and this book is a literary tribute to the goddess, even in its style. He also says, "The early Gentile Christian borrowed from the Hebrew prophets the two religious concepts, hitherto unknown in the West, which have become the prime causes of our unrest: that of a patriarchal God, who refuses to have any truck with Goddesses and claims to be self-sufficient and all-wise; and that of a theocratic society."[33] I might add, an Apollonian society at that!

So, in our own society, we've translated some of these mythic images, such as *hubris,* into various social dicta, such as the Peter Principle – that is, don't rise above your station. Stay where you are and do not transgress certain moral codes or family laws or religious dogma or political strictures, and so forth. Now, we all struggle with these things, and the planet that represents this realm and makes us struggle with them is Jupiter, because an important function of Jupiter is to instil a sense of correctness of the right place to be. The myths and stories of Jupiter are far too numerous to cover today, so I'm not going to reiterate all the stories of Jupiter-Zeus, but some of them are quite relevant to how we can perceive the archetype, the Jupiterian archetype, within ourselves and astrologically.

First of all, we can see there's something about Jupiter that is highly impressive, tyrant or not. As the story is told, his rise to power actually liberated a new mythology, so there's also something avuncular and benevolent about this tyrant – it's the image of the benevolent dictator. Therefore, if we have transits of Jupiter, it assists in giving birth to new perspectives. If we're having a Jupiter transit, it can deliver an entombed, or nascent aspect of one's own self. Jupiter transits are very tidy – every year, once a year, it changes signs. It spends twelve years and one month circling the zodiac, so about every twelve years there's a rebirthing opportunity. Just as Zeus liberated the swallowed offspring of Kronos, the transits of Jupiter can liberate a new way of being, a new truth or realisation. In short, it urges the delivery of a new mythology within an individual.

---

[33]*Ibid.*, p. 485.

There's always something within us that is excited and wants to give birth – that knows that there's something greater inside, that we can be more of who we are. Saturn, of course, says you can't, but Jupiter is the one who comes in and says, "I'm going to take what's my due. I'm going to give birth to the new order." And so his sense of omnipotence and exuberance actually talks about his own divine child origins.

The divine child myths are relevant to Jupiter and his origins. Again, we all feel,to some extent, that divinity is immanent, that it is both within and without. Children experience it quite personally, in that, if they have been punished or treated unfairly by their parents, they often think, "Oh, my real parents left me with these people just for a short period of time, and one day they will come and get me and everything's going to be all better." Or there's such an attachment to the concept of divine parents that the archetypal parents play more of a role in the formation of the child's psyche than the real parents. This is something that is inherent within all of us. To some degree we're all divine. But a strong Jupiter actually confers a psychic component of divinity that has a very personal aspect to it, so that there can be confusion between the inherent immanent divinity in all beings, and actually being a divine person. I'll talk a bit more about that later.

Often, when parents treat the child as divine, it backfires. What the doting parent is effectively saying, when he or she anticipates the child's every need, acts on it, and does everything for the child, is, "You aren't competent to do these things, such as getting your own glass of milk, cleaning your room, taking out the trash, picking up your toys, etc. Therefore I must do them for you."

A strong Jupiter can give a person a feeling of specialness, divinity, or *hubris!* This is frequently upheld and reinforced by childhood treatment, when the child is literally told he or she is special, divine, or better than other children. Or the child is isolated by illness, or survives a life-threatening situation or a tragedy, and this can also result in a Jupiterian feeling of omnipotence. It may, in fact, be true, but one never really knows. However, if a normal, healthy child is treated as a god, then as an adult he or she can become an insufferable tyrant to others, not recognising mortal limits until misfortunes in personal relationships, business, or creative efforts brings him or her up short.

Zeus was the kind of god, being the head of the Pantheon, who could do anything he wanted – he was above *hubris*. He was the one who meted out justice to those who offended this particular law of transgression. He was a figure who seems, by association or marriage or internal incorporation, to have actually acquired a sense of civilisation. He was not a civilised individual as a god; he was a rampant kind of character who went about doing what he wished and administering justice here and there. Indeed, Zeus was the only god who begat other gods! He was the father of Apollo and Artemis, Hermes, Dionysos, Athene, and Persephone. By Hera, his wife, he fathered only Ares and Eileithyia (the midwife).

Zeus was always having relationships with goddesses and mortals alike. He did have a significant relationship with the goddess, Metis, whose name means wisdom, wise counsel or prudence. Like his father before him, he was warned by the Fates that he would produce a son who would overthrow him; again like his father, his way of dealing with this was to swallow Metis immediately. Having done that, he incorporated wisdom, wise counsel, and prudence, implying that it wasn't there before. He had to take it in and gestate it within himself – before the swallowing of Metis, he must not have had this prudence or wisdom. He then developed a splitting headache, at which point Hephaistos came along with his silver axe, split his head open, and out flew Athene.

Athene today stands as the representative of the court of justice. So it's really by association and by assimilation that Jupiter stands as a planetary symbol for justice, because Jupiter in himself wasn't strong enough, or moderate enough, to see the wisdom and the prudence of mortal experience. He had to marry it, incorporate it, gestate it, and give birth to these civilised traits through a female medium.

Therefore, though in some ways Jupiter might appear to be justice, in fact it is his daughter who is. She represents an intellectual way of doing things. A new form of justice emerges with Athene's birth – it is not justice in the archaic sense. Zeus' justice (Athene), like his wisdom (Metis), was only a by-product. The arrival of jurisprudence – a Latin word – is actually a much later concept than the early Greek. The original word for justice in ancient Greek is *Dike* – a goddess – Zeus' daughter by Themis. There is some relationship between archaic justice – Dike, an abstract concept of righteousness, balance, correctness and cosmic/natural law – and Athenian justice or jurisprudence, which has to do with social order and human law. But it is an evolutionary step. In its rawest sense, justice has to do with our ability to see ourselves as behaving in a way which can only be called righteous in accord with higher forms of law. And anyone who transgressed this during the course of mythic history was always punished by Zeus. But jurisprudence – the law of the courts – was founded by Athene, Zeus' daughter.

The birth of Athene marked a significant turning point in modern times. Her relationship to the system of justice as we perceive it today is the basis of common law. Unfortunately, Athene was not popular with the 1920's suffragettes, nor with today's feminists, because she took the side of Apollo in the trial of Orestes, who murdered his mother. Athene cast the deciding vote that Orestes was free to go, and she then reduced the avenging Furies to safe little goddesses of the Athenian household and renamed them the Eumenides (kindly ones). Greek myth has her as the founder of the court of Areopagus (Ares' hill) in Athens, which is the cornerstone of the court system we have today. Does your Jupiter listen to the laws of the land or the laws of nature? Do you have a split there? How do you reconcile the fact that we need both, but on occasion, especially in times of personal or moral dilemma, nature must out?

Audience: I can relate to that problem. There is a lot of that evident today, in our medical system. As a nurse, I see people being kept alive on drugs and life-support systems, and being monitored long after I think that their natural appointed hour has come. This is the kind of dilemma that occurs when nature and culture find themselves at odds. Part of me wants to let the person die, especially if they are very old, or infants in terminal condition, but I know that this is wrong according to the Hippocratic oath, or at least as it is applied today. The problem I have with it is, I know that, a lot of times, the people are kept alive because the medical profession needs to learn something from them, they experiment with them. It is horrible. We read about it all the time. I can really relate to that problem very personally.

Erin: Where do you have Jupiter?

Audience: You'll laugh, it's so obvious. I have Jupiter at 28° and Pluto at 26° Leo, in the 8th house, square to Saturn in 26° Scorpio in the 11th. [1 July 1956.] I get very upset over this, maybe because Mars is in Pisces – I get angry and sick from it.

Erin: No wonder you know what this is about! I would laugh, but it is so close to the bone. I'm sorry, I am quite stunned by the configuration and your concerns. I must think for a minute. Have you ever thought of moving into the field of medical ethics law? You're still young enough to continue training. By nature you are more in tune with earth-law, natural law, than with the Athenian laws. And, you could be very effective in such work. You know, it is as if you are so closely in touch with a collective ethical problem, one which is peculiar to our times, that you may be called to do something about it. You would then step up your knowledge (Jupiter) to wisdom, and you might find the fight satisfying.

Mars in Pisces could absorb the sickness of what you see, with no recourse but to be victimised by it yourself, but if you fight for victims, you could stop being ill from it. The problem as I see it – and I have seen it very close up, having nursed a couple of people in their last days – is that, if we keep people alive beyond their body/soul calling, Pluto comes above ground and hangs around "up here". I said this to a friend of mine who was being kept alive by drugs – a friend who knew what I was talking about. It is very unnatural. And with you having Jupiter conjunct Pluto, you are very susceptible to this unnatural stance of Pluto – and with Saturn in Scorpio and 8th house planets, you are like the *psychopompos,* the soul guide.

Audience: I have thought about it – ethics, that is. Perhaps I shall look into something more heady and not so emotionally and physically distressing. Something must be done.

Erin: Thank you, let me know. Look, this is a good time to take a break, think about what has just been said, and pull in a bit. I don't want to wade into anything new without some reflection on what you have said to us.

[After the break]

One dialectic in Athenian philosophy occurred between the terms *doxa* and *sophia* – opinion versus wisdom. Well, Jupiter is *doxa*. It might lead to wisdom, but only if we gestate knowledge, and allow it to come to its term. It is at the root of the word orthodox (straight, or accepted opinion). Orthodoxy is death to creativity. The received opinion (not wisdom) of cultural law can kill the potential for receiving wisdom from natural sources. We could look at our Jupiter to try to determine our own tendencies toward *ortho-* or *heterodoxa*. Do we think "straight" or do we think "other-wise"? Jupiter and Saturn, for instance, struggle between the old orthodoxy and the new heterodoxy. Oddly, once Zeus took succession, his heterodoxy became the new orthodoxy. But, then, that's the way it goes: Today's heresy is tomorrow's status quo.

Zeus could act willfully and spitefully. He was known to confuse the mind with a state called *Até* – and there's really only one way to interpret this: ruin. *Até* is a Greek word, and is a "she", a personification of "ruin" – the kind of ruin that comes because you're confused about what you're supposed to do, and you dally too long at the threshold, or you engage in something that trips you up where you don't quite get the clear picture. You may become irrational and act too quickly, or become frozen or paralysed, and become a victim of your environment or of others. Your passions or your desires overrule your capacity to reason or think. In other words, you have lost your sense of inner justice, and can't distinguish between right and wrong, advantageous and disadvantageous courses of action. You are infused with *até*. This was one of Zeus' curses.

Astrologically speaking, *até* can come upon one because a transit from Jupiter brings too much to bear on a given planet or situation – having too many possibilities and avenues for action can be as difficult as being limited to one path. For instance, how do you cope with decision-making when there are too many options, too many choices or things to do? You might almost think, "Well Jupiter has now brought me far too many decisions – I cannot possibly do it and therefore I will collapse into a stupor and not make any of them." In which case, the deed has been done. You would have been served with *até*, which will then lead to ruin. We need to ask ourselves: What is this? How do we cope with this aspect of ourselves? I think the confusion of mortals and heroes renders bad judgement, and actually results in an inability to "Know thyself", and in carrying on in a way which really transgresses the law of "Nothing too much". So, there is that aspect of overindulgence, or overactivity – of too much – of simply not knowing your dimensions.

It strikes me that being afflicted by *até* is not always such a bad thing. That's how we learn, especially when we're younger. A fourteen-year-old person afflicted by *até* or confusion is not in as much danger as someone who is, say, forty-eight, who runs up against his or her limits and doesn't know where they lie, and who needs to draw back and examine his or her life in a better way – to really see clearly what's right, what's correct, what's just.

This too has to do with Jupiter's capacity to act as a channel for wisdom. It's when we lose the sense of personal wisdom, or we forget what our *moira,* our lot or portion, is, that we experience the kind of tragic flaw where we run up against a condition or circumstance in our life that creates a kind of crack in our reality. Then we end up overburdened, crushed by too much – having taken on too much, not knowing when to draw the line. Jupiter is not wisdom personified, but acts as a conduit through which wisdom might come. I think that the incorporation of wisdom through marriage and through relationship adds a dimension to Jupiter's astrological character, and our relationship with the planet as "justice" within. Jupiter does have the sense of being able to make right decisions based on inner moral law. This sometimes means going against the status quo.

As I mentioned briefly before, Zeus was the father of the Muses as well. Their name means "reminders", and their mother's name means "memory". So there's another implication of an assimilated trait, one which is not inherent but is acquired or created through a union with the feminine. The Muses are the inspiratrices for the arts and sciences. For instance, their name, Muse, is the root for "museum", which was a place connected to the Muses *(mouseion)* for the arts and learning. The Muses are always invoked in the traditional sense, not to inspire, but to recollect. This is a rather Socratic idea about learning – that we recollect that which is already known in the soul, we don't learn anything new. Ancient poets would always call upon the Muses to remind them of all that is, was and ever shall be. Hence, the higher mind and the inspirational tone of the astrological Jupiter come to us yet again, indirectly from his marriages and children!

Jupiter and the god of ecstasy

The indulgent side of Jupiter comes, I think, partly from the Dionysian side of him, where his relationship with Semele produced Dionysos. Hera was jealous of Semele's pregnancy by Zeus, so, in disguise as a human, Hera persuaded Semele to pray to Zeus to visit her in all his splendour as a god. He tried to talk her out of it, but then relented, and she was reduced to a cinder in a flash of lightning. Zeus managed to save the foetus, which he then sewed into his thigh – which is interesting, because Jupiter and Sagittarius rule the thighs. Again like his father, he became a surrogate parent, gestating his own child and giving birth to it. He gave birth to the god, Dionysos. Dionysos symbolises the capacity for the astrological Jupiter to reach states of ecstatic transcendence. This was done in ritualistic ways in the ancient Greek world, because they believed that if they enacted rites of passage symbolising important turning points in the life, that life would be better endured, and the gods appeased.

The Bacchanalia, as it was called, was performed to reach states of transcendence – to enter a religious state of ecstasy, which literally means "standing outside" of oneself. The methods to achieve this were, first of all, to drink copious amounts of a special kind of wine (which likely had some psychedelic properties), tearing around in the woods, behaving licentiously with all sorts of creatures, and achieving a state of what was called *enthusiasmos* – which means being "filled with the gods".

Taking in of a magic ingredient – whether it's mescaline or psychedelic mushrooms in the case of Meso-American Indians, ayawaska in the Amazonian region, peyote in the Pueblo rituals, or the moly root of Circe which turned Odysseus' men into swine – is an old, old custom. In Indian myths, there is a parallel god, Soma, who was sewn into the thigh of the sky-god, Indra, and who invented and named the intoxicating drink after himself. These customs of altering the relationship between the mind and the environment were meant to be religious – they were shamanic or healing.[34]

Shamanic ritual often involves intake of spirit though natural sources, and release of inhibitions and the return of the repressed act as healing agents. Certainly, the Dervishes, though *sans* drugs, whirled themselves into an altered state. However, the Dionysian ritual of the Bacchae goes right back into the Minoan culture – Dionysos himself is a newcomer to the Pantheon, though his status as an Olympian is legitimate.

So the Dionysian act – a Jupiterian ritual of going to the mountains, reaching a state of *enthusiasmos* or ecstasy, purging oneself of social strictures, confinement of the status quo, and cultural repression, and becoming one with animals and nature – allowed the cult of Dionysos to experience *participation mystique*. This form of religious experience has become both pedestrianised and pathologised today – the natural need for taking in spirit has resulted in serious drug and alcohol abuse by everyday citizens in search of an ecstatic experience. There is an instinctive need at work, in taking in of a natural substance to reach a transcendent state, to put us back

---

[34] Arthur Evans, *The God of Ecstasy*, St. Martins Press, 1988. This book is wonderful - all about Dionysos and the Bacchae. It is very scholarly, but not turgid. There is a new translation of Euripides' *Bacchae* in the back, with pictures of the actors in the Valencia Rose Cabaret production. One of them, the "slave", is Jack Fertig, a San Francisco astrologer and gay activist, better known as Sister Boom-Boom of the Sisters of Perpetual Indulgence.

in touch with the divine. For instance Jung's support and endorsement of Alcoholics Anonymous is quite well known, and in a letter to the founder of it, he recognized that an alcoholic person is a religious person, a person who needs to take in spirit in order to feel divine. We even call alcohol "spirits".

The pathology of Jupiter can incorporate an over-excessive indulgence in something – a substance or behaviour pattern or ritual – a taking in and purging in order to reach an ecstatic state, to be outside the self, to participate with nature and gods. It's no accident that the theatre in Athens was called Theatre Dionysos, because the citizens would go there, get blind drunk, carry on, and vicariously participate in stage plays all day and night. There was a tragic trilogy, a comic trilogy, and at the end a satyr play. The satyr play, from what we know, is an obscene satire, which also relates to the Bacchanalian aspect of Jupiter. The satyr play enacts crude animalistic desires on stage, so that everybody would get to watch it, but nobody would have to do it.

There is also an implication of Dionysos being important in the Orphic mystery cult, as Dionysos Zagreus. A variant on the Dionysos birth has him as a son of Zeus and Persephone. Zeus came to her in the form of a snake (again, the earth wisdom symbol), and they had Dionysos – but, when he was an infant, he was torn to shreds by the Titans. However, his heart remained intact, and Zeus sewed it into Semele, who gave birth to him as Zagreus. This guise, as Dionysos Zagreus, places him as a chthonic god, an underworld associate, to whom is attributed kindly judgement after death, freedom from punishment, rebirth, and eventual blessedness. Now, Zeus himself is also referred to as Zeus Chthonios, because of his position as father of Persephone, goddess of the underworld. Orphism and Dionysos are deeply connected – the women of the Orphic cult were called Maenads, as were the woman who worshipped Dionysos. Euripides wrote about them in the *Bacchae*.

In the play, Pentheus is king of Thebes. Ironically, he is also Dionysos' cousin, in that their mothers are both direct descendants of Cadmus. Pentheus' mother, Agave, has rejected the worship of Dionysos, and in revenge the god drives her mad, and she goes to join the Maenads in the revelry. Too, Pentheus has made the Bacchanal illegal in his territory, because it is licentious, and he is revolted by the revels and the rituals they indulge in. Basically, he is terrified of a shadow-aspect of himself. Now, the conflict in the tale lies here: Although he is repelled by the cult and outlaws it, secretly he really wants to see what they do. So, he talks his servant into dressing him up like a woman, so that he can go out and pretend that he's one of the Maenads, and he can watch all these awful things go on. His desire for voyeurism, to secretly observe for prurient reasons something he ordains as sinful, flies in the face of Dionysos. So, Dionysos, angry because he isn't being propitiated, decides to teach his cousin a lesson. We all know of this phenomenon, where someone declares a war on a way of being, yet is part of that very thing himself or herself.

Well, Pentheus' servant is, in fact, Dionysos in disguise! With great glee, he dresses Pentheus up as a Maenad, and off they go to the hills and woods where the Bacchic rites are to be enacted that night. The king stands there and watches the whole time, terrified, but secretly gratified by his participation through voyeurism. He's able to both participate and experience the acts, and at the same time feel disgusted and horrified. Well, he's spotted by one of the Maenads and recognised as not being who he really is, a hypocrite, and he's torn to bits, shredded by her. In the morning his head is paraded on a stick and stuck outside his castle. Unfortunately, the horror of this story, which is very typically Greek, is that this particular Maenad is his mother.

An outstanding example of this kind of voyeuristic Jupiterian/Dionysian character rests in the Sun-Jupiter (retrograde, obviously) opposition from Capricorn to Cancer of J. Edgar Hoover, founder of the FBI and its offspring, the CIA, in America. He was absolutely rabid about homosexuals – they were outlawed from the FBI, and if he could have, he would have condemned homosexuality as a federal offence. The weird thing is, J. Edgar Hoover, if not actively homosexual, was secretly a cross-dresser. We now know he enjoyed dressing up in ladies' underwear and night clothes. As a secret transvestite, Hoover was acting out the Pentheus archetype. The projection of one's shadow in such stark light demonstrates extreme hypocrisy. If this duplicity becomes an addiction or habit, there will be some kind of betrayal of mortal – and moral – limits, and a form of retribution will come down. Unfortunately, Hoover's political power was so great that his hypocrisy was never exposed, so to speak, until after his death.

A Jupiterian conflict can arise – hopefully not in this extreme – in anyone. If someone is violently repelled by a certain kind of moral behaviour, you can be certain that it is a well-nourished complex of the shadow variety. Any overwhelming attitude that falls into a Jupiterian domain – political, sexual, religious, intellectual, social class, race – is the result of an uneducated, undernourished Jupiter function, which can flip into a form of extreme prejudice against anything "different" from oneself. A form of xenophobia results.

Transits of Jupiter can bring upon one a need to break out, to cut loose, to explore dimensions that have never been explored. In the course of the civilisation of cultures and individuals, there is always something repressed – there really has to be. If we could retain or access more elements of our primal selves, of childhood, it would be good. But there has to be some form of repression in order for our civilisation to occur. However, when Jupiter comes along in transit to a planet in the chart, you may find that you shake off the cloak of conventionality and break out, delivering yourself into the hands of the gods. You find that you need to get in touch with the side of yourself that is wild and free, animal and primal, and that can be a positive side of the Jupiterian experience.

Audience: So, Jupiter in the chart can be "in drag".

Erin: Indeed, look at the past American president, George Bush. The great proselytiser of family values, an anti-homosexual, right-wing fundamentalist Christian with a high moral tone – and a Jupiter singleton retrograde. And, an international arms dealer, a warmonger – yes, that too is a form of drag! Tsk, tsk.

But if we are engaged today in reconnecting to our mythic or creative era roots, and we are conscious of this reconnection, then it might well be that we have a way of dealing with the idea that "something out there made me do it". In other words, these days, we have to take responsibility for our own feelings, our own behaviour, our own actions. So something "out there" didn't make you do it – something "in here" did. Knowledge coupled with awareness, and the ability to recall your own self and know who you are, are very much part of Jupiter and Jupiter's domain. The struggle for balance with Jupiter, of truly listening to your instinctual nature and then balancing it with your place in the world, can sometimes be quite difficult, to say the least. All of your instincts may want you to do something, but the outside world says it is foolish or ridiculous. It is then a moment to explore what truth is to you personally, and how well you can live your truth and still feel responsible.

You want to employ or propitiate your Jupiter, in order to give you the wisdom from the inside, from the intuitive self, to create the right decision, the correct decision – not the socially correct one, but the one that's right for you, that has more cosmic reality. I think maybe that's part of the Jupiter-Saturn issue, actually – controlled expansion. The role of Jupiter as benevolent protector is also really important.

Stranger in a strange land: the traveller

We hear about travel, exploration of other cultures, the ability to speak other languages, love of ethnic and tribal ways – this is all very Jupiterian as well. Now, that also comes out of myth, because one of Jupiter's many roles as a god was to protect individuals in transition. Each god had very specific roles – Aphrodite had to take care of love, Artemis took care of the animals, Dionysos took care of the bestial nature, Saturn took care of the heroes that returned from battle, and Jupiter took care of the traveller, the journeyer. His epithet in this instance was Zeus Xenios, the protector of strangers. This guise speaks of our traditional interpretation of Jupiter, because it rules people who are in between known departure and an unknown destination. This is the state of being in between – in other words, you have left the known place, like Odysseus leaving Troy, and are heading "home", but the path is fraught with unknowns.

The sacred place that we occupy, when we are without identity and egoless, and are between the known departure point and the unknown destination, is one that needs to be treated with a great deal of respect. This "space" is a psychological, spiritual, and physical state of being. It speaks of a kind of ambulatory *temenos,* or a place in which one undergoes the loss of ego identity in order to give birth to a new self. This gives rise to the image of Jupiter as the midwife of the new mythology, of the new self.

One of the most powerful cultural codes in the ancient Greek world was the guest-host relationship. When a stranger comes to your door, you are beholden to that stranger, you must give them everything they need. You must look after that stranger because that person is in a state of grace. If you don't, then Zeus will send retribution – you'll lose all your gold, or your daughter will run off with a lesser prince, or a disease will befall you and your people. This protective side of Jupiter is something that each of us has within us, and when we ourselves are in a state of transition we might want to propitiate or give some kind of gift to Zeus, because it is his domain to protect us in an unprotected state.

When we go through an identity shift, there is a major crack in our perception of reality, and we can no longer relate to who we used to be and are not yet who we will be; it is in fact a religious state of being, and all sorts of things happen. We start to look for signs and portents. Everything looks very shiny and magical. Even if it's difficult, even if it's a state of pain, we might still arise each day with an excited feeling of adventure. But when this is going on, one is also very vulnerable, because one is open to attack. This is where it's important to realise that there is a place of safety in this liminal state, and that one's own Jupiter might show how one experiences transitional states.

In the *Odyssey,* there are many meaningful, if brief, stories that are directly related to liminality – Odysseus exemplifies this law of sacred transitional reality, of nonidentity. However, he transgresses one of the most important laws effective when one is a journeyer. Odysseus and his men enter the cave of the Cyclops, Polyphemos, who is Poseidon's son. Polyphemos eats two of his men. Odysseus is trapped in the cave another whole day, while four more of his men are devoured. He makes the Cyclops drunk, and burns out his eye, then sneaks his surviving crew out under the belly of sheep. The Cyclops is roaring and screaming and calling to his neighbours, "Help, help, I'm blinded, I'm blinded!" and all his neighbours call back, "Well, who did it?" And Polyphemos shouts down to Odysseus and says, "Who are you?" and Odysseus says, *"Outis!"* which means, "I am no-man!" (It's a word-play on his own name.) It's perfect. And the Cyclops says, "No-man did it, no-man did it!" and they all go away, leaving him to be tormented by Odysseus.

When I read that, I had an experience much like Freud must have when he read about "sons lying with their mothers in dreams" – I was floored! Of course, I thought, when in transition, especially on the seas of liminality, one should be nobody. It is a law of nature. Do not have an ego, lest it betray you. Apparently the Greeks thought this as well. But Odysseus is a young man, very excited, filled with the vigour and heroism of war, and suddenly he blows it, because he realises midway what he has accomplished in damaging the vicious Cyclops – he wants acknowledgement for what he's done.

As the Cyclops continues to bray out at him, "Who are you?" Odysseus turns around and shouts back, "Odysseus, son of Laertes!" and immediately his fate turns. From that point on, Poseidon has it in for him, all the way. Up until then he was fine. He defied one of the most sacred laws of transition, and that is, do not identify yourself, let go, remain in a state of egolessness. As soon as you seize upon an identity and it's inappropriate, you're doomed. During times of transition, the ego softens, becomes malleable and needs to be fluid. To assume an identity before the fact is *hubris*. Jupiter's domain again!

Cavafy wrote a poem called "Ithaka", and I'll read a few lines from it that illustrate the concept of the egoless traveller:

> When you set out for Ithaka
> ask that your way be long,
> full of adventure, full of instruction.
> The Laistryogonians and the Cyclops,

> angry Poseidon – do not fear them:
> such as these you will never find
> as long as your thought is lofty...
> Have Ithaka always in your mind,
> Your arrival there is what you are destined for.
> But don't in the least hurry the journey.

We need to trust the side of ourselves that is in harmony with the traveller and the journeyman – know our destination and let the gods guide. There is a destination, one does get there. Through unplanned, circuitous routes, perhaps – Circe, clashing rocks, the Sirens, Scilla, and various other creatures notwithstanding, there is a destination. And it is toward a new ego function. But the more you struggle under the impression of ego, the less functional you are in the course of the whole journey. People who find themselves frequently in transit – compulsive travellers, people who absolutely must go to another country, or cut themselves off from their roots – have significant Jupiter aspects. I have a streak of this myself, I confess, and I've often felt, if you have a strong Jupiter, a planet in Sagittarius, or a heavy 9th house, that you don't need an analyst, you need a good travel agent. That's how you solve your problems, you can just go somewhere else and see another dimension of life. It's not always escape.

This is where the pathological side of things can be exaggerated – it's only a problem if it's a problem. In other words, I would not say, "Oh well, you travel a lot, so therefore you are an escapist," unless travel for the person was an escape, rather than a necessity or a life-style. Some people are made like that; some people need the passing of the horizon, they need a new challenge, they must speak another language, they simply have to go into another culture to discover themselves. And the reason for this is because they are global citizens – they think globally, not locally.

There are two sides to Jupiter. There's the exuberant, outgoing, extroverted, travelling global citizen, and then there's the rank tyrant or the dogmatic fanatic. This is the Jupiterian split. People who have a strong Jupiter and Sagittarius prominent, or a loaded 9th house, paradoxically, simply must put themselves in unfamiliar territory in order to feel at home. Sometimes it is because they feel like they are strangers in a strange land anyway, so they may as well go somewhere where it's going to make it real. It's like seeing your inside on the outside – it externalizes an internal condition. The person who is truly governed by Jupiter – that is, Jupiter has precise aspects from the Sun, Mars, the Moon, Jupiter rising, singleton retrograde, or focused in a stellium – is a stranger by nature, and is often more comfortable creating his or her own territory, than adopting the one he or she was born into or brought up in. The test is to create your own world – this is a highly creative circumstance, but it can be despairing because we can fall into strong ego conflicts.

Explorers of all realms are Jupiterians. Jupiter is the part of us that wishes to discover and know far-reaching horizons. Very often, even having a Sagittarian IC or Jupiter in the 4th house will take an individual into new cultural realms, seeking a commonality with another collective. They find themselves moving, relocating, emigrating and sinking roots into foreign territory by circumstances or necessity. In doing this, of course, they have created home. Depending on personality type, socio-economic conditions, one's own nature, and so forth, this can be portrayed in many variations on the theme.

For example, recently I did a chart for a woman who had a very isolated Jupiter – singleton retrograde – and I knew I was walking into loaded territory, because the woman was born deep in the English countryside and had never left her birth village. And I thought, How do I touch this? I know this woman feels like an alien, and that she is lonely and distressed and thinks there's something wrong with her. And there actually isn't anything wrong with her at all. The only thing wrong was that she had never ventured out from her own little world, and if only she could study, travel, or explore new horizons in some way, she would know that she was not strange, but a "stranger" in search of a familiar. Then she wouldn't feel so weird.

There can be sense of distance, isolation, and alienation around your Jupiter – people who have a strong Jupiter are, in fact, very powerful, and need an arena for it. They love to experience other worlds, but if they are fearful or timid or there's a counteraction to this desire to explore new horizons or break new ground or be self-starting, then it does create a sense of incredible isolation and disassociation, wherein they feel there may something wrong with them – everybody else is fine but they are weird.

Audience: What did you say to the woman you mentioned?

Erin: I did finally broach the subject of her feeling isolated and displaced. And I talked about the value of philosophical exploration – I told her some of the stories about Jupiter that I am relating to you today. She was fascinated by the correlation between the Greek myths and her own inner feelings. She decided to do some reading – I recommended some books that would rekindle her early recollection of school mythology class! Oddly, it was perfect. She was an introvert, so study and adventure in the mind were her outlets for her Jupiter situation. It does mean, perhaps, in the case of an introverted person, that a foray into an educational arena would be helpful.

This is where education comes in. You don't have to leave your house to travel – you can read, you can expand your mind, you can go beyond the limits of your own experience intellectually. Again, Jupiter drives you to do that. So it's the desire to know, and possibly to recall – to be inspired by the daughters of Zeus, the Muses, to be able to be poetic, to be romantic about life itself. That is very Jupiterian. He was a romantic. These tough characters in ancient myths were also portrayed in tender ways as well. This benevolence and self-love is quite important, especially in these states of experiencing oneself as an alien. If it's taken to extremes, this business of being a stranger in a strange land, then it can lead to a disconnectedness or negative type of ecstasy, where you're outside of yourself to the degree that you're actually in spiritual peril. Spiritual emergency can take over. These are things that you need to be in touch with within yourself.

The whole idea of disorientation and alienation from one's own culture, race or religion leads me to believe that there is a collective pool that we pluck identity from. Generally (and thankfully, for it would be pandemonium otherwise), most people are quite comfortable within their milieu, but occasionally there is a throwback or a mutation in the family system, wherein the individual is actually foreign. He or she truly has emerged out of long latent origins – a single facet of the family which has been forgotten, repressed, or was so long ago in the dynasty that it has "died", but is then reborn and enlivened in a member of the family. In this case, the family of origin is seen to be foreign and uncomfortable. Perhaps there is a quantum level experience here, where the logic of genetics and psychological inheritance has a warp.

Jupiter and the saviour complex

There are certain kinds of travellers who are travelling for a collective purpose; perhaps they are a testing ground for the human experience, or are taking insight into new areas. Their personal journey is undertaken on behalf of many. Their work, whether it is writing, teaching, counselling, revolution, or healing, has a ring of real truth to it, and hundreds, thousands, sometimes millions of people respond to it. Their fate would play a role in this – and this is *not* measured in the horoscope – and they would become a spokesperson for the collective. They embody an archetype and thus are removed from the personal realm. I once had the privilege of meeting a radical Central American Jesuit priest, who has spent his entire life fighting for his people, living the revolutionary cause, travelling the world under pseudonyms, saying mass in war-zones, smuggling people across borders, and actively participating in the political arena of the revolution in his country. When I spoke with him, when he was on a trip to the place I was living, I asked him many questions about himself, and none of his answers were personal.

My close friend, who had the misfortune of being in love with him and having his child, took many years to realize a truth which I could see the second he walked in my door. He belonged to the collective, he was not "human", he was divine. This man is not a household name, he is not famous like the gurus of our era – that is not his mission. He is a living embodiment of his cultural anxiety, and is also its healer. I am not easily impressed, and I was not impressed with him – I was awed and fascinated by the *charisma* (literally, in Greek, "gift of grace,", "free gift", generally a gift from the gods) of his spirit. After the interview, I had to confirm to my girlfriend, to my sorrow for her personally, that this man belonged to no one. He belonged to the gods. His Sun and other personal planets were in Sagittarius in the 9th house, and his MC was also Sagittarius; and he had Jupiter on the Ascendant.

So, this guerilla priest, as he is known, is a grounded, solid Jupiterian type, who incorporates and embodies various aspects of intelligence, wisdom, truth, justice, and a powerful reconnection with nature and the divine. Jupiter can often come up with a spiritual teacher. Of all the gods and all the planets, the function of Zeus, the god, and Jupiter, the planet, can embody more characteristics at once, and thus it is potentially the most complicated planet in the horoscope. If we incorporate into our own Jupiter all of the attributes that are assigned and allotted, then we can ourselves become a kind of conduit or bridge between the sacred and the profane.

This is where you can find true teachers, people whose personal experience of their own divinity is not split off and projected onto a guru of one type or another. They experience their relationship with the divine as an equal one. And therefore they can, in fact, teach truths, because they are not polluted by the dogma of *doxa* – opinion. Jupiter then acts as the divine inner guide, to explore territory outside the known reality, in participation and in collaboration with the gods. One is thus protected. In that instance it is safe to go into this territory because it's not out of *hubris* and it's not out of egocentricity. It's out of a true desire to learn. It's not about knowing things, it's about learning things.

If your own Jupiter function is "clean", then you will instinctively know when wisdom becomes dogma. I can't put it into words, but I think you'd get wind of it – you'd sense something questionable and you'd want to turn your back on it. It's a form of pollution. The idea of going outside the normal reality, and being in touch with the divine, is Jupiterian, not Uranian – let me put it that way. In other words, it hasn't got anything to do with being split off and in the ideal world of forms that Plato outlined, where everything down here is a cheap replication. It involves a real connection and collusion between the sacred and the profane. The strong desire within us to find a rational, intellectual method of explaining why God exists, how God exists, and to define God, is also Jupiter.

When we look at specific aspects and placements of Jupiter, we say, "Well, how do you image this in your mind, what conclusion have you come up with, what rationalisation have you come up with, how do you approach this desire to know the unknowable?" And that's through a Jupiterian experience as well. However, there's a real pathological side to this one – I'm sure you already know about the dogmatist – Jupiter gone bad, so to speak.

The omnipotent and omniscient side of Zeus, which is powerful and helpful, benevolent and kind, can also be absolutely disastrous if it becomes an autonomous function in the psyche, and is not cooperative with the other planets. If Jupiter inflates and takes control, then a high moral tone is poured over everything. The result is usually a rejection of all things outside one's own belief system, and the imposition of one's own will and dogma on anyone who will stand still long enough.

An inflated Jupiter could actually be quite mad, or it could be a compensatory device in the unconscious of a person who suffers terribly from feelings of inferiority. That's where you get the split between others and the self – this is me, that is you, I'm OK, you're not. That would be, of course, a form of xenophobia – it's the shadow function of Jupiter, the pathological side. Ideally, Jupiter would lead one to accept the fact that individual people and cultures are different but also correct and just in their own right, and that beliefs are relative. The ruthlessness that Jupiter exhibits at times, especially as a religious or political fanatic, or simply as an insufferable bore, is incredible.

I'll bet there isn't a person here who never has got on their high horse and lorded it over everybody else about how much they knew about something and how right it was, and what was spiritually correct. It's just part of growing up, really, isn't it? It's part of growing. It's natural, it's instinctive, but it's also something to watch for, this inflated concept of self-divinity. It does lead us back to the aspect of the divine child, who never matures out of that phase. But there are many people who do this, and there are also many kinds of divine children, because they've had all the requisite experiences: the endangered childhood, the struggle with the parents, the painful wound/discovery/experience, the fight for freedom and vindication of their generation, the opportunity to revive culture – in short, the whole cycle of Jupiter's heroic origins.

But as an aspect of the religious fanatic who is ruthless and believes that he or she is right, Jupiter is very dangerous. Witness the issues of religious and moral ethics surrounding the Ayatollah and what's happened with author Salman Rushdie, as a perfect example of Jupiter gone mad – the *fatwah* placed upon the author who writes a "blasphemous" book. The Ayatollah had a Jupiter-Venus conjunction in Sagittarius in the 3rd house. Another example of exceptional intolerance and self-righteousness is the Fundamentalist Christian movement in the U.S. It is just hair-raising, and fully endorsed by the former U.S. President Reagan, and made sacrosanct by George Bush – who, as I mentioned, has a singleton Jupiter retrograde. Here is the inflation of an individual who believes that his moral code is right, and that's it, off with everyone else's head. When Pluto enters Sagittarius, it is likely we will see a lot more of the religious wars.

So there are things to watch for – for instance, Jim Jones, the San Francisco cult leader, and the mass suicide of his followers in Guiana in the 1970's. And then there is the most recent one, in Waco, Texas – David Koresh, who declared that he was God, the mass messiah, and the divine child. This is an archetypal thing. You can run into it a lot, especially if you're working in areas like astrology and any of the associated healing professions – to greater or lesser degrees, of course. This is one of the bugaboos of our own work as astrologers. It has the occupational hazard of identifying with the knowledge as a source of personal power – an intellectual *hubris* – and imposing dogma and Jupiterian lordliness over everyone.

England had its own Jupiterian, David Eyke with his turquoise jogging suits and messianic beliefs – good colour, really, like turquoise – divine colour, in fact, isn't it? Isn't he a sports commentator, or something?

Audience: Yes, he was a television sports presenter.

Erin: There you go, Jupiter-Sagittarius. A true spiritual translator, a teacher or transmitter of universal truths, has quite a strong balance of Jupiter. His or her sense of justice is benevolent and global, recognises distinctions, but doesn't discriminate. Or if one does discriminate, one remembers that it's a mind-trick and that it's OK to be a white, middle class professional, or it's OK to be an untouchable in India. It's OK to be a Mestizo Indian in New Orleans. However, it's not OK to think there's something wrong with any of those distinctions. So it's alright to be defined and bounded as Saturn depicts in his story, but to honour the differences is the task of Jupiter.

Audience: Can't Jupiter show signs of being self-indulgent and lazy? Would that stem from a philosophical origin, too?

Erin: Hmm. Yes, it is more like a psychology, rather than a philosophy, that says, "I'm special, so look after me." It's not a terribly well developed outlook, if it is truly lazy, but there are ideologies that rationalise living off others' sweat. That can be taken to extremes as well. Let it all unfold and be on the dole. That kind of OK-ness isn't OK with the people who are supporting them. However, there is a distinct line between social need and social irresponsibility. I should think that Jupiter would play quite a role in that kind of psychology. This is not to say that those who have should not help those who have not – certain levels of taxation are quite fair and correct, in this respect. Religious tithing was instigated to support the church, which doesn't suit everyone. Another type of tithe is possible, and one which I believe has value in the greater whole. There is benefit to be given and gained in putting back time, love or money – whichever is your greatest asset – into the community that supports you, that you live, work and relate within.

The charisma of Zeus – the etymological source of the word means "bright" – is brightness, brilliance, and luminosity. There is a special charisma about the Jupiterian person, and anyone who falls headlong into their aura may have a problem with their own underdeveloped Jupiter. As one matures toward the middle years, Jupiterians seem to become more kindly, more mellow, and less in need of the energy of others to feed them – just as Shakespeare described in his soliloquy, a kindly, avuncular nature can develop with time. Individuals lacking discrimination, either because of the excitement of youth, or suffering from the mortal flaw of *ate*, can be swallowed by Jupiterian people. They can become endangered and in spiritual peril.

So we must always keep a check on Jupiter, perhaps develop a little more Saturn to balance out Jupiter. Jupiter's message is to be able to experience ourselves as holy and divine and sacred, but in the context of our profane lives. In the words of the oracle, "Know thyself", and "Nothing too much". So the ultimate goal of Jupiter and self-development would be to embody all of the complex archetypes Jupiter symbolises, and work towards a focused but balanced attitude, always keeping in mind the big picture.

Jupiter in aspect to the natal planets

Sun and Jupiter

The Sun and Jupiter are both rather similar – astronomically Jupiter is likened to a "mini-solar system", with its moons and gravitational pull. Both are rulers of fire signs, both are agencies for the greater good, health and well-being of the whole person and both are "bright". The Sun-god, Apollo, is Jupiter's son, remember, and if they are in collusion, there is something operatic and epic about their experience of life. Regardless of the contact, Jupiter will enhance any characteristics of the Sun. For instance, if you have a Sun-Saturn square, but the Sun is trine Jupiter, then you have the potential for very solid stages in ego-development. Sun square Saturn means you will have seven-year critical turning points in the deconstruction and reconstruction of the ego, but with the trine to Jupiter there is always a sense of being favoured, and it would lend a much less gloomy and subordinate vision to your sense of self and ego. The individual would likely feel more spiritually supported during his or her crisis periods, and hope, optimism and faith would not flag dismally in times of difficulty. It doesn't take away the difficulty, but Jupiter would add a dimension of movement, liberation and choice which Saturn prohibits.

Basically, the Sun-Jupiter conjunction is "good". Jupiter favours the Sun, as I said, and can bring added brightness and luminosity to the personality. The Sun would channel grandness, thoughtfulness and charisma through Jupiter, which obviously can be overdone. Certainly there is a basic feeling of immortality and the potential to act in extreme ways, to prove oneself or challenge oneself and one's ego – and in the case of sports or physical endeavours, challenge the body. Mountain climbing, car racing (with a bit of Mars), downhill skiing, flying, paragliding, and so forth, are Sun-Jupiter (and Mercury) activities – all have a high risk, a dependency on luck (the god's domain), and *hubris!* I always think of Icarus when I think of Sun-Jupiter – flying too close to the Sun, getting too bright, outshining all else, compelled by the desire to go higher and higher.

The greatest danger of overamped Sun-Jupiter contacts – especially the conjunction – is *hubris,* taking on too much, or being too grand, or expressing too much *largesse.* Although it is a relatively benign and good-hearted aspect, people can instinctively resent Sun-Jupiter people, thinking them insensitive or out of touch with the masses, the *hoi polloi.* There is such a magisterial aura around a strong Sun-Jupiter person that it masks the normal, everyday self-consciousness and insecurities that all people entertain about themselves. This can mislead others into believing they are invincible and indestructible, and are exempt from the mortal fallibility that everyone else experiences. It is not so much the signature of the showman, but when the spotlight is on, they do shine a bit brighter than anyone else. The saving grace of Jupiter is humour, always.

I have always found it interesting that Emmet Kelly, the "sad clown", had four planets in Sagittarius, including a tight Sun-Saturn conjunction in this sign. His own Jupiter was in Scorpio, just to add a twist to the act. He was the first clown to break from the French silky, cone-hatted clowns who were beautiful and lyrical. Kelly established the tradition that Chaplin took up, and was followed by clowns of all kinds. The sad clown is the melancholy of Saturn, but it is also the cosmic pain of Sagittarius. There is always a hint of world-weariness and jadedness in the Sagittarius humour, as if a glimpse of the world has made it sad, realising that the grandness of the ideal world is a cosmic joke on us mortals.

Where there is Jupiter there is bigness, but it's the conjunctions, squares and oppositions that run into potential problems with inflation. Inflation does not always manifest as self-aggrandised personality. It can come cleverly disguised – Zeus was the master of disguise – and can appear humble, sweet, kind, generous, and loving, when in fact, it is using those personality demonstrations as guile. More often than not, this is deeply unconscious.

Audience: I was just going to ask that. I know someone with his Sun in Leo square Mars-Jupiter opposed. This man has all the appearances of being gentle, kind, loving, generous, and magnanimous, and in fact, is quite giving on the material level. When dealing with people he doesn't know well, or on the phone, butter wouldn't melt in his mouth. But, in fact, he is very self-centred and monomaniacal, but does not see this. His affection feels false, it is so evenly distributed around, always "loving" people. He is fearful of repose and introspection, too, and very cynical about psychological development. He prefers to jump a level and concentrate on what he calls spiritual development. He declares himself never to get angry, but I have seen him hostile, vicious and ruthless. But he says it isn't "really him" when he is driven by others to anger.

Erin: Well, who is it then? And, secondly, how could he see it when he's on the inside of it? It is a repressed part of his deepest nature. I should think this man has a received wisdom that kind, gentle behaviour is equal to a kind, gentle person. We know that is not always an equation. Too, it may be that he had an exceptionally benevolent but beleaguered father – Sun-Jupiter does bring to mind a father larger than life, but, with Mars, a conflict about father and fathering. Sometimes generosity is masking a fear of intimacy – if

Venus and Jupiter

you can give things to people in lieu of affection or real committed feeling, then it is also a way of controlling them, keeping them paid off so they can't ask for more. I wouldn't know if your friend is this way, but there can be a defence mechanism called "generosity". Carelessness with resources can be Sun-Jupiter, also, where there is a fobbing off of personal responsibility, allowing the universe to take care of you. It does – but not always in the way which one fancies.

Also, at Sun-Jupiter square, Jupiter is moving slowly, preparing either to go retrograde in a month or having just gone direct a month ago. So you get a different tone altogether. It could indicate a laziness, a desire to gain consciousness without the hard work involved. Too often I have found that people on spiritual paths are looking for a short-cut, or hoping to by-pass the hard work of psychological maturation. I am not talking about psychology as a model – that can be another form of dogma – I am simply speaking of consciousness, to the degree possible, at all times, of what one is doing, and why.

The Sun-Jupiter square is rather like receiving an arrow from an angle just outside one's sphere of vision, whereas, with an opposition, you can clearly see, you can see what is "out there" or coming at you. A conjunction is something that is happening within, it is self-generated energy. The trine is a fairly graceful angle – trines capture light and refract it out in a harmonic that is peaceful. But a square comes at you from the periphery, so if you are blinkered and staring straight ahead, you don't see what is coming. You get hit sideways by surprise. A Sun-Jupiter square can be possessed by or obsessed with, or at least overly concerned about, beliefs and ethics and moral codes as part of the personality. You don't know how conscious someone is by looking at their chart, so you can only know by talking to them and understanding their experience, exactly how they deal with it. Never impose an attitude or a moral bias on somebody because of their horoscope. Someone could have absolutely horrendous aspects and be a saint. Other people may have nothing but trines and sextiles, and all they do eat and drink and sleep – by the way, that's not a general interpretation of trines and sextiles!

The Sun-Jupiter square is in danger of being invaded by inflated ideas and self-aggrandised beliefs, only because they suspect that there's something out there that will tyrannise them. As a result, they themselves can become tyrants. Now, a good tyrant is a good thing – this is what a competent administrator or an insightful leader is. The word *tyrannos* is the root of "tyrant" and is the Greek word for king, so this is not always a terrible thing. But in an unconscious individual, or someone who is insecure, disturbed, or has endured a negative primal experience in their life regarding authority and justice, it can become a divine, messianic sort of characteristic – imposing his or her will right and left, without any kind of mediating influences. Life can be unjust, life is unfair at times, and if you have a Sun-Jupiter aspect, injustice is taken personally. For example, if a parent dies too young, this can felt to be a moral insult, a personal injustice; if a child is bullied, a victim of injustice, a Jupiter-victim, then this is unjust and is fed into the Jupiter moral development.

However, a positive Sun-Jupiter square person is one who is filled with a sense of divine destiny, and who acts as a pretty clear channel for truth and wisdom. But they have to be very conscious and rigorous – there needs to be constant vigilance, a need to put a governor upon the Sun, the ego, to watch that it doesn't get carried away with itself. You can never say, "Oh well, Sun-Jupiter square – you really think you're terrific, don't you?" It's very unlikely that it's wholly the case, because no one does. Everybody goes through moments of lack of self-worth, and, indeed, the Sun-Jupiter person can internalise Zeus and come down very heavily on himself or herself – the extremes, you know. But you would be safe in saying to a Sun-Jupiter square, "I'll bet you really have to work hard not to overcompensate or overdo things, or to build yourself up more than is necessary in order to validate your experience of yourself."

So the down side is about ego inflation. There are tendencies to throw the ego and the godhead all into one pot. But Sun and Jupiter are, by and large, a most agreeable pair – very agreeable – they both think highly of themselves, if you will, and have a lot of respect for each other. Because Jupiter is the social organiser and the Sun is both centre and circumference – the self and the ego – there can be an ability to really see the big picture. Sun-Jupiter contacts are generally rather benevolent to the individual who carries them. But I like the idea of the big, fat, roly-poly dispenser of food and drink, yelling and joking from the head of the table, which you mentioned earlier. Well, you've got to get it out somewhere.

Audience: What about the quincunx?

Erin: The quincunx is spiritually torn – there's usually an edge to it that Sun-Jupiter doesn't normally portray. It has to do with a feeling of having a purpose in life, but not being really sure what path to take to find it. There can be a relentless quest, and an annoyance with things that don't further immediately, and it can mean a lot of false starts and a lot of storming down the wrong paths. A Sun-Jupiter quincunx takes a lot of forbearance from either side, and they are slightly different. The forming (applying) quincunx – a 1st-6th house aspect – can give one the feeling of having to fight with god all the time via the physical body. There can be weight problems, sugar problems, metabolic problems. But the separating quincunx – a 1st-8th house aspect – can feel as if the gods are conspiring to make the path a tricky, deceptive trail, filled with spiritual peril, challenges fit for gods.

Audience: What do you mean by "1st-6th house aspect"?

Erin: If you place the slower moving planet in the Ascendant position, and then count around to the faster moving planet making the quincunx to it, the faster planet will be either applying toward an opposition with the slower planet (1st-6th house) or separating from an opposition with it (1st-8th house). In this way, aspects have a house connotation. For example, there are two kinds of sextiles, one of which is formed when the faster moving planet is separating from the slower one (1st-3rd house sextile) and the other which is formed when the faster moving planet is applying to the slower one (1st-11th house sextile). This adds a dimension to aspects that is not readily seen in a chart, but informs the aspect about its purpose. In other words, the sequence goes: conjunction (1st house), sextile (3rd house), square (4th house), trine (5th house), quincunx (6th house), opposition (7th house), quincunx (8th house), trine (9th house), square (10th house), sextile (11th house), and conjunction again.

That first quincunx has to do with the body and its issues. Sometimes it can be the problems I mentioned, or it can be problems with the liver or circulation, and reflexively, the kidneys. Those issues have to do with the ability to process poison and to expurgate. That's the purgative side of Jupiter. It can mean health problems. Moderation is really the key to anyone who has a strong Jupiter. You often don't learn that till it's almost over.

The other quincunx, the one following the opposition, is more mysterious, and has more to do with risk-taking and 8th house matters, like sexual issues. Overindulgence, guilt, excess, puritanism, religious attitudes, fears – all these things can manifest through Jupiter in that quincunx to the Sun.

Audience: Would the Sun-Jupiter at the MC attract a lot of attention, maybe even attention you don't ask for or want? I have it there in Capricorn, and all my life, people have shown jealousy and resentment toward me in my work – especially at work. I cannot think why. Actually, it is not with the superiors, but with my equals. People under me don't show this. I guess it is just with peers, really.

Erin: That's true when you have things up in the top of the chart. You really are up for grabs. People talk about you. They have something to say. People feel they have to comment on you, project their own undeveloped or unrealised traits upon you. What you have to watch, with Jupiter high in the chart, is being a victim of gossip, oddly enough. Other people are jealous, for some reason, of whatever it is that you have. You may not understand it because it's yours and you are quite unaware of its full value and worth, but others might see it, and if it reflects a trait underdeveloped in themselves, then unconsciously you can stir up resentment in them. Or you might actually have some kind of talent that they don't have but desire to have. It does mean you have to be extra-benevolent toward others, and accept a certain kind of responsibility – it's often incumbent upon the Jupiterian person to be nicer and more understanding than anybody else, even when you'd rather cheerfully rip their heads off!

Now, the problem is actually seeing others – I mean, seeing them in their own lights. Jupiter doesn't notice the small things – it tends to be chauvinistic and elitist, noticing only that which is beautiful, large, successful, or high-profile. Also, Jupiterians need to be aware than they exude confidence, and thus must help others grow into their own confidence. Otherwise they can be seen as arrogant and controlling, tyrannical and full of themselves, when they are really simply having a good time and making the most out of their environment. However, others might think, "Well, who do they think they are?" So it really is a test of your humility, I suppose.

You may be too busy to notice the small things that people need to be recognised for, and they feel you are above them, or they perceive you as thinking you are above them. Some choices need to be made for yourself – either you don't care about this, or you have to extend yourself to them and reach out, letting them know you do know they are there! The other factor is that there is a genuine luck that goes with Jupiter, and this makes people mad. But remember, "luck" is dispensed by the gods, so luck can turn. Propitiate it. Burn many thigh-bones to Zeus!

Audience: Well, it is quite lonely at times, and this is meant genuinely, I feel very left out – it isn't as lucky as they would have it! I would trade it for just being "ordinary".

Erin: I know what you are saying, but you don't really mean it. What you mean is that you need to be accepted by mere mortals. It's one thing to hobnob with the gods, but one has to work with ordinary people. You have to confess that there is an element of hierarchical elitism, and it can be fun. It doesn't always mean that one is a snob. In fact, people with Sun-Jupiter can be very shy – because they are often noticed! But you do know that certain things are done in certain places, and there are certain people that can go here and go there – you really appreciate the roles we play, and the finer things in life. Jupiter is an elitist planet. So it identifies what is good and beautiful and wise and true, and anything that is sordid is to be ignored – unless it has that Dionysian streak, in which case there is a fascination with the catabolic elements of society, the down-and-outs, the street people, the strangers and wanderers among our society.

Jupiter and Mercury

Jupiter and Mercury have the combination of omnipotence and loquaciousness. There is a talent in the delivery of messages, and the ability to translate, facilitate and mobilise ideas – these are people who are real orators. Now, by orators, I don't mean that they necessarily speak well all the time, but in their minds they are translating images and symbols constantly. Mercury-Jupiter is excellent for academic types of work, but it's also very good for empathy, for being in touch with the inner integrity of others and sensitive to their personal codes of ethics. You might think in terms of people who are advocates for other people, who can divorce themselves from their own belief system and act in accord with the needs of other people. For instance, this makes a good lawyer, a good barrister – somebody who may be quite capable of defending a guilty person, because Mercury brings an element of impartiality to bear on any circumstance they find themselves placed in. It is a playful aspect between the two of them by nature, but it also confers a serious element to the mind.

In the Homeric Hymn to Hermes, Hermes is an *enfant terrible* – he is up to no good from the moment of birth. He steals the cattle of the Sun, Apollo's cattle, and, to make a long, wonderful story short, his adventures end up in an informal "court", with Zeus as judge over his infantile but clever crimes. Now, Zeus is merciless when he is tricked, but he finds Hermes charming and witty. Hermes becomes Zeus' favoured son. There is a collusion between the two of them which creates the trickster-mind, the clown, the mind of rapier wit and repartee – generally, Mercury-Jupiter is amusing.

And so there's a great enjoyment of the exchange of information, of the hierarchical situation, because Jupiter, in fact, being head of the pantheon, must have a sense of supremacy. Our Jupiter tells us where we are supreme. Therefore, it has to be admitted that, with a strong Jupiter, there is an element of elitism about how we feel about others. But Mercury-Jupiter conjunct is a natural facilitator and translator. They can translate obscure information and render it so that others can understand complicated concepts through simple language. The reverse, as usual, can be true – they might find the most convoluted way of saying the simplest thing!

Audience: Doesn't Mercury-Jupiter show up in the charts of linguists, actual translators?

Erin: Well, not always. But certainly there must be a fascination with language and linguistics and translation of symbols, where the mind is trying to figure things out all the time, finding meaning and reason behind everything. Remember me talking about the rationalization of myth? Well, that wasn't just an exercise in method, but a way of experiencing the lengths that Jupiterians will go to find an answer to the most simple thing. Love of history, the past, cultural origins, religions – Jupiter pursues the things that make human beings culturally different, though collectively they are identical *en masse*. It is the Zeus-Jupiter function to bring meaning to life. To be able to crack the communication codes that sharply distinguish one culture from another is very Mercury-Jupiter.

Mercurial Jupiterians have to be especially careful not to latch onto dogma. Remember *doxa* versus *sophia?* Well, opinions run very high with the Mercury-Jupiter person, and they must dig deeper for wisdom. Opinions can override wisdom, as the mind can be too easily influenced by glib conventionality, run-of-the-mill philosophies, and modish platitudes, which are not truths but stereotypes. Now, there is a truth lurking in stereotype, as it is a popular, current expression of an archetype. So, the inherent indulgence and laziness in Jupiter must be overcome so that the Mercury-Jupiter can discipline itself to go deeper and not take shortcuts to understanding by adopting current opinions instead of truths.

Audience: I would think it was a good aspect for teaching. But, is it a writer's signature? I want to write books but I'm not very disciplined. I work with shiatsu and reflexology, and I want to combine them with astrology.

Erin: That's a good idea – synthesising healing disciplines is very Mercury-Jupiter conjunct. It's facilitation, the desire to teach others what you have learned. It could be a writer's signature, but there the

9th house is important; in thinking, Mercury Jupiter is expansive, and needs to write and disseminate knowledge, but for manifestation and the ability to do the actual work of writing, the boring, disheartening part of it, I think a shot of Saturn is essential. Oddly, I've seen a lot of writers with Mercury-Pluto contacts – squares and oppositions quite strongly, but also the trines and sextiles. But the 9th house is for publishing and for having your ideas disseminated abroad.

Audience: Wouldn't Mercury-Jupiter tend to take on too much, or have an inclination to be a dilettante?

Erin: Yes. It can be information overload, and you have to be very careful that you don't get too scattered. There can be a difficulty in discriminating, recognising what is germane to an issue and how to contain information in limited packages. You can be very certain that people don't want to read everything you think, even though you think they might. The applause must come after the performance! Sometimes with the indiscriminate types, you get what I would call an education junkie. Once they've finished one degree, they've got to get another. Or, I'm going to do this course and I'm going to do that course, and the idea, I think, at some stage in the game, is to bring Saturn into it. Let's round it all up, put it together and turn it into something solid. The myth-making ability with Mercury-Jupiter is strong, and they can be eloquent and timely, or they can be a legend in their own mind. The ideas might be heavenly, but they have to be rendered here on earth!

One thing I can say across the board is this: There is something about Jupiter, Sagittarius, and the 9th house that wants credibility and acceptance. This can take the form of academics, or simply being acknowledged for one's accomplishments. It is a burning need, a longing, an erotic desire – and if it can't be got one way, it will be got another. If it can't be done in an orthodox fashion, then heterodoxy will do. Jupiter can be very creative in finding ways to gain credibility, credentials, and recognition. Whenever I see a list of degrees behind someone's name, I smell Sagittarius/Jupiter and the 9th house. It's like I said about not needing an analyst, but a travel agent – another degree will do as well!

In myth, Hermes could "maze the minds of men", put them into a kind of trance so they would not notice what was going on, and Zeus instilled *até*. Between the two of them, one could be rendered positively witless! There is a perception problem that can arise, because Mercury rules the metaphorical "trees" and Jupiter the "forest". Mercury-Jupiter confusion can be irrational, scattered, overcommitted, and generally fuzzy about specifics. Breadth can supersede depth, and although I think it would be a mistake to write off a Mercurial Jupiterian as superficial, there can be a feeling that one is not being fully appreciated on an emotional level, a feeling level, with these people.

Audience: What do you have in your 9th house?

Erin: Mars, Saturn, and Pluto, and that's enough about that.

Audience: My husband is a repository for other people's problems. Strangers on trains tell him the most personal and sometimes appalling troubles. He has Mercury and Jupiter in the 12th house. It is a problem, because on a personal level, with friends, neighbours, and family, he feels too much empathy.

Erin: Weird. But, listen, he has it in the 12th house! Strangers (ruled by Zeus Xenios) tell him their secrets (12th house) while in transit. Both Jupiter and Mercury rule travellers, and they protect the traveller. Clearly, your husband is a Mercury-Jupiter figure to people in transition. He should do it for a living. He has an innate ability to offer advice, or simply be the silent oracle to dispense wisdom to strangers. It's a remarkable manifestation. Why does it bother him? Or does it really? His fascination with the troubles and fortune of the collective is embodied in his 12th house aspect. Mercury and Jupiter are actually fairly neutral, in the sense that Mercury is really plainly a conduit, a channel – it has nothing to say, it is the messenger, it isn't the message.

But the lack of ability to control talks about another kind of problem. That's how it comes out, right? So we would be able to say, perhaps, that here's a man with a problem in saying "no". And this is the form it takes. He hears all their long sad tales of woe, but that isn't the Mercury-Jupiter problem. So the problem lies elsewhere. Maybe he deflects his own concerns and doesn't pay enough attention to himself. That would be a harsh judgement. I don't know the man, so I wouldn't want to ever say that, unless I saw evidence of it. But it's possible. That's an interesting point to bring to that problem, because what it demonstrates that the aspect is not itself pathological, but the way in which it is experienced, or the context within which it's offered, can be. 12th house planets can remain sleeping or dormant, deeply unconscious, and he may not realise he has to draw boundaries around what he picks up from others.

Now, the squares and oppositions can be hard, because they can take on far too much, and not realise it until they are swamped and burned out. The aspect "thinks" it's omnipotent, it can handle everything, and maybe it can, but it can't all the time, so inevitably there is a fall. Somewhat like the Sun-Jupiter opposition, it thinks it can take on the world, when in fact it really can't. These people can promises that can't be kept, not because they're evil and want to con you, but because they think, "Well, I can do that. Sure, I can meet you and you and you in three different parts of town within fifteen minutes." And it doesn't work. So, there's a problem in drawing boundaries with Mercury in a hard aspect to Jupiter. There's a problem with discrimination. Mercury is not exactly known for discrimination anyway, and Jupiter is omnipotent, it can do anything, any time, anywhere.

Audience: Does it make a difference if they are in their own signs, like Mercury in Gemini or Virgo, with Jupiter in Sagittarius?

Erin: Ah! Notice that they rule the mutables – they rule Gemini, Virgo, and Sagittarius. This is clear a circuitry of information, assimilation and dissemination. It is part of what I call the communication circuit (ending with Pisces, the collective pool of ancestral wisdom), so if they are found in rulership loops and in their fraternal signs, then it can magnify the need for strong belief systems and structure programs for intellectual activity. Hermes-Mercury's very essence is indiscriminate. But the sign Virgo has to do with very discriminate, precise parameters. Drawing boundaries around things is what Virgo is needed for. It makes sense, it is intelligent, it has to do with making sense out of Gemini, which collects data indiscriminately. Let's say you're doing a research project, you've read all the books, you've made all the notes, and then you must sit down and do a Virgo on it. And then, in order to further perfect it, you do a Sagittarius on it. And then the final editing is always the Pisces – someone else does it, who has objectivity, because once you get to Pisces you've lost your own vision on the project. Through the function of Pisces it is distilled into its perfection, or it disappears because it is not viable. You yourself don't see this part of it as clearly, if at all.

As for Mercury itself, planets are totally and completely different from the signs they rule. You can think of signs as an evolution – in the case of the mutables, they move from data-gathering (Gemini) to rendering it intelligent and systematic (Virgo). Mercury isn't discriminating, but Virgo is. It has to be, it will choke, it can't digest masses of information without digestion and assimilation. Then it is sent over to Sagittarius, where it becomes a full-blown credo.

Audience: I did not talk until I was about four years old. My parents thought I had a serious problem. However, these days I talk for a living. I am a fund-raiser for major corporations, and I travel around the world talking people into investing in ecological projects. My own Mercury is in late Scorpio, but conjunct Jupiter early in Sagittarius in the 4th.

Erin: A networker – there you go. What you've described is an interesting pathology around communication. It sounds like you didn't have much to say to your family until you absolutely had to. It's as if you were a watcher, an observer, a witness to your family's interaction, and you may well have waited until the last minute to participate. I would say there is something that has been passed on to you from way back in the generational line, that you needed to connect with before you'd be able to talk or want to communicate. As soon as that happened, as soon as your child-mind found its relevance in the family group, then eloquence followed.

Audience: Both my sister and I have Mercury-Jupiter conjunctions, but mine is in Capricorn and hers is in Aquarius. We are thirteen months apart, and we drive each other mad, because I like logic and order and she operates on wit and is very spontaneous and takes a lot of risks. She also is scattered, but gifted, whereas I always feel a bit dull. I am focussed and have to have security. I have a degree, she does not, but she's more "successful" than I am in her work.

Erin: That's absolutely perfect. It speaks for itself. It's one of those things that you wouldn't dare say. Everybody would say, "Oh, that's so obvious!" I guess astrology must work, so I'll press on for another thirty years. That's a beautiful example, those are really good examples that we've had. What a lot of Mercury-Jupiter conjunctions!

One of my clients has Jupiter in Capricorn, and she's a brilliant orchestra conductor. That Jupiter is squared by Mercury in Libra. She travels around the world conducting, she's very famous already at the age of forty, and is now writing two books on two different aspects of the music world, both historical. This is really super-Jupiter-Mercury, and exceptionally productive. She is all the things positive – buoyant, gifted, "shining" – but there are some relationship problems, because of all the moving about. With the Uranus-Neptune conjunction transiting over Jupiter in Capricorn, something's going to have to stop, something will change to give the energetic outlet a different form.

Jupiter and Venus[35]

Both Zeus and Aphrodite are the most prominent members of the Olympian pantheon – their powers are equal. In the *Iliad,* Homer has a line of introduction for Aphrodite, calling her "Aphrodite, daughter of Zeus".[36] However, we also know of an older myth, wherein Aphrodite is parthenogenically born to Ouranos, and is the eldest of all the gods and goddesses. Regardless of her parentage, throughout mythology, Aphrodite and Zeus are equally powerful, licentious, gifted, benign, but also ruthless when crossed,

---

[35]See Part One, pp. xxx for additional material on Jupiter-Venus aspects.
[36]Homer, *The Iliad,* op. cit., Book III.274.

unpropitiated, or tricked. Both gods have magnificent powers of enchantment, and both are dedicated to maintaining their ascendancy. Aphrodite has a warrior side to her, she was a staunch defender of the Trojans, and employed her tricks on both Helen and Paris, and on Zeus himself, casting spells of love and desire upon them so their senses would be dulled by desire and lust, thus weakening them. Zeus was a shape-shifter, be it into a swan, bull, or shower of gold, and in his guise as such, lured many a woman into love. Aphrodite is the goddess of both love and war – and when Zeus and Aphrodite are put together, almost anything can happen.

Both are fruitful agencies in the horoscope. Both Venus and Jupiter have been called "benefic" – Venus the lesser benefic and Jupiter the greater. There is an aesthetic harmony about the two planets that is very strong when in conjunction, trine or sextile. People with the Jupiter-Venus contact in the traditional soft aspects do have a charisma, a grace about them which can be enchanting or bewitching. Obviously, it can be too much of a good thing, but, as Mae West, who had a widely squared Venus in Cancer to Jupiter retrograde in Aries, once said, "Too much of a good thing is just right."

The famous excesses of Jupiter and Venus can be physical, emotional, or spiritual – the "too much" factor is largely a product of angularity, simply because there is less ease of flow between the two planets, and the stress of oppositions, squares, quincunxes, and their derivatives creates anxiety. Anxiety creates dis-ease, and thus can constellate in the body as overweight, diabetic or hypoglycaemic tendencies (especially if it's a family dynamic), food allergies, hormonal swings, and so forth. It can be excessive in emotional investment, and dogged in its pursuit of happiness, then discarding when the emotions are sated. Spiritually, there can be *hubris* or inflation as a result of angularity and lack of assimilation of the stress of the planets angling – ogling? – each other.

The supremacy attitude of Jupiter can make it very difficult for the Venus-Jupiter person to put themselves in another's shoes, and if they do, might be so offended or repulsed by any sordidness or scariness that they quickly step out of them, to pursue their own path. Although they can appear insensitive, they are actually overstimulated by others and other people's energetic fields, and thus run hot and cold. Introverts tend to move the Jupiter-Venus into more artistic and literary, or philosophical, pursuits, while extraverts move the Jupiter-Venus around in more social circuits.

Both planets are associated with loftiness – Venus as Aphrodite/Urania, and Jupiter-Zeus, speak of the high-blown rational mind, and strong philosophical, spiritual, and ethical beliefs can dominate their thoughts and behaviour. Essentially, there is a bit of the elitist – even if in the shadow form – in the combination. Dogma can be either benign or malignant. I have known Jupiter-Venus people to be excessive in their penury! They may be too much the underdog, too much the poverty-stricken victim, too much the victim of their own desires, needs, and self-destructiveness.

If there is a harshness or darkness in an individual, Jupiter and Venus may not lighten it up at all, but create excess there as well. Remember, the Ayatollah, with his Jupiter-Venus conjunction in Sagittarius in the 3rd house, could not for a minute be considered as benign, but he could be considered as effective, powerful, high-minded, religiously maniacal and fundamentally orthodox, a global figure, a man of conscience and belief. Right? His vision of how the manifestation of God should take place is singular, and in accord with the most rigid dogma. This is an extreme of the orthodox – the straight thinking that cannot incorporate the heterodox, the possibility that there are other, equally valid moral codes, spiritual beliefs and social mores.

Wherever we find Jupiter, we find epic feats, and Venus has her dual nature – Urania, the celestial goddess, and Pandemos, the worldly goddess. It seems that fiery and airy combinations of Jupiter and Venus (which automatically suggest trines, sextiles and oppositions) are made up much more of the dreamer and idealist, whereas the earthy and watery combinations have more of the worldly, human-animal, Pandemos aspects of Venus' dual nature. The extremes of ideals and visions that Jupiter-Venus brings to the mind and spirit of an individual need to be brought into "earth form" – otherwise, both Jupiter the sky-god and Venus Urania keep ideas, projects, relationships, and spiritual feelings up in the ozone. To bring the ideals of the higher mind into the reality of daily life is the greatest task set for the Jupiter-Venus person.

So, you see, through their elemental harmony, the trines, sextiles, and oppositions are more workable, in the sense that there is agreement between the heavenly and earthly natures of the two planets – for although Zeus-Jupiter is a sky-god, he does have domain over the "affairs of humans", and Aphrodite-Venus has two distinct sides, her mortal-loving one and her heavenly, immortal nature. Thus, if there are squares between Venus and Jupiter, where elements are at variance with each other – fire and water, earth and fire; water and air, air and earth, and so forth – the squares bring a tension and confusion in how to bring the idealism of the mind into the realm of the social, ideological, practical world. Clearly, if there are releasing aspects – one of them trine to the Moon or Saturn, or another embodying planet – then the combination of so-called uncomplementary elements will collect around the modes, cardinal, fixed and mutable, producing a meeting-place between idealism and realism. Then, manifestation of ideals can come through action. Modes are action and elements are the essential nature underlying the action. That's why it's good to have a nice combination of hard and soft angles in the horoscope.

Deep in the hearts of Jupiter-Venus people is enacted a fairy tale of a perfect world, wherein all differences can be balanced by love or philosophy. Neither planet is against war or difficulty, but equally, neither planet is one to give in to defeat. We have very, very strong characters in their planetary archetypes, and their manifestation in the personality is always evident through strong attitudes toward love and relationships, art, literature, religion and spirituality, sociology, politics, finances, education and learning or teaching. The Charites, daughters of Zeus – also known as the Three Graces – are personal attendants of Aphrodite. *Charis* is the root of charisma, meaning, on the gross level, graceful, but on the celestial level, gifted by the gods. Hence we have a deeply attractive force between Venus and Jupiter. The Graces, the Charites, are said to be the personifications of the things that enhance life, that give life a real meaning and sooth us with small or great luxuries. Somewhere in all our horoscopes lie Jupiter and Venus, and even if they are not in classical aspect, you could look to them to find the pleasures in life that will ease the hard edges and the roughness of experience.

But when they're assigned to each other, in a particular angle, then the seeking of the sublime is stronger and more at the forefront of the deeper self's intent. Jupiter-Venus intends to have comfort, beauty, harmony, and agreement in its life – even if it means withdrawing from the sordid, daily aspect of life, and retiring to a place either within the self or in a distant land, an isolated territory of the world where the sense of peace and grace can be cultivated and maintained. People who need drugs to remove them from the harshness of the world often have Jupiter-Venus prominent in their important configurations in the horoscope, and people who ascribe to rigorous religious practises and faith also have this as a strong impetus in their charts.

Beauty is in the eye of the beholder. The story of Beauty and the Beast is a lovely allegory that illustrates the ability for us to "see" beneath the surface of things and find the core essence of perfection and grace that lies at the centre of creation. Creativity for the Jupiter-Venus person might still be as painful and strife-ridden as birth always is, but there is an innate ability to see the beauty at the heart of anything, whether it is a stone, a poem, a street-person, or an idea. Theirs is a world of potential perfection and harmony. Obviously, this perfection and harmony might be created only in their own image or imagination. Beauty, like love, has its cultural vogue and its collective agreement. Some people seem to be on the first wave, or closely associated with the things that are in synch with the social or collective trend in style, fashion, ideology, or political movement. You will find that they have a strong Jupiter-Venus alignment in their horoscope.

This kind of collective and individual sympathy often involves the Moon, for the public – for a famous example, we have Marilyn Monroe, with her Moon in Aquarius, very close to the Descendant, opposite Neptune rising in Leo. Venus is also angular (like the Moon) at her MC. Her angular Venus (in the Gauquelin zone in the 9th house) is exactly sextile to Jupiter. Now, her reputed paramour, John F. Kennedy, was a Jupiterian as well, with a strong Venus, but not because it was in a classical aspect to Jupiter – it wasn't. He had a Moon-Venus square (the Madonna/Magdalene split in the male) and a Mars-Mercury-Jupiter conjunction which trined the Moon in Virgo. In other words, his Jupiter was trine the Moon, which in turn squared Venus, and we find him to be a man excessive in his emotional and sexual needs. See?

Audience: Yes, in other words, even though his Jupiter and Venus aren't in aspect, the fact that Jupiter is tied to a strong aspect to Venus means that he has a sort of Jupiter-Venus connection once removed.

Erin: Exactly. You see, you need to be creative with aspects and use your own intuition, and see how they might manifest in ways that we can't "cookbook"! Even more fascinating – the reason I have brought Marilyn and Kennedy into this – is that his Venus-Ascendant line in his Astro*Carto*Graphy® map runs right through Marilyn's birthplace – Los Angeles! So, she activated his Venus (and clearly it was his Venus rather than his Moon in the split), by location and by astrological sign. His Venus in Gemini is near her Sun in Gemini. There is far more to their horoscopes than that, but it's a good illustration of the movement of planets amongst each other. In fact, Kennedy had a Mars-Jupiter conjunction (with Mercury), which falls in with the next aspect we'll look at – and he was an invader, really, a man with a mission, a warrior and an orator. His Mars/Jupiter/Mercury-Ascendant line ran right through the Philippines and Vietnam under his Saturn-IC line – all hooked up!

Jupiter and Mars

Now, Mars was not a very well developed character in the Greek myths. He is mentioned, but not that often, and when he is, it is usually in the middle of a battlefield, a riot, a revolution, or as a background god to trouble. He is generally depicted as a kind of divine swashbuckler, not highly thought of, and at times he appears as little more than a butcher. The more profound moral and theological aspects of war were taken over by other deities, for example, Zeus or Athena. In the *Iliad,* Zeus says to Ares: "Do not sit beside me and complain, you two-faced rogue. Of all the gods who dwell on Olympos you are the most hateful to me, for strife and wars and battles are always dear to you."[37]

After that attack, Zeus does spare him pain, but only because he is Hera's and his (Zeus') own son. It is interesting, this lack of well-articulated character, but then it is also descriptive of the Mars function – primitive, raw, powerful, but undifferentiated unless in context of something else.

Audience: What about with Venus?

Erin: Yes, he is the lover of Aphrodite, and their child Harmonia is the product. However, Jupiter and Mars produce no such mythological child. They produce nothing. They are not terribly well connected, even though Jupiter follows Mars in the sequence of planetary individuation. It is as if, after desire (Mars) is instilled, civilisation and rationalisation must follow (Jupiter). The Greek god Ares is largely known for his massive tantrums, and the Roman god was transformed into the agrarian god of agriculture and cultivation. The sword became the ploughshare. The Romans had deeper religious and philosophical connotations for their Mars – he was propitiated in the spring, and the month of March was named after him, and actually began the Roman year under the pre-Julian calendar.

Jupiter's function for Mars in the chart is to provide an arena for its primal force – to give it a context and an outlet for expression. When they are together in an aspect of one kind or another, there are definite characteristics that need to be differentiated and released. How this is done is not only dependent upon the specific type of astrological aspect, but also on the level of characterization that the individual has in himself or herself – in other words, just who the person is and how versatile their possibilities are for outlet.

I think Jupiter and Mars need a variety of outlets on as many levels as possible, without becoming depleted and scattered. Jupiter and Mars

---

[37]*Ibid.*, Book V.889-91.

contacts show that these people need to revitalise themselves on a regular basis, utilizing their abundant energy to the fullest. Physical outlets may be necessary for physically robust people – in other words, playing sports, doing weight training, having a regime where the body is pushed to its limits and where instinctual anger and rage find a productive way of working together. Let's say the person can't, or is not inclined to, engage in physical activity. Then there has to be an arena in which the anger and rage can be enacted in a way which is helpful, supportive and benevolent, and contributes social benefit – even if that simply means being self-contained! A Mars-Jupiter person is not usually not a team player, unless they are considered to be a star – if it is athletics which attracts them, then usually it's "personal best" – competitions like skiing or running, where the competition is with themselves, trying to best themselves. That's Mars-Jupiter – it's not really good at team sports, unless you are in fact killing other people on the other side for the team, and you are recognised as leader.

Because Mars has a lot to do with "fight", that is, simply survival, any number of things can bring Mars up. Whatever threatens you – whether it is loneliness, fear, loss, being controlled, loved (yes, loved), disliked, poor, in the dark – figuratively or literally, will bring Mars rushing to the surface to attack the offending circumstance. Some people are very threatened by someone caring for them, and their instinctual survival has been nourished on pain and rejections, so even when it seems irrational, a person can become angry and hostile when they are in a safe, loving relationship. The thing to do is to connect with whatever threatens you and look at it. One way of connecting to whatever threatens you is to examine what enrages you!

I think of Mars as being about two years old – that's when you have your first Mars return, and when you enter the stage in life where you begin to pull away from safety, from the safety of mother. The antics of the two-year-old are renowned. Anything within arm's reach is up for grabs, literally. The "terrible twos" are about saying "no", and carving out an identity separate from what others have in mind. This takes incredible will. Mars is an essential function in distinguishing your own primal needs from those of more civilised, older people.

When Mars is up, you are two years old. Think carefully – when you have an irruption of rage, how old are you inside? When you don't get what you want, how old is your reaction? It isn't infancy, necessarily – that's a whole other domain. It really is about age two. How your demands were met, how "no" was said to you, and the degree to which your newfound assertive toddler explorations were tolerated and met, are pretty much how you are when you meet similar circumstances at thirty, forty, fifty and forever.

Audience: Yes, exactly. I have thought that myself! I have Mars square Moon-Jupiter, and I was the "victim" of a mother who did everything for me. It made me furious. I had to fight for independence, and now, I always find myself having to go back to that feeling and "bring myself up", if you know what I mean. I am sure, when someone wants me to do something, or questions my behaviour, that they are trying to thwart me, and part of my maturing process has been to rationally understand that that is not what is happening, but it is what happened in the past. So, even though I am returned to this baby place, I still have to work at it.

Erin: Yes, you see, Mars isn't something you really can grow out of, but you can learn to craft, contain, and civilise it, which is what it sounds like you have had to do – and likely, will always have to do, to some degree. I think it is a form of spiritual path, the path of the warrior. You see, the contact between Mars and Jupiter makes the person aware of aggression and competitiveness, but they are not themselves always competitive or aggressive by personality. Rather, the contact makes them highly sensitive to the martial energy, which may make them shrink from situations in which they have to engage in hostile or personally aggressive acts. Unconsciously, they might even stir others to behave aggressively, whether that is in the realm of ideas and philosophy, or physically. This is where the subtlety of placement enters into the analysis.

Jupiter and Mars can mean excessive bouts of rage – global, undifferentiated rage – where the iron will of Mars meets the wrath of Jupiter. It can be a terribly moralistic and judgemental combination, and I've found that, even though it's an active psychodynamic aspect, a significant amount of the martial stress is expressed through the body, through things like headaches, metabolic fluctuations, acute anxiety attacks, clumsiness when tired or under emotional stress, accidents due to hastiness and plain old carelessness, or vague sharp pains. So something has to be done with the body, that is, you go to work in a way where you can actually deal with this in some way, shape or form. Many people with the combination find that Chi Gong, or Tai Chi, or various forms of highly stimulating yoga, have done wonders for the mind-body balance. If it isn't the type of body that enjoys traditional sports, then those channels will work as well. Ritualized aggression is a significant social outlet for collective Mars-Jupiter energy – group sports.

Audience: Oh, yes, actually I do both – Tai Kwon Do and Tai Chi – an aggressive and a receptive form of mind-body-soul unification. And it is perfect.

Erin: Just as easily, the aspect can be employed by the challenging study of subjects that have to do with revolution. There can be a fascination with war – which doesn't mean that the person is pro-war. It means that he or she is interested in the history of aggression, of cultural turbulence, lost civilisations, and is fascinated by how others have dealt with martial and philosophical conflict, either collectively or individually. I have a friend, a very old man now, who was a forensic psychiatrist, and worked intimately with the criminally insane, particularly murderers. You'd never find a kinder, more hilarious man than him – he had a Mars-Jupiter conjunction! One evolved method of dealing with one's own shadowed aggression is to make a living from it.

Mars-Jupiter is fascinated with cultures, peoples, and civilisations which have moved from their primitive origins towards increasing progress. It's a relationship of planets which is interested in the philosophical and psychological side of historical development. But when you think of Mars, you think of infantile rage, which is essential in individuation. It's essential to making statements about yourself as you continue to mature, becoming increasingly more of yourself as you age and develop. When Mars is configured with Jupiter, in some way this process of individuation has to take place in a social context. For example, most people who are heavily involved in civil rights are super-aggressive people. They get out there and get involved in active participation, in ritualised, socially acceptable violence – demonstrations, protesting, exhorting leaders to step down – it's a very politically sensitive and aware contact. By political I mean aware of how the interaction of human beings with human beings establishes social order. So somewhere in the Mars-Jupiter person, there has to be a way of using that. It can be done by sword or pen, or simply by having very powerful and personally motivating beliefs. Their political beliefs can cause them to move or change countries, or force them to do so due to upheaval or uprising, or even philosophical and social conditions in their homeland.

A conjunction would take a great deal of maturity to actually understand what this high level of aggressive energy is about. There need to be mediating aspects, or other contacts that connect the conjunction to purposefulness. Unless it is very well supported by, say, a Saturn sextile or a Sun trine, or something that really gives it a focus or a channel, like involvement with a stellium, then a Mars-Jupiter conjunction can be hyperactive and obsessive, but without direction. But with focus and some significant way of channelling it, it then becomes an excellent medium for making social statements. But there will always be an underlying anger that is being marshalled and civilised through the work they choose to do.

The harder angles, especially the square or opposition, can result in denial of the primitive Mars, and an overemphasis on Jupiter – on the social side of things. Psychologically, the individual can deny they ever get angry, because they don't "believe" in it – because they're too benevolent, they're too spiritual, too enlightened. It could be passive-aggressive – in other words, everybody else gets really angry around them, but they don't. Passive aggression is very economical – you don't waste your energy, but everybody else is in complete turmoil, and you just walk around looking peaceful, wondering why everyone around you is tearing out their hair, shrieking and acting so hysterical! To people who are sensitive to the interior emotional tone of others, the energy that emanates from an unbalanced Mars-Jupiter feels like a coiled serpent in their solar plexus, waiting to spring. Essentially, what has happened within this individual is that they've arrested their Mars development, and it never really matures into something productive. They are chaotic, unsettling, hyper, and even though they can be brilliant, they are unfocussed and live by faith alone.

As I mentioned, the mythological evolution of Mars originated in the great ten-foot-tall Greek god, who threw tantrums in the middle of the Trojan fields, or who was only seen at wars and riots and inciting people with violence. Then as the myths moved through Rome, and Rome adopted Mars as being an important symbol for its civilisation process, Mars actually became a more benevolent god, and started to represent things like agriculture and cultivation, as I mentioned. One of the myths of Rome is that Ares-Mars was the father of Romulus and Remus, and, as you know, the other myth is that Aphrodite was the mother of Aeneas, who also was a founder of Rome.

So we could look at the process of moving from the Greek to the Roman archetype of Ares-Mars as analogous to the way that we develop, from screaming infants, cutting teeth and stamping our feet at the age of two in order to say who we are, into someone who can say, "That's me, that is you, and that is where the line is drawn. And you've just crossed the boundary. I'm not going to kill you, but don't do it again." So individuation, self development, actually goes through those stages where you learn to say "no". You don't have to get into a huge scene about it, wielding axes and things like that. But a Mars-Jupiter opposition would be a tendency to be over the top about anger. But there is a whole moral thing – there can be a lot of guilt around anger, if you've got Mars-Jupiter contacts.

Audience: John Mackinroe has a Mars-Jupiter opposition.

Erin: He does? How perfect! I wonder if he ever lies awake at night torturing himself over what a scene he's made on the courts! He's obviously entertaining – I hope he finds himself entertaining. It would be awful if he imposed some kind of moral guilt upon himself for behaving this way, just because everybody else doesn't.

Audience: Yes, I was watching him being interviewed on television, and he didn't express any regrets over his image or actions, but felt quite justified in his anger toward referees and the social restrictions he finds in the tennis world.

Erin: I wonder if he does curl up and say, "Oh my God, is that me!" This is where he can't control it – that's the Mars-Jupiter opposition. Maybe he should go to one of those workshops you were talking about! Maybe you could take charge of writing him a letter saying, "You go, because you have a Mars-Jupiter opposition – you need to project your Jupiter onto somebody else and become more civilised." But there you go – I am sure a lot of his anger is really at his own lack of perfection, and he is out for the personal best. He is clearly not a team player. Jupiter people act out important social rituals for others. If they're big, larger than life, they get to do things other people unconsciously would like to do, but can't or don't. Then others can be vicarious participants, like Pentheus at the Bacchanal. I would think that someone like Mackinroe makes everybody else look good. That's the other aspect of it.

Audience: Do you mean that oppositions can create a situation where the personal actually embodies a collective feeling, and acts it out for them?

Erin: Yes, a kind of "you do it" syndrome! In the case of Mackinroe, and his Mars-Jupiter opposition, he does play out something that allows others to vicariously experience rage without paying the penalty for it. That is, "You're known for being nasty, I'm not. So I'm going to get you to do it, and then I'm going to feel good." This is the projective thing. If you've got an opposition in your chart, then you're not only the recipient of this projection but you're also potentially throwing it out.

Jupiterian types can act out the role-playing for others. Mackinroe is a lovely example. Everybody else looks so mild-mannered and polite and civilised next to him. But, on a personal level, it also justifies behaviour, because the powers that be, the justice of the game, exacts its penalty. It's like asking a paranoid when they started to become paranoid, and they say, "When they began to follow me."

Jupiter and Saturn

Jupiter and Saturn are father and son. This is where we are today, stuck between Jupiter station-direct and Saturn station-retrograde. It is a reenactment of the mythological battle between the old order (Saturn) and the new order (Jupiter). *The Clash of the Titans* is a great classic movie to watch, keeping this aspect in mind! There is an inherent antithesis between the agencies of the two planets, which, as in Hegel's philosophy, can be eventually synthesised in the psyche of an individual by recognising that there is a time for change in one's own social and moral structures. Jupiter-Saturn trines and sextiles have a more rhythmic ability to throw out the old, outmoded self and allow a renewal of patterns, behaviours, beliefs and ethics. However, the hard angles are not so fortunate. The squares between these powerful gods create a lot of interior and social tension. Sometimes the squares literally speak of having to battle social hierarchies which exist in their birth-culture. I have seen it represented in the charts of a couple of people who have had to deal with their social "class" in a way which is classic.

For instance, a young man, exceptionally bright, won scholarships all the way through school. He then entered Oxford University under a scholarship, and did exceptionally well. He then became an alcoholic, and proceeded to recidivate back into the council estate consciousness which had been his legacy for many generations. He had a great hostility for the "upper classes" – a great amorphous enemy with whom he had developed a very personal inner relationship. Not only was he fighting a class structure in his "cultural psyche", but it was being enacted within his psychic hierarchy. He could not, or rather, would not, rise above his station, and guilt at leaving his father behind eventually won out, which is a very sad thing.

Audience: Wouldn't Saturn and Jupiter in a positive relationship have an inherent wisdom about how to go about making structural changes in society and business?

Erin: I think they're two of the best business partners you can find in the horoscope – on the board of directors, Jupiter and Saturn make the deals. And when they're getting on with each other, your life investment is well protected. Sometimes you don't have to think in terms of exact aspects – you can loosen it up. You must think in terms of exact aspects if you want very specific challenges to be defined in the horoscope, but when you think in terms of the elements alone, you can find they operate well enough that way. In other words, taking a random example, let's say you have Jupiter in Libra and Saturn in Sagittarius. Then you would have a fairly harmonious engagement – they were there in 1957 – and because they are in mutual reception, as well as Saturn being exalted in Libra, there would be an inherent ability to respond positively and with inner wisdom to social change, just based on elemental harmony.

When you've got a precise aspect, you've got a very specific charge put upon the two planets to act something out. But you can think loosely, in terms of harmonious elemental relations. There's no planet unaspected, if you think of midpoints, harmonics, phase relationships, and so forth. Jupiter and Saturn can agree to collude in controlled expansion – Jupiter can have free license, as long as Saturn can come in and put a stop to it if it gets too much. And Jupiter can push at the resistance of Saturn and, in turn, Saturn will bow down periodically and back off, and let the new social order take place when they are engaged in dialogue.

Because Jupiter stands for the originator of new social order, a new mythology and theocracy, and Saturn stands for idealistic outmoded history, people with strong Jupiter-Saturn aspects have an innate sense of the necessary succession of regimes – of how society and cultures and the protocol of the hierarchy of succession is enacted. It is the very tension that the antithesis engenders which makes the aspect particulary psychologically stressful. They are often politically active. It can mean they are in positions of diplomacy, where they have to mediate, where they're the best people to look after the crew – they're the management heads or they head a team. Often they deal with the disagreements that go on in human relations, public relations, and that type of thing.

It's a really pragmatic aspect – a good, solid, earthed contact. The square or opposition can mean that the person's social ability is undermined, and they have low self-esteem, because their individuality has been swallowed by the status quo. Thus their creative impetus can be suppressed, repressed, or indeed, dead. It requires a tremendous amount of energy to disgorge their buried or entombed sense of personal creativity, and much courage to speak up about their wisdom and challenge the received information of their cultural, religious or family ethos.

It can also be a push-me, pull-me feeling. Even if you have a grand trine between Sun and Jupiter and Saturn, it means that both Jupiter and Saturn are at slow motion, if not actually stationary. Sun trine any planet from Jupiter outward means that planet is retrograde. In this case it means that one of them is going direct and the other one has just turned retrograde. So you end up with a push-me, pull-me kind of aspect. I actually knew someone with this aspect.

There's a great desire to grow and expand, to get out there and do everything. You believe that you can do it, and in your most confident moments you can probably accomplish anything. However, Saturn comes in and says, "Who do you think you are? What have you got to offer?" So there's a kind of wet blanket, or lead balloon, if you will, that comes onto Jupiter, which thinks it can do everything – and realistically, can't. Somewhere in there lies the truth.

Audience: When the Sun trines Jupiter but is in a grand trine with Saturn, would that act as a more motivated or directed path? I know someone with this too, born in 1948.

Erin: Yes, I know someone with that, as I mentioned and I'll illustrate that in a minute. First: A grand trine is a closed circuit. The energies of the planets run round and round, keeping an internal feedback loop going between all of them in the trine. This is exclusive of the rest of the horoscope. There is a kind of ostracising going on in the grand trine – it shuts out dialogue or feedback from the rest of the planets. But when the Sun is involved, it is a very special grand trine. I call it a Solar Grand Trine, and in the

Retrograde book there is a great story about "Paul", who has exactly the same configuration you are asking me about.[38]

When the Sun is involved in a grand trine, one planet is stationary-retrograde and the other is stationary-direct – always, within a few degrees. For instance, if the Sun is trine Jupiter within 4° to 6°, then Jupiter is either stationary-retrograde or stationary-direct, and you get a really slow, ponderous type of Jupiter. The Sun is the focal point, and its secondary progression will give you precise timing for events and the unfolding of the grand trine.

Secondly, as to your question about it being more motivated or directed – yes, in distinct stages. The planet that is stationary-retrograde will indicate what needs to be internalised and gestated, while the planet that is stationary-direct acts as the externalising agent. In the case of Paul, Jupiter was stationary-retrograde, and he had "learning difficulties" – or, rather, communication difficulties (it was in the 3rd house). These were partly overcome when Jupiter actually turned retrograde at age four. But when his Saturn stationed direct at age six, he made a major breakthrough – his "problem" cleared up, and he was thenceforth an applied student, a scholar, and eventually became a well-renowned teacher. He said he felt he only "incarnated" when he was six. Perfect for the Sun-Saturn image, isn't it? Subsequently, the progression of the Sun ticked off sequential breakthroughs and precise changes in his life. For example, when he was twenty-four, the progressed Sun made its predictable square to Saturn, and he finished his university degree, and emigrated to England. Paul's real name was Howard Sasportas. He won't mind if I tell you now, I know that.

Good planning and awareness, recognition of content, context, and the whole social issue, knowing what one can actually do, being aware of timing, the recognition of limits and acceptance of the fact that you are mortal – the combination of the two planets can be so productive. It's a really solid, productive aspect. Wherever Jupiter is,

---

[38]Erin Sullivan, *Retrograde Planets: Traversing the Inner Landscape*, Arkana Contemporary Astrology Series, Penguin, London, 1992, pp. 128-29 - Paul's story. But for the most astounding solar grand trine metamorphosis, see "Martina", pp. 146-151.

there follows Saturn, so it may take time. It may take the first Saturn return, for instance, and beyond, for the individual with the Jupiter-Saturn conjunction to mature emotionally with their own ambivalent and action-reaction way of being. It's actually found in the charts of people with pathological bipolarism (the old term was manic depression) in their families.

Oddly, I have got a couple clients who have been diagnosed as bipolar (manic depressives), and have been greatly aided by medication – one whose mother has a Jupiter-Saturn conjunction while her son suffers the wild, seasonal swings of a manic depressive. He has the opposition. Families enact group or collective fate in which certain individual members of the family are the star focus. There were many victims in the dynastic line of the House of Atreus, but it was Orestes who was the transformer of the pollution. It all funnelled down through him. We start to get into really strong family themes when we move from Saturn outward. These are unconscious threads that run down through family lines. So there's a Jupiter-Saturn potential for dynastic miasma, where the "sins of the father" fall on the head of the son, or those of the mother on the daughter, or any other parent-child relationship possibility.

And so a person who may not experience an illness as extreme as classified bipolarism will still experience a mild form of manic depression – cycles where everything is wonderful, but then the elation subsides. The back-and-forth mood of Jupiter and Saturn creates a feeling that there's always hope and optimism, but every time it emerges, it gets squashed. Jupiter with Saturn can manifest in the body, where the condition of the soul is rendered in the body in psychosomatic expression.

Audience: What about the squares? And quincunxes? I think the quincunx sounds like it might be a karmic aspect, where God points the way but makes it harder than the person is capable of dealing with.

Erin: Even more likely, that individual is carrying some long line of dynastic power struggle. There is even a strong possibility that the imbalance began back in the ancestral realm of a person with such a conflict of Saturn and Jupiter, and he or she actually does need to look back into the family legacy to see what they might do to purge (Jupiter) the ancestral blockage, or lift the "curse", to use traditional language. Purging a family curse is a drag – however, it's a dirty job, but someone has to do it!

Every so often, an individual is born to do this for an entire culture – they are the Jupiterians in the Saturnian world. They embody, or are possessed by, an archetype, and thus lose their individual power as they become a voice of the collective and a tool for collective transition. One of those Jupiterians was the American comedian of the late '50's and very early '60's – Lenny Bruce. Lenny Bruce once said that the only justice in the Halls of Justice is in the halls! He spent a lot of time in the system of jurisprudence, and Athene showed no mercy toward him, so he must have known!

He was desperately funny, but he was rude, obscene, and exposed the underbelly of the super-moral McCarthy era in the U.S., when the investigations into unAmerican activities were taking place in the 1950's. He was hunted down, harassed, arrested on stage during his acts, convicted repeatedly for obscenity and drug possession, and generally was "killed" by the system. He died of a heroin overdose, but it was a kind of Marilyn Monroe syndrome. He was ahead of his time, but not by much. He was a harbinger of the new consciousness. In the 1960's, following his death, the Uranus-Pluto conjunction, with Saturn in opposition, brought out a huge number of people to change the system, and Lenny Bruce, with his sex and toilet jokes, is pale by comparison to the devils we face today.

Jupiter and Saturn conjoin every twenty years, and the ancients called that configuration the Golden Triangle, because its cycle is such that it conjoins in each mode or element for a full cycle-and-a-half, give or take a conjunction. It inaugurates a new social order every time, and when the Jupiter-Saturn conjunction moves into the next element, for example, from earth to air, it is called a Grand Mutation. In the last two hundred years, every American president elected during a Jupiter-Saturn conjunction has died in office, except Reagan.

Audience: Is that because the conjunction moved from earth to air? Do you think there is new social order being inaugurated in preparation for the age of Aquarius?

Erin: Yes, it is part of the complex weaving of new aspects, new signs, new images and symbols as we abandon the epochal signature of Pisces. And, indeed, that Jupiter-Saturn conjunction occurred in Libra. And Reagan has an Aquarius Sun. (The previous conjunction, the one Kennedy was elected under, was in Capricorn – the next one occurs in the last degrees of Taurus in 2000, and again in 2001 in early Gemini. It's a slow mutation from earth into air.) Now, remember, there was an assassination attempt on Reagan – he did get shot, but he survived it.

Nancy Reagan and their astrologer Joan Quigley were in consultation on a daily basis at particular times in his reign, and she was very sharp about these things. Say what you will about these media types, but Ms Quigley retained a dignified and professional silence until she was betrayed by the Reagans, at which time she did begin to reveal her role in their lives. (She was a keynote lecturer at the largest professional astrology conference in the world, the United Astrology Congress in Washington in 1992, where she discussed her involvement with the presidency.) But that's a really good social example of an aspect mutating its historical outcome.

Jupiter and the outer planets

When we get beyond Saturn, Jupiter tends to interact with Uranus, Neptune and Pluto as more of a facilitator to reach transformative levels of mental experience. It's not quite so physical or mundane in its manifestation, but more of a psychodynamic function. When Jupiter jumps the Saturnian rings of the social, physical and visible realm, Jupiter's role changes somewhat – it becomes more of an agency for transcendental change and experience. Jupiter is more "heady" in the trans-Saturnian realm; his higher functions operate – for better or worse – in a more obvious fashion. Jupiter is now the bridge across the physical boundary of Saturn and into the upper aethers, especially in his first contact with Uranus, his mythological grandfather. Generally, just as people tend to have "cleaner" relationships with their grandparents than with their immediate parents, so it seems to be with the gods!

Jupiter and Uranus

Jupiter and Uranus have a very special connection. Ouranos was the upper air, the aethers beyond the stratosphere, and he had no connection to the affairs of humans at all. His reproduction ended, really, with the Titans and the Hekatonchires. Once severed from Gaia, he remained in the lofty realm of the ideal world, of the imaginal realm, and thus, he is our spiritual and psychological symbol for the ultimate realm of perfection in the imagination, the watcher rather than the participator. Zeus' manor, however, was in the heavens and the Olympic range, overseeing earthly activities and the interaction of the gods of his realm. Think back on what has been talked about today. Jupiter never really put his hand to the affairs of men, but incorporated many attributes which have to do with intellect and mind. We might find how the astrological Jupiter in contact with Uranus facilitates the mediation between inspiration, imagination, and the function of witnessing, and the individual's response to the social *Zeitgeist* and his or her need for personal identity within that context.

The Jupiter-Uranus square doesn't necessarily mean that the person is at odds with philosophy or society, but it means that something from outside might come in and shock him or her into some kind of awakening or an awareness. We're at the stage where Jupiter now makes all the aspects – in other words, it's Jupiter's motion that applies to Uranus, Neptune and Pluto. That means that the aspect lasts as long as the Jupiter transit lasts.

The conjunctions of Jupiter to Uranus are about every fourteen years, and, in themselves, aren't generational aspects. But they are sharp statements made within a generational motif. Jupiter moves 4° on average in one month (6° at its fastest when conjunct the Sun, and 0° at station-retrograde, and it's retrograde for four months of the year). So a Jupiter-Uranus conjunction will only produce a small number of people within the generational stamp of Uranus' sign.

Therefore, we can't really call it a generational aspect, but it does enhance the tone of that Uranus type. Uranus is in a given sign for seven years. And in the course of that seven-year period, Jupiter will cover half the zodiac (well, seven signs). You might want to consider it this way: Whatever sign Uranus is in, there will be several types of Jupiter-Uranus aspects to Uranus that sign during the course of that time.

So when you're looking at a Jupiter-Uranus aspect, try to consider how is it that this individual person is meant to benefit personally from the wisdom of the ages, which is very Uranian – the wisdom of time. Will they benefit both themselves and others through it? It can be a very humanitarian contact, but it can equally be self-serving to the highest water! It can be very eccentric, and find very odd ways of expressing this humanitarian bent, this desire to serve and help, to be at one with the universe, to be able to deal with the collective, and to find identity in the collective.

Because it is group-orientated and tribal, its shadow function can be xenophobic if the opposition or square is involved. The two of them together talk about finding a collective voice which mirrors one's own individual imagination and resultant philosophy. So the individual seeks out a religious group, a study group, or something that will actually conform to what their inherent standards are – as opposed to conforming to an outside influence. In the case of being born into a particular religion – Catholic or Muslim or whatever – you have to conform to the religion. However, some people break from that – Jupiter-Uranus types are more likely to break from the conventional or family religious patterns to seek out a new religious expression or dogma, or a place to go that will allow them to worship the divine in their own way.

Uranus, in its brief tradition (relative to the established intra-Saturnian planetary group), has been called transpersonal. Yes and no. The outer planets are deeply personal in that they force one to come to terms with aspects of one's own personal unconscious, and make it conscious. Uranus becomes a personal planet whether one likes it or not, especially in mid-life, and from the Uranus opposition on, one is required to individuate more and more rapidly, to find out who one really is. Jupiter-Uranus types don't seem to work through personal issues more quickly, but I think they do it more thoroughly when they are pressed into making changes. There seems to be a search for spiritual groups or intellectual collectives that will really encourage their development to quicken. You might think they are very independent, but the 9th and 11th houses are both to do with tribalism and collective beliefs within a social context. However, Jupiter-Uranus is spiritually radical. Independence and individualism are measured against some collective standard – it is only in the context of the group that we can say we are individualistic!

Audience: What about the Jupiter-Uranus conjunction in Cancer in 1955, when it was square to Neptune? Then, Jupiter was involved with two outer planets, which seem to be giving double messages.

Erin: It produced some seriously conflicted people. It is an aspect that longs for separation and individuation, while at the same time is called to merge with the collective in a way which disintegrates personal ego. The Jupiter-Uranus conjunction says, "I'm going to be my own person, I'll find my own way," but there is a lure from the Neptune square to get lost or be spiritually involved with collective issues. Therefore, it could be very good if it was involved in some kind of activity that served the collective in a big way – in other words, going out and doing good work for people, search and rescue, feeding starving people, working with people with AIDS, dealing with mass collective problems. They can also make very objective advisors and counsellors – they aren't terribly feeling, unless there is water around the chart, but they're certainly perceptive and clear.

Jupiter and Uranus together, and involved with that square to Neptune, could actually produce the most enlightened ways of being in the world, of being socially active in the world. It also produced some very good astrology, for at that time in the mid-1950's, the collective mood began to shift. Yes, it was terribly conservative at the time, but its product over time was to revolutionise spirituality, religious expression and political action. Remember, in the beginning, we talked about "today's radical aspect is tomorrow's status quo"? Well, that's what happened over time.

On planet Earth, there was a knee-jerk reaction in society that tried to smooth everything out, as if the collective was anxious about what the aspect of Jupiter conjunct Uranus in Cancer square Neptune in Libra was going to do. Everyone tightened their ties and pulled up their socks and went ultra-conservative, hoping that would "cure" it. But the people born under that aspect were the "loosening" of the fabric of society, that would unravel completely by the Uranus-Pluto conjunction opposed by Saturn in 1966!

The next Jupiter-Uranus conjunction that took place after the Cancer one was in 1969, in late Virgo and again in early Libra, and the first men on the Moon marked a quantum leap in communication and travel. The next Jupiter-Uranus conjunction after that took place in 1983, in the early degrees of Sagittarius. The early 1980's were exceptionally expansive, a reaction to the highly forgettable '70's. Do you know there were no major conjunctions at all in the '70's? No new starts! A Jupiter-Uranus conjunctions brings society and its belief systems – its regulatory systems – into a new place. Communications, global networking – computers finally became "PC's", and increasing numbers of people became computer-literate and had them in their home. There was great hope for the future of economic and political growth.

Now, wasn't that the buzz-word of the '80's – networking, how very Jupiter-Uranus! I think the key to all aspects lies in the nature of their conjunction. Rudhyar was first to develop the psychological sequence of phase relationships, and in that seed of conjunction, we find the secret message of the two planets concerned, in their successive, developmental relationships.

People with Jupiter-Uranus contacts – all of them – have to watch their energy, because it can leak out. This is quite true of Jupiter and Neptune as well, by the way. It's hard with Jupiter and Neptune to differentiate between what your needs are and what everybody else's needs are, and that's where I think there is great potential for getting lost and giving over too much to the collective need. This is why the Jupiter-Uranus in Cancer square Neptune in Libra is having such a profound mid-life experience right now, as Uranus-Neptune transits opposite their natal Uranus. Over the next few years they really have to come to terms with society's dissolution, and their own personal disillusion within that as well!

Through the Uranus-Neptune conjunction, which is an antithesis, they, as individuals, are going to have to learn how to survive with integrity, ego, and occupation intact. The confusion brought to bear with the Uranus-Neptune conjunction could be thought of as if you have taken a huge dose of sleeping pills, and the alarm clock keeps ringing. Once we are through that aspect, and Pluto enters Sagittarius and Uranus passes into Aquarius, it will be interesting to see what is left standing in the way of orthodoxy! Pluto in Sagittarius will be the holy wars. We'll talk a bit about that when we get to Jupiter and Pluto.

With Jupiter and Uranus, it's a little bit more articulated, because there is the capacity to coldly observe one's own behaviour. Uranus is the inner witness. Uranus in the chart pinpoints the part of you that observes yourself participating in your own world. You might be amazed at your own behaviour – sometimes appalled at what you are doing. "Why am I doing this, when I know better?" I'm sure there are times, in fits of rage or something, when you've actually had a running conversation within yourself – "This is not necessary. Why are you behaving this way?" You know this is "beneath your evolution" in the scale of behaviour possibilities, and yet, there you are being human again. People with strong Jupiter-Uranus aspects have far-reaching, lofty goals – wanting to achieve great things for themselves, others, their peers, and the future society, which often they foresee, while still having an acute awareness of their own flaws.

But it's a problem if you give away all your energy to the collective, because then you end up as a kind of empty shell, and have really nothing to give anyway at the end. And I'm not confusing Uranus with Neptune, because they're vastly different. But there is a possibility of becoming a victim of the collective, as opposed to a voice of the collective, when you've got personal planets or social planets bound up with Uranus, Neptune, or Pluto. Choices have to be made, and those choices are sometimes forced upon one by circumstances, because the outer planets are more likely to act upon you if you aren't acting in accord with them. You don't have to use them, but they will certainly use you at some stage in your life if you don't. Jupiter and Uranus need to find the way to bring the idealism of the upper air into the breathing space of mortals – in other words, to work toward improving relations between what is truly unique to them and what is going to further them in the social, tribal and relational world.

But you have to have the opportunity to take advantage of the options in consciousness that Uranus, Neptune, and Pluto offer. Let's face it, more than three quarters of the world doesn't have the opportunity to sit around in workshops and philosophise about their psychological state. As a result, if you have entered that realm and opened the door of perception into the world of personal individuation and spiritual transformation, you can be personally affected by collective experiences. In what were once called the Eastern Bloc countries, and in Bosnia, Ethiopia, Israel, the entire Middle East – the majority of the world, for that matter – are they capable of individuating through the process in which they are embroiled? They are victims of a global aspect.

Those of us who are here today are highly privileged individuals who have choices – most people don't – and so some of what we say today is invalid in practice, virtually impossible to put into action in the context of what's really going on in the majority of the world. I would be hard pressed to do a psychological session for a woman in a bombed out flat in Bosnia, who wanted to know when she would see her children again, if she would ever see them again. I would find that very difficult. I don't know that you could talk easily about spiritual growth and the process of individuation without witnessing your own Uranian position in the Jupiterian realm of world politics.

We, in this room, are not experiencing those Jupiterian atrocities individually, or in our society. However, we are part of it, and it is happening to us. We are not free of it in our conscience, nor in our consciousness – and we are experiencing it in the collective unconscious. That we have both the faculties and facilities to think, and the time to ponder life's mysteries, does make us responsible for using the information we have as an opportunity to make something out of it. That's when it works. That's when we are in touch with those planets, and they are personal.

Collective configurations like Uranus-Neptune conjunctions and Saturn-Pluto squares do affect us personally, but the greater effect is global. And we are part of that – the individual is responsible for the collective. We are experiencing global aspects in a personal way, because we are part of the world. Although we are not being invaded in England and America by outside tyrants (although maybe being tyrannised by inside agents), we still do connect to outer planets. Even though we are not being bombed, blitzed, or starving, we are intimately related to the people that are. Indeed, the enemy might be closer to home – within us, or simply within our own society.

As the planets array themselves in the heavens, they touch us in a deeply personal way. Jupiter offers an opportunity to work Uranus into the status quo, by outright revolution or subversive tactics. Take your pick. Transpersonal contacts to Jupiter create more individuality, rather than less. We are more individual because of them, therefore they are personal planets. When we talk about Jupiter-Uranus revolutionaries, there are a lot of people with Jupiter-Uranus contacts who are not revolutionaries, but rather, are victims of revolution. They will be acutely aware, in their own experience, that somehow their own social order is very tied in with the new way of being. Jupiter-Uranus people are front-runners, leaders.

If a Jupiter-Uranus aspect is connected to the Sun, Moon, Mercury, or Venus, then the whole configuration is the avenue down which you can take your unique beliefs. If Jupiter and Uranus are square or opposite, then there will always be an encounter with higher authority, or with people in positions "above" you, which will irritate and cause anxiety. Unfortunately, this is part of the path – the obstacles to getting to the deeper self are almost always social and hierarchical, and because of Jupiter's mythic history of killing off the feminine, the struggle usually lies in the realm of ideas. Feelings are not much good in this arena, and if it is a feeling person with a revolutionary aspect, then it can hurt them badly when they are called to confront their beliefs.

Jupiter-Uranus trines are very productive in bringing new and innovative ideas to the people. They can even create schools of thought – not always literally, obviously, or there would be millions of them. Actually, there might well be millions of them, but I don't know of them all! But people with a strongly placed trine, especially if configured with personal planets, will have the opportunity to spread their philosophy fairly widely. This puts upon them a need to separate out from the masses, to be as strong an individual as possible, so as to not be easily invaded by the collective or the group. It is a thinking function, Jupiter and Uranus, and with the trine, it thinks creatively and clearly. There is a dash of dogma involved, but it will have the personal stamp of the individual propounding it.

The square is a bomb-thrower – either they are getting bombed, or they are tossing it. This is because it is coming from family patterns, or from a dissonance with the social norm – or both. Someone back in the family line is a defunct revolutionary, and the Jupiter-Uranus square person is taking up where the thread was broken off. They may have come from a line of law-makers and law-breakers. Too, they find they have to defend their beliefs constantly, partly because their deeper self demands conflict to further refine their codes of ethics and beliefs, and partly because fate has it that they should encounter threats to their independence in the group.

Jupiter, Neptune, Pluto and everything

Audience: There was a point when Jupiter was involved strongly with Uranus and Neptune and Pluto and Saturn!

Erin: 1964/65 – yes, I remember it well. Many people don't, however. It is something that I'd like to get my teeth into, because it invokes a lot of information, but it means cutting our time a bit short for Jupiter-Pluto. Is that OK?

Audience: Yes!

Audience: No!

Erin: Well, I can't please everyone, can I? Let's see, the ephemeris...Right, there it is – June, 1965, and it was back in orb in February, 1966, so it had about a year of transitory effect. That's plenty of time to take root. We had Jupiter in Gemini in a square to Saturn in Pisces, which was opposed to Uranus and Pluto in Virgo. And Neptune is tied in there, because it was sextile to the Uranus-Pluto and trined by Saturn. What a time! Let's break it down and give Jupiter the supreme focus, as this is his day and we don't want him immolating us with thunderbolts.

Jupiter is the focus of the T-cross – what does that do? It exaggerates and amplifies the struggle between a deep, nuclear power and a resistant, existing status quo. Saturn, the old order, is opposing the new, young, Uranus-Pluto revolution. And, conversely, the new revolutionary aspect is breaking down the status quo. The fact that this is facilitated by the trine/sextile from Neptune suggests to me that this aspect was being infused into the psyche of each and every individual living at that time – that the aspect permeated all levels, absolutely everything, from the most mundane to the most elevated. And, indeed, history bears this out.

We're all walking headlines of the moment of our birth, so we represent in body the spirit of the world, the *spiritus mundi*. That means that it has to be brought to fruition, to consciousness. So the major configurations that you're born with, especially when they are challenging and implicate the death of an old social order, mean that you have to work extra-hard to separate that out, sort it out, individuate it out, and find your own place in the world of change.

As I feared, we are running into the last few minutes of today's seminar. Jupiter with Neptune needs to be glanced at, if briefly, and Jupiter with Pluto – we wouldn't want to leave Pluto out, would we? Perhaps we can use the last bit to weave Jupiter in and out of Neptune and Pluto, and take care of any loose ends or questions you have.

Audience: Do you think that the real power of the current aspects we have today will really only manifest with the coming-of-age of the people born with them?

Erin: Yes, I do believe that. Even today's aspect, that is, one which is currently in the heavens, and thoroughly effective now, continues to mature over time as it manifests through events and circumstances, both collectively and in individuals that are born in that moment. For example, people born with the Saturn-Pluto conjunction in Leo in the late 1940's generation are now receiving the Saturn in Aquarius-Pluto in Scorpio square to that conjunction, which occurred in 1946-48. So the Saturn-Pluto generational stamp, coupled with the sextile to Neptune, marked the birth of the nuclear age. This has fully matured, and now we live, not so much with the threat of nuclear war as such, but more with the threat of devastation of the planet, but with depletion of resources and breakdown of the old ways.

Therefore, people born with the nuclear aspect of Saturn conjunct Pluto are acutely aware of this, as are the subsequent generations. And the oddest part is that so many of that generation seem to forget that they are actually part of the creation of the ecological and sociological breakdown. It is, in fact, that very generation who demonstrated against nuclear warheads – they are the same generation who have perpetrated the situation in which we all now find ourselves.

Everybody out there whom we think is "us", as opposed to "them", is, in fact, generally within our own age grouping. It does mean we have to examine – on every level, with the greatest generosity of ethics and moral codes – what our resources are, tribally, personally, and collectively. And that's what Saturn and Pluto are about – how do we get to the true level of resource that we have, whether it's time, or love, or money? And certainly global resources are in question and deeply threatened at this time in our existence. Just think in terms of things like fossil fuels. That's very Saturn-Pluto, isn't it? Fossil fuels are the ancient, archaic remnants of an earlier time which are buried beneath the earth, and which have, in fact, given us the warmth and resources that we need. Saturn-Pluto give us the very image of mining and drawing resources from the bosom of the earth, which has nurtured these organic materials so secretly – where dinosaurs have become tar-pits and oil mines!

There is always something occurring at a subterranean level which we don't fully understand – the image of the dinosaur-*cum*-fuel brings to mind a parallel in the psyche which says our own individual "mines" have resources yet to be revealed, yet to be matured to the point of usefulness on the conscious level. It is possible that the Saturn-Pluto square right now, being coupled with the confusion of the Uranus-Neptune conjunction in Capricorn, is bringing us closer and closer to the breaking point. However, having said that, the separation of Uranus from Neptune actually marks the clearing of the fog, and after Uranus moves into Aquarius, Pluto into Sagittarius, and then Neptune into Aquarius, we shall see the product of history and begin, yet again, a reconstruction for the future. But first, the deep correction of balance must begin, and I would have to say that sometime after January 5th, 1994, the correction can begin.

Another major date in the future, already forming in the heavens, is mid-February 1997, when there is a conspiracy of aspects at 5° of fire and air – an amazing configuration between Pluto at 5° Sagittarius trined by Saturn at 5° Aries, with Jupiter and Uranus at 5° Aquarius at the midpoint of those two, and Mars retrograde at 5° Libra. Since we are now in times of earth and water configurations, it feels heavy and is about deep issues of security and feeling – whereas when the shift moves into fire and air, we take the collective ethos to another level. For now, it takes a lot of energy to move through these times – we'll talk more about the major configurations toward the end of the day.

Audience: Just one more question about the effect that the Uranus-Neptune conjunction is having...

Erin: That's what's going on now. It's the death of illusion, it's the recognition of the importance of the ability of the individual to actually do something about collective issues. It's no longer a fanciful, airy-fairy concept. However, it's going to take time. When you have massive configurations of that type, that is, Uranus/Neptune/Pluto conspiracies, which touch personal planets in the chart, it really does take time to come to terms with it. Pluto is the last planet in the solar system, and by nature of its place in the ordinal system, it is the last planet that we grow into. And it's probably a good thing, because if we were all empowered by Pluto at the age of ten, it would be like *Lord of the Flies*. It takes temperance, and at a certain age your body can't take too much, so your mind starts to work more, or your soul starts to work more. You start to grow into Pluto. I think you first get to Saturn and everything's fine, and then, after the Uranus opposition, you get to Neptune and then Pluto, if there is time and consciousness. And really, a person doesn't grow into Pluto until well after forty-five, or into their fifties.

Audience: Does the Pluto square to Pluto in the chart bring that kind of awareness in?

Erin: It doesn't always. Anyone born, say, from 1930 through about 1958/59, experiences the Pluto square to itself smack in midlife – as the Uranus opposition begins to occur – whereas my parents' parents, my grandparents, died when Pluto squared Pluto, because it was part of the death transits, it was part of the culmination of life. Transiting Pluto square natal Pluto was the gateway to the other side! For instance, in 1915 Pluto was at 0° Cancer. People born then had their Pluto square Pluto in 1971-72, at age fifty-six. Someone born in 1885 had their Pluto square Pluto in 1958 or so, at age seventy-three! The War- and post-War generation has to live through the Pluto square, and incorporate it and its deeper meaning into consciousness, along with the irruption of Uranus, which is a regular, generic feature in adult maturation – highly challenging.

This is because of Pluto's eccentric orbit. It has a fixed return – 245 years – but its path is elliptical against the zodiac, and it spends thirty-two years in Taurus and eleven in Scorpio. How we see Pluto's transit against the backdrop of the zodiac as it begins to elongate again, as it moves into Capricorn, Aquarius, and so on, will gradually extend the Pluto square Pluto time into later and later years in an individual's life. So, it is the Pluto in Leo and Virgo generations who experience their Pluto square in mid-life, between thirty-eight and forty, adding a dimension of life-and-death to the mid-life transition. It is actually quite a painful transit, as all the old illusions crash and death anxieties rise. It means saying goodbye to a way of perceiving life. It is very much a "truth transit", because people's eyes are opened in very shocking ways when Pluto squares itself. It does terminate a way of being, and, depending on Pluto's natal place, it can be a real rent in one's emotional, spiritual and psychological fabric.

Audience: So, what you were saying about coming into Pluto power – do you mean to say that we might never come fully to that planet in the whole of the lifetime? Does that mean that Pluto always remains unconscious?

Erin: But that's not totally what I mean – I mean that, in the hierarchy of the individuation process, you start with the Sun and you work out to Pluto. And the mysteries of Pluto, and the depths of Pluto, and the kind of power that Pluto actually contains, are destructive in full measure anyway. But in the wrong hands, and especially if you're too young, it can play havoc with power in the most core sense. It really is a matter of psychological maturation. It's really interesting, because as I get older, my clients are becoming younger... I mean, I see a lot of people now in their thirties and younger, and they have strong Plutos in their charts, and it's completely innocent. They don't fully recognize their impact and the ultimate intent of their deepest self as it sturdily marches toward its constellating future! It is quite refreshing, frankly. They don't even know how influential and powerful they could be, and likely will become, if they are already examining their deepest core nature in their twenties and thirties.

They are truly and completely unaware of this, and very humble, but they are aware of something greater than their own ego. Unlike the collective consciousness of the Pluto in Cancer people, whose fate was to lead them with a security-minded and territorially focused intent, the Pluto in Libra people are already tapped into the collective, and wanting to know how they might individually support it. As a generation, they're filled with a sense of humility. And I may say, "You have the capacity to do great work and to be centrally focused, and to have quite an influence and power – not only within yourself, but also in the community [in accord with their own chart]...It's something you will mature into, you will grow into..." They say, "Well, I don't feel that. I've no contact with that at all." And, I think to myself, "Just as well, just as well, soon enough, soon enough."

I have noted that the Pluto in Scorpio generation is already showing a phenomenal amount of worldliness and the "new brain" is emerging in them. The mental mutation necessary for survival in the new world-consciousness has been established with the Pluto in Scorpio generation.

These people are certainly intelligent. It's not denial when they say they are unaware of this coiled power in them. They're not lying, they're not suffering from lack of self worth – they are truly not in touch with it yet, but will be over time, once having achieved a certain level of Saturnian confidence, Uranian uniqueness, and self-identity, Neptunian loss of identity might be necessary, oddly enough – to melt down into something completely amorphous, and reform an identity, before you can get to the Plutonian stage of real central power, core power.

Pluto's very interesting, because its glyph is also the symbol for plutonium, which is the by-product of the nuclear reaction. A nuclear reaction is something that is very safe on the Sun, because that's what the Sun is – it's a series of powerful nuclear reactions that send out radiation, giving us light and life. But if you bring it down to this planet, it gives us death. And so there's nothing wrong with it in its right place, in its right context. Pluto power is something that is truly better served during and after the crisis of midlife identity, and into another stage of their life, where perhaps the ego isn't so much involved – in other words, where the life crisis is not so much about being successful, or making the most of the earning years, but where it's about being truthful and honest and clear and aware. OK, I will say a few things about Neptune and Pluto with Jupiter before we close.

Jupiter and Neptune

I do want to say a bit about Neptune and Jupiter combinations, because they are also fraternal. Brothers and equally powerful, they rule the domains of the earth and the sky. By the way, Poseidon does rule the oceans, but also the freshwater streams and tributaries under the earth. There's nothing really horrible at the core of this combination, but it can be deluded – all for the good, of course. Both rule signs and houses in the horoscope which deal with ancestral and collective issues, and they do collaborate to create a synthesis between the mind and soul. Jupiter-Neptune conjunctions occur about every thirteen or so years, so evolving aspects from that point are about the infusion of new styles of group spiritual work. People with Jupiter-Neptune conjunctions are usually preoccupied with the state of the soul – either their own or their neighbour's. There is such a strong desire to blend belief with true spiritual feeling that there can be something messianic about it. The opposition can become a psychological complex, however, and is the more difficult of the two. Even though I always say an opposition is a split conjunction, this meeting of opposites is rife with potentially inflatory ideals which are then pressed onto others.

The great dream of the Jupiter-Neptune person is Utopia – that somewhere it exists, or that at some time they will achieve this elevated place. And they might well do so. I think they are terribly concerned about the cares of society and the sad things that go on, where individuals lose their humanity or their sense of dignity. This configuration, like Jupiter with Uranus or Pluto, can bypass the human being and deal with people as groups. The sensitivity to the underdog, the loser, the homeless, the disaffected, the insane or imprisoned, is very high – so high that they suffer for those people. They are easily disenchanted – obviously because they are easily enchanted!

When Jupiter and Neptune are conjunct in the heavens, it is a meeting between the great spirit, the league of ancestors, and the social container in which those intangibles can be met. There is a strong need in people to find safe places to put their spiritual longings. Churches, synagogues, mosques, places of divine worship like stone circles, glades in the woods, and shrines on hilltops have existed as long as we know people have. Jupiter is the shrine or the container for the divine spirit, and Neptune is the symbol for the thing we can't contain. Neptune is around and within and has no limits, no boundaries. Thus, we build places to corral it, either in our minds with dogma, or on the earth as a shrine. Great wars are fought over ideology and theology. People kill each other for what they believe and think, more than for the land they occupy.

If Jupiter is dominant, the Jupiter-Neptune person can be an unbearable bore with his or her spiritual path. If Neptune is dominant, then it's all too ineffable for words. They are living in a fused state with god – there is no reason or rationale. Clearly, the squares are more susceptible to splitting off and taking one side or another. The trines and sextiles are gentler and more creative – this aspect is also of the artist, the sublime creator of images and symbols. Music, painting, film, and imagery of all kinds help the Jupiter-Neptune person express their longing for union with the divine. If social life needs to be sacrificed for a more hermetic life, a monastic life, for instance, then this aspect will enhance the romanticism of it.

Jupiter and Pluto

Pluto is probably the most inevitable of the gods. I mean, it's inexorable, isn't it, the end? Hades in the Greek world-view was not the Christian Hell, it was a place of transition, a place for the soul to reside and refresh itself in between its incarnations. Pluto can be very nurturing on the existential level, because it is in that mysterious place that you get cared for after corporeal life has ended. As the place of the shades, or the souls, it has a rather restful connotation, but when we are in full vigour of life, we don't consciously court death, or desire to go to this place before our time. But people with Jupiter-Pluto aspects are very curious about this particular journey, and are less fearful of its inevitability. Jupiter's sense of adventure knows no bounds. Jupiter-Pluto contacts are magical, deeply, profoundly magical. In fact, there are all the earmarks of sorcery around the two of them, and the Jupiter-Pluto aspect is one which can do magic. Therefore it is an aspect that needs to be highly respected. And it can be charismatic and brilliant and catalytic; there is power to transform lead into gold.

I see Hades as a state of mind, a place where we go when something familiar has ended. Jupiter can only shed light here – remember, they are equals, brothers, and polarities in manor, Jupiter of the skies and

Pluto of the underworld. They balance out the extremes of life, the endless possibilities of Jupiter and the inevitable terminus of Pluto. We don't know what it is that lies beyond Pluto's orbit, but there are now hints of some phenomena that speak of a cosmic zone. If those realms are explored in our lifetime, we are in for the biggest event in consciousness! Meanwhile, we remain unconscious of what lies outside or beyond Pluto. And, analogously, we remain unconscious of the depths, breadth and full capacity of Pluto in the psyche. If we are attracted by the mysterious, then Jupiter will gladly escort us to the edge, but not beyond – he was not privy himself to the realm of his brother. We go to Pluto alone. But, if you have a Jupiter-Pluto conjunction, you might well not mind that kind of aloneness, because there is a sense of fraternity between you and the unknown.

Jupiter-Pluto people feel the existential world – they know they are alone and their path is singular. The alchemist knew this very well too; his only companion was Hermes. There is something hermetic about the closed container of self and soul that these two planets create – a kind of alembic in which all sorts of magical transformations are undergone in secret. They do exude an aura of powerful mystery. The problem is that they can be attracted to the dark forces. Now, there is always something fascinating about the shadowy realms, the dark forces, and black magic. And because evil does exist, it needs to be seen, and there is nothing wrong with peeking over the edge at it. But if one falls in, then the path back is fraught. Mystery writers, healers, magicians, people who work in the criminal world, and those who can heal the evils they are both attracted to and repelled by, can use the Jupiter-Pluto connection to their best result. It's not a bad contact for astrology, either, being the interpretation of mysterious symbols involving the study of personal and global transformation.

Although this has brought us to the end of the day, it isn't the end of the subject! Thank you.

Bibliography

Detienne, Marcel, *The Creation of Mythology*, trans. Margaret Cook, University of Chicago Press, 1986.

Evans, Arthur, *The God of Ecstasy*, St Martins Press, 1988.

Graves, Robert, *The White Goddess*, Faber and Faber, 1961.

Homer, *The Iliad*, trans. Richard Lattimore, University of Chicago Press, 1951.

Kirk, G. S., *The Nature of Greek Myths*, Pelican, 1974.

Sullivan, Erin, *Retrograde Planets: Traversing the Inner Landscape*, Arkana Contemporary Astrology Series, Penguin, 1992.

The Oxford Companion to Classical Literature, Oxford University Press, 1990.

Xenophanes, "Xenophanes on Drinking Parties and Olympic Games", Illinois Classical Studies 3 (1978).

Acknowledgements

Thanks to Jenny Rawlinson for transcribing the hours of tapes of the two seminars. And to the CPA students for being so stimulating!

About the author

Erin Sullivan is Canadian-born and has been a consultant astrologer and teacher since the late 1960's. She has lectured worldwide, and led workshops and symposia on many aspects of human development, using mythology, psychology and the rich language of astrology. At Cold Mountain Institute, and P.D. Seminars in British Columbia, she did retreat workshops on "The Gods Within" and "In Midlife", and was also the resident astrologer for the New Horizons Programs in the 1980's for the Cold Mountain Institute. Her work has led to specializing in the area of life transitions and rites of passage, and she works with both individuals and groups, facilitating life changes. She now continues to do workshops on transition for P.D. Seminars on Gabriola Island in British Columbia, Canada.

In 1989 her work brought her to London, where she is a tutor for the Centre for Psychological Astrology, and the Series Editor for Penguin's Arkana Contemporary Astrology Series. She is the founder and co-director for Southern Cross Academy in Johannesburg, South Africa and an adjunct faculty member for The Central American Institute of Prehistoric and Traditional Cultures at Belize.

Erin has authored several books: *Saturn In Transit: Boundaries of Mind, Body and Soul, Retrograde Planets: Traversing the Inner Landscape,* and *Dynasty: The Astrology of Family Dynamics* (all with Arkana, C.A.S.). Her chapter on "Hermes: Trickster, Teacher, Theos" appears in the Llewellyn book, *The Planets.* She has also produced a three-volume set of teaching videos, *Astrology, Mythology and the Psyche,* available in the U.K. through Midheaven Bookshop and in the U.S. through Spectrum Videos and her own company, Southwest Furthers. Her website home page address is: http://www.brookeline.com/astrology/sullivan/sullivan.htm.

Erin lives in London half the year, usually from June through October, writing, teaching and consulting, and has a winter home in Arizona, where she consults and conducts workshops. She has two grown daughters and one grandchild.

About the Centre for Psychological Astrology

Directors:
Liz Greene, PhD, D. F. Astrol. S., Dip. Analyt. Psych.
Charles Harvey, D. F. Astrol. S.

The Centre for Psychological Astrology provides a unique workshop and professional training programme, designed to foster the cross fertilisation of the fields of astrology and depth, humanistic, and transpersonal psychology. The main aims and objectives of the CPA professional training course are:

a) To provide students with a solid and broad base of knowledge, within the realms of both traditional astrological symbolism and psychological theory and technique, so that the astrological chart can be sensitively understood and interpreted in the light of modern psychological thought.

b) To make available to students psychologically qualified case supervision, along with background seminars in counselling skills and techniques which would raise the standard and effectiveness of astrological consultation. **It should be noted that no formal training as a counsellor or therapist is provided by the course.**

c) To encourage investigation and research into the links between astrology, psychological models, and therapeutic techniques, thereby contributing to and advancing the already existing body of astrological and psychological knowledge.

The Centre's course is based on the academic module system, in which credits are collected for each seminar attended. The student is required to attend fifty one-day seminars and forty one-and-a-half hour case supervision groups, and submit term papers on selected themes. Seminars, examples of which are listed below, are grouped around nine Core Themes, with a minimum number required for each Theme. Each Core Theme is usually covered by at least one seminar each term. Of the fifty seminars, four are compulsory. These are the "Psychological Approaches" seminars, which include exploration of the work of Freud, Jung, Psychosynthesis, Gestalt, and other overviews and techniques, and the "Counselling Techniques" seminar. The remaining forty-six seminars are made up from selecting seminars out of each Core Theme, using the indicated "required number" as a guide. The course runs on a three-term system, new terms commencing in September, January, and May. There are roughly ten seminars per term. The regular course tutors are Liz Greene, Charles Harvey, Melanie Reinhart, Darby Costello, Erin Sullivan, and Juliet Sharman-Burke. The CPA regularly invites visiting tutors, including Suzi Lilley-Harvey, Warren Kenton, Michael Harding, Richard Tarnas, Nick Campion, Jan Lee, and Lynne Bell. Beginners and Intermediate Courses are also offered by the CPA. These are not part of the Diploma Course, but can be used as preparation for the course.

In order to facilitate students with daytime commitments, the one-day seminars are held on weekends, usually Sundays, and the case supervision meetings are held on weekday evenings. All the supervisors are both trained psychotherapists and experienced astrologers, and each student has the opportunity of presenting case material from the charts he or she is working on. The groups consist of roughly eight people, and never more than ten. Three times a year, an in-depth oral assessment is conducted in a small group of no more than six people, which counts toward case supervision hours. On completing the required number of seminars and supervision groups, the student is entitled to receive the Certificate in Psychological Astrology.

In order to be awarded the Diploma in Psychological Astrology, the student must, on completing the seminar and supervision requirements, submit a 15,000-20,000 word paper. This may be on any chosen subject under the general umbrella of psychological astrology, provided example charts of individuals interviewed by the student are used to illustrate any theory or historical investigation. Many of these papers may be of publishable quality, and the CPA may consider them for eventual publication under its own imprint, the Centre for Psychological Astrology Press.

THE SEMINAR CURRICULUM

Attendance at the Orientation Meeting, held each September, is required for all new students. This is followed by a student/staff meeting, thus providing the new student with an opportunity to meet the teaching staff and established students. The nine Core Themes around which the Diploma Course is based are given below, with some sample seminars. New seminars under each Theme are constantly being added, and repeating seminars are constantly being changed according to further research and experience on the part of tutors.

Core Theme 1. Cycles. 6 seminars required.
Life Cycles
Retrograde Planets
The Mid-Life Crisis
The Transits of Saturn and Uranus
The Progressed Moon Cycle
The Astrology of the Collective Part 1 (current transit cycles)
The Astrology of the Collective Part 2 (generational and historical cycles)
Pluto in Sagittarius – the Marriage of Heaven and Hell

Core Theme 2. Planetary Archetypes. 11 seminars required.
Sun and Moon – the Roots of Character
Sun and Saturn – the Development of the Ego
Mercury as Transmitter and Communicator
Venus – Aspects of Love
Mars and Desire
Jupiter and Saturn – Guardians at the Threshold
Uranus and the Art of Stealing Fire
Saturn and Neptune – the Imminent and the Transcendent
Neptune and the Quest for Redemption
Chiron and the Wounded Healer
Pluto and the Underworld Journey

Core Theme 3. Prognostication. 3 seminars required.
The Ethics of Forecasting
Progressions
Transits in the Birth Chart
Horary Astrology
Solar and Lunar Returns
Fatalism in Action: Greco-Roman Prediction Techniques

Core Theme 4. Relationships. 7 seminars required.
Synastry
The Composite Chart
Male and Female in the Birth Chart
The Moon and Primary Relationship
Childhood and Development
Parental Images

The Parental Marriage
Family Dynamics
The Ascendant and the Four Angles
Relating to the World: Astro*Carto*Graphy
The Aries Point and our Relationship with the World

Core theme 5. Models in Interpretation/Philosophy. 4 seminars required.
The God Image in the Horoscope
Platonism and the Music of the Spheres
Wiliam Lilly and "Traditional" Astrology
Fate and Free Will
The Four Elements and the Psychological Types

Core Theme 6. Astrology in the World. 3 seminars required.
Techniques of Counselling
The Astrologer, the Counsellor, and the Priest
The Uses of Horary
Vocational Astrology
The Twelve Houses (Parts 1, 2 and 3)

Core Theme 7. Body/Mind, Illness and Health. 4 seminars required.
Astrology and Illness
Symbols of the Body in Astrology
Sanity and Insanity
Depression
Neptune and Hysteria
The Horoscope and the Defences of the Personality (Parts 1 and 2)
Complexes and Projection

Core Theme 8. Image and Symbol. 4 seminars required.
Astrology, Myths, and Fairy Tales
Myths of the Zodiac
The Sun and the Creative Process
Astrology and the Mythic Tarot
Neptune and the Artist
The Imagination and the Element of Fire

Core Theme 9. Deeper Geometries and Perspectives. 4 seminars required.
The Psychology of Midpoints (Parts 1 and 2)
The Harmonic Chart (Parts 1 and 2)
Using the Fixed Stars
The Nature of Aspects (Parts 1 and 2)

QUALIFICATIONS

Fulfillment of the seminar and supervision requirements of the In-Depth Professional Training Course entitles the trainee to a Certificate in Psychological Astrology. Upon acceptance of the thesis, the student is entitled to the Centre's Diploma in Psychological Astrology, with permission to use the letters, D. Psych. Astrol. The successful graduate will be able to apply the principles and techniques learned during the course to his or her professional activities, either as a consultant astrologer or as a useful adjunct to other forms of psychological counselling. Career prospects are good, as there is an ever-increasing demand for the services of capable psychologically orientated astrologers. The Centre's Diploma is not offered as a replacement for the Diploma of the Faculty of Astrological Studies, or any other basic astrological training course. Students are encouraged to learn their basic astrology as thoroughly as possible, through the Faculty or other reputable source, before undertaking the In-Depth Professional Training Course. The CPA offers Introduction to Psychological Astrology courses on weekday evenings.

The CPA Diploma does not constitute a formal counselling or psychotherapeutic training. Students who wish to work as ongoing counsellors or therapists should complete a further training course focusing on these skills. The Faculty of Astrological Studies runs a specially designed two-year post-Diploma course in Counselling for Astrologers. There are also many excellent courses and schools of various persuasions available in the U.K. and abroad. CPA students who have successfully completed the Diploma Course and have qualified with a recognised psychotherapy or counselling training group can, if they wish, be placed on our referral list of counselling astrologers.

SEMINARS IN ZÜRICH

Certain seminars from the Centre's programme are available in Zürich. These are open to the public. Please write to Astrodienst AG, Dammstrasse 23, 8702-

Zürich-Zollikon, Switzerland, for details. However, those who wish to enter the In-Depth Training Course will need to attend seminars and supervision in London in order to obtain the Diploma, and should apply for this through the London address.

THE HOWARD SASPORTAS SCHOLARSHIP

A scholarship is available to one student per year, for either the September or January intake, covering all CPA Diploma Course fees. This Scholarship is awarded on merit, and students who wish to apply for it must first take the Faculty of Astrological Studies exam (Certificate or Diploma level). This must be done before beginning the CPA course. The successful applicant will have passed one of these exams at the highest level and, having obtained their results, should then pass them, together with a completed application form, to the CPA for consideration.

INDIVIDUAL THERAPY

In order to complete the In-Depth Professional Training, the Centre asks that all students, for a minimum of one year of study, be involved in a recognised form of depth psychotherapy with a qualified therapist, analyst, or counsellor of his or her choice. The fee for the Centre's training does not include the cost of this therapy, which must be borne by the student himself or herself. The basis for this requirement is that we believe no responsible counsellor of any persuasion can hope to deal sensitively and wisely with another person's psyche, without some experience of his or her own. Although it is the student's responsibility to arrange for this therapy, the Centre can refer students to various psychotherapeutic organisations, if required.

CRITERIA FOR ADMISSION

The following guidelines for admission to the In-Depth Professional Training Programme are applied:

a) A sound basic knowledge of the meaning of the signs, planets, houses, aspects, transits and progressions, equal to Certificate Level of the Faculty of Astrological Studies Certificate Course. The Centre's own introductory and intermediate courses will also take the student to the required level of knowledge.

b) Being able and willing to work on one's own individual development, as reflected by the requirement of individual therapy during the programme. Although a minimum of one year is required, it is hoped that the student will fully recognise the purpose and value of such inner work, and choose to continue for a longer period.

c) Adequate educational background and communication skills will be looked for in applicants, as well as a degree of empathy, integrity, and sense of responsibility.

ENROLMENT PROCEDURE

Please write to the Centre for Psychological Astrology, BCM Box 1815, London WC1N 3XX, for fees, further information, and an application form. Please include an SAE and International Postage Coupons if writing from abroad. The Centre may also be contacted on Tel/Fax 0181-749-2330.

PLEASE NOTE

a) The Centre does not offer a correspondence course.
b) The course does not qualify overseas students for a student visa.
c) The course is for European Community residents only, although exceptions may sometimes be made.

ABOUT THE DIRECTORS

Liz Greene holds a Doctorate in Psychology, has completed the Diploma for the Faculty of Astrological Studies, and is a qualified Jungian analyst (Dip. Analyt. Psych. from the Association of Jungian Analysts in London). She works as a professional astrologer and an analyst, and teaches and lectures extensively throughout Europe. She is a Patron of the Faculty of Astrological Studies. She is the author of many books on astrological and psychological themes, including *Saturn, Relating, Astrology for Lovers, the Astrology of Fate, The Mythic Tarot* (with Juliet Sharman-Burke), *The Outer Planets and Their Cycles, Mythic Astrology*, the *Seminars in Psychological Astrology* series (four volumes, with Howard Sasportas), and *The Astrological Neptune and the Quest for Redemption*. Most of these books have been translated into German, French, Italian, Spanish, Portuguese, Danish, Dutch, Hebrew, and Japanese. She has also written the text for several astrological computer programmes, including the Psychological Horoscope Analysis, Relationship Horoscope

Analysis, and Children's Horoscope Analysis. These programmes, designed with Dr. Alois Treindl of Astrodienst AG, Zürich, have also been translated into several European languages.

Charles Harvey has worked full-time as a consultant astrologer since 1966, when he obtained his Diploma from the Faculty of Astrological Studies. He has taught regularly for the Faculty since that time and was its Vice-President from 1977 to 1986. He was President of the Astrological Association from 1973 to 1994, and is now its Patron. He has been a trustee of the Urania Trust since 1970, and its Chairman since 1982. For many years he worked closely with John Addey on developing the use of harmonic concepts in astrology, and with the Ebertins on developing the use of midpoints. In 1991 he was presented with the Astrological Lodge's Alan Leo Award for service to the astrological community. He teaches and lectures widely throughout Europe and North America. As well as writing numerous articles for astrological journals, he is author of *The Astrology of the Individual and the Collective,* co-author of *Mundane Astrology* (the authoritative work on the subject), *Working with Astrology* (on the psychology of harmonics, midpoints, and Astro*Carto*Graphy), and *Sun Sign – Moon Sign,* written with his wife, Suzi.

About the CPA Press

The seminars in this volume are two of a series of seminars transcribed and edited for publication by the CPA Press. Although some material has been altered, for purposes of clarity or the protection of the privacy of students who offered personal information during the seminars, they are meant to faithfully reproduce not only the astrological and psychological material discussed at the seminars, but also the atmosphere of the group setting.

Since the Centre's inception, many people, including astrology students living abroad as well as those attending CPA seminars, have repeatedly requested transcriptions of the seminars. In the autumn of 1995, Liz Greene, Charles Harvey, and Juliet Sharman-Burke decided to launch the Centre for Psychological Astrology Press, in order to make available to the astrological community material which would otherwise be limited solely to seminar participants, and might never be included by the individual tutors in their own future written works. Because of the Centre's module-type programme, many seminars are "one-off" presentations which are not likely to be repeated, and much careful research and important astrological investigation would otherwise be lost. The volumes in the CPA Seminar Series are meant for serious astrological students who wish to develop a greater knowledge of the links between astrology and psychology, in order to understand both the horoscope and the human being at a deeper and more insightful level. The volumes are not available in most bookshops, but should be ordered directly from the CPA, or purchased over the counter from Midheaven Bookshop, 396 Caledonian Road, London N1.

www.ingramcontent.com/pod-product-compliance
Lightning Source LLC
Chambersburg PA
CBHW052048220426
43663CB00012B/2492